FUNERALS IN AFRICA

Funerals in Africa

*Explorations of
a Social Phenomenon*

Edited By

Michael Jindra and Joël Noret

berghahn
NEW YORK · OXFORD
www.berghahnbooks.com

Published in 2011 by

Berghahn Books

www.berghahnbooks.com

©2011, 2013 Michael Jindra and Joël Noret
First paperback edition published in 2013

Library of Congress Cataloging-in-Publication Data

Funerals in Africa : explorations of a social phenomenon / edited by Michael Jindra
and Joël Noret.
  p. cm.
  Includes bibliographical references and index.
  ISBN 978-0-85745-205-4 (hardback : alk. paper) — ISBN 978-0-85745-206-1
(institutional ebook) — ISBN 978-1-78238-128-0 (paperback : alk. paper) —
ISBN 978-1-78238-129-7 (retail ebook)
  1. Funeral rites and ceremonies—Africa. 2. Death—Religious aspects. 3. Africa—
Social life and customs. 4. Africa—Religious life and customs. I. Jindra, Michael.
II. Noret, Joël.
  GT3287.A2F86 2011
  393'.9—dc22

                                                                        2011003895

British Library Cataloguing in Publication Data

A catalogue record for this book is available from the British Library

Printed in the United States on acid-free paper

ISBN 978-1-78238-128-0 paperback   ISBN 978-1-78238-129-7 retail ebook

Contents

⁂ Illustrations

Maps

Illustrations

Foreword

Funerary rituals fascinate people in most cultures in part because they are so full of contradictions. Nothing is more natural to human life than its cessation, yet nothing is more culturally specific and arbitrary than the disposal of the dead. At certain moments in funerary rituals, the dispositions and funerary techniques in play seem to be as globally standardized as the layout of airport terminals, yet at other moments nothing can be more parochial and better reflect local thought and practice. Hence nothing is more familiar to us and nothing more exotic than funerals elsewhere. Moreover, funerals are about the dead, yet intended for the living. No other ritual focuses more intensely on the individual, yet at the same time celebrates kinship and neighborhood to such a degree. Funerals are tearful, yet fearful: the rituals attempt to assuage grief through the induction of the deceased into the collective memory, yet at the same time they are a means to bid farewell. Often the living hasten to cut all ties with the newly dead, yet as soon as these same dead are on their way to become ancestors, the living nevertheless also want to communicate with them. Funeral rituals tend to be carefully planned and often are a triumph of rationality, yet they allow for the strongest and sometimes most spontaneous expressions of grief, and they are designed to sublimate the strongest emotions.

Funerals often trigger a crisis among the surviving kin and neighbors (who killed this dead person?), yet the rituals also tend to knit these groups closer together and to increase their solidarity. Funerals deal with the ethereal, yet they often also involve great expense and a considerable calculation of material expectations. Funerals are as much about death as they are about the manifestation of ultimate reality and the ultimate meaning of life, even as they are coping with the most concrete and evanescent details of the here and now. Hence no rituals are more static, stodgy, and conservative than funeral rites, yet nothing is more dynamic, inspired, and innovative than these rites that always change on one point or another with every new occasion. Funerals transcend fashion, yet slavishly adhere to it. Many paradoxes surround funerals, if only because by definition death tells us about life, society, and culture. No wonder, then, that funeral rituals fascinate, and, as the editors of this book put it, that they are often "the key cultural event" in tropical African communities. Levi Strauss might have said: funerals are "good to think."

Precisely because they are so good to think, funerals act like an isotope in the bloodstream: they allow us to better understand communities and their culture when we see them in action. Hence a book of essays about funerals in tropical Africa happens also to be an excellent introduction to the overall diversity of tropical African societies and cultures. The editors have brought together essays about nine cases, every single one of which is presented in its specific and contingent social and cultural surroundings. Moreover, the uneven spatial distribution of these cases is particularly well designed to facilitate an analysis of the funeral phenomenon in and of itself. Readers are presented with two clusters of funerary traditions—southern Ghana and north-central Kenya—which shrilly contrast with one another in almost every particular, while two further West African cases complement the first cluster, and finally one essay from Zimbabwe contrasts with all the others. Thus on the one hand, readers can appreciate the detailed dynamics and relative importance of small changes within each cluster, while on the other, they can also focus on the huge contrasts that exist between funeral practices in one part of Africa and in another, contrasts almost as stark as could be imagined between funeral traditions anywhere in the world. Perhaps nothing better illustrates how diverse societies and their cultures can be, even within tropical Africa.

Most of the contributors to this book are members of a new generation of anthropologists and historians. From this point of view, the most striking feature of this work may well be the considerable continuity of their research with previous practice, a continuity that stretches back a full century in relation to some descriptive matters and also in relation to the interpretation of funerals as a rite of passage. The focus of these authors on careful, detailed ethnographic analysis as a means to approach and understand societies and cultures—in other words, these authors' hermeneutic approach—inevitably recalls the anthropology of Clifford Geertz (as does, in some essays, the practice of thick description as well) and implies the blunt rejection of the views of those who, a generation ago, berated all ethnographic accounts as spurious and useless.

At the same time, these essays signal a major shift in the approach these younger scholars take to social and cultural anthropology in general, a shift implicit in the major goal the editors have set for this collection: "Specifically, this volume highlights how and why mortuary practices, meanings, and beliefs associated with death have changed over the years …" In a break with earlier anthropologists, these younger scholars no longer believe in perennial institutions and reified cultures that obey hidden universal laws of society, which anthropologists can unveil by fieldwork. These editors and authors are so far removed from such attitudes that the absence of any attempt here to provide a universal or even a pan-African typology of funerals, an absence which will forcefully strike anyone who entered the profession two generations ago, will seem uncontroversial to them, and they are to be congratulated for this. What has changed is the acute sensitivity all the contributors to this book show toward the role of contingency, of the constant changes in every single instance that funerary rituals are enacted. The contributors are aware of how culture and community are freshly created at every instant, and hence of how much change matters. For every new funeral slightly alters the rituals in one detail or another, as each funeral interacts with a slightly different situation and the slightly different needs, stresses, and expectations within the social groups that give rise to such liturgies and endow them with cultural meaning. As a result—and for the first time in the history of anthropology—it has become almost impossible to distinguish between the ethnography of the social historian and that of the social anthropologist, a major breakthrough in the handling of knowledge, and all of these essays are shining examples of this new ethnography.

One example of the effects of this "new ethnography" is the treatment these authors give to the by now classic theme of the confrontation between Christian funerary practices and so-called "traditional "ones. First, one observes that this question is not the most dominant issue that most essays raise. Second, one discovers that both Christianity and "traditional" practices are moving targets. In many ways, Christian funeral rites change just as frequently and as much as their local counterparts do. One could say that they are Christian according to the local rite, just as Anglican funeral services in England are Christian according to the current Anglican rite, or as Catholic funeral services in the Democratic Republic of Congo observe current local versions of the Democratic Republic of Congo rites. Whether in Ghana, Kenya, or Zimbabwe, local communities have poured both Christian and non-Christian usages into very similar molds according to their insights and needs. What once looked in the abstract like a wholly unbridgeable gap between two incompatible systems has dissolved into many small adjustments of nuance and preference. While previous scholarship could not cope with these phenomena, the new ethnography easily accounts for them.

Indeed, this book has much to offer to many different audiences, ranging from professional scholars—like anthropologists, social historians, or students of religion—to lay persons attracted by the topic, including practitioners such as clerics and morticians who are responsible for conducting funeral services in tropical Africa itself, but also many others. Readers will find much to keep them spellbound in this collection of essays, indeed even more than they expect, because there is so much of interest beyond the specific topics that draw them to this work in the first place. They may be fascinated by the plethora of data that forcefully illustrate both the huge diversity and the never resting dynamics of local cultures and societies at work all across tropical Africa, and they may also be intrigued by the insight into the novel practices of ethnography these essays provide, as well as the fresh perspectives the essays give on the changing fundamentals of the discipline of cultural anthropology itself. May they make the most of their reading!

Jan Vansina
MacArthur and Vilas research professor emeritus in history
and anthropology at the University of Wisconsin-Madison

Funerals in Africa

An Introduction

Michael Jindra and Joël Noret

In Africa, the events surrounding death are often described as the key cultural events of a particular area. Entire neighborhoods and villages are drawn to them, and family members and friends who have migrated to other areas and countries are lured back. The funeral service and burial may only be a small part of such funerary events. From mourning practices to dancing, drumming, drinking, and eating, the events may, in some regions, involve planning post-funerary activities over many months or years. Many have heard about the tremendous resources funerary events often consume, one example being the fantastically carved and decorated coffins of southern Ghana, but this phenomenon only touches on one aspect of a much more complex and involved process. Most visibly, there are status concerns, family bonds, and succession issues at stake, but under the surface—or perhaps better described as hovering above—are the ancestors and other spirits and powers that add to the cultural importance of these events, which across large areas of sub-Saharan Africa have indeed become huge affairs.

These events continue to provide crucial insights into the state of society, as they are integral to social, economic, religious, and political life. For Westerners, among whom death is normally a private and family affair, this is sometimes hard to fathom, but in the African context, funerary rites are often the communal event *sans pareil*, with ramifications going well beyond the events themselves.[1] It is hard to overestimate their impact, as anyone who has lived for a time on the continent can attest. In many African societies today, funerals and commemorations of deaths are the largest and most expensive cultural events, with families harnessing vast amounts of resources to host lavish events for multitudes. Government and church officials alike often decry these events and try to regulate them, often with little effect. In fact, these elites are regularly the same ones that involve themselves in huge funerals, since burying beyond one's means and literally "at all costs" (Noret 2010) is often the implicit social rule. On the world's most economically frail continent, development experts lament the resources channeled away from productive investment and used instead in consumption of food, imported drinks, entertainment, and funeral finery. "This is not an efficient allocation of resources," laments a development economist (*Economist* 2007; see also Monga 1995). Yet in many places these events keep getting larger.

This edited volume brings together scholars who have conducted research across sub-Saharan Africa on funerals and post-funerary events. Specifically, this volume highlights how and why the practices, meanings, and beliefs associated with death have changed over the years, aspects of social change that are little known or understood. The causes are complex and numerous, and vary depending on the region of sub-Saharan Africa. The essays in this volume discuss events from throughout the mortuary or funerary cycle, which can last for years depending on particular regional practices. When funerals are held very soon after death, they may be relatively small, but grand preparations are often made for an event held months or years after the death to "remember" the dead or to mark their passing to the land of the ancestors. In other regions, as in the southern part of the West African coast, the increased use of mortuaries in which bodies are kept frozen means that burials may be delayed while elaborate preparations are made for funerals that can take place weeks, months, or in some cases over a year after death.

In most African regions, certain deceased have long been important because they were central figures in building institutions (especially lineage structures), and thus played a key political role. This social and political prominence was expressed in elaborate death rituals. The social and religious changes of the colonial and postcolonial periods, however, brought about the development of new (and sometimes competing) social hierarchies and further differentiation of the social and religious worlds, and led to an increased variety of important dead being buried in honorific ways by those groups who wanted to build their own status. In a sense, we are arguing in this book that there has been a continuing (though changing over time) political significance to dead bodies in Africa, a significance which involved more and more people as the religious and social differentiation increased on the continent during these later periods. Additionally, in contrast to older, Durkheimian-inspired understandings of funerals in Africa as moments of social communion in the face of death, we intend to show that funerals are major occasions for the (re)production and the (un)making of both solidarities and hierarchies, both alliances and conflicts (see also Posel and Gupta 2009; Smith 2004 ; de Witte 2001: 51–80; Vidal 1986). With this perspective, we also intend to highlight issues of succession and the reorganization of social and familial positions in dynamic social configurations, rather than social reproduction *stricto sensu*.

Other areas we address include changes in religious beliefs (e.g., the growth of Christianity and Islam) and social structure (e.g., changes in social hierarchies and social breakdowns), along with processes of colonialism and industrialization, urbanization, technological changes (e.g., the use of mortuaries), and the more recent onset of AIDS pandemics, all of which appear as key features in many parts of the continent. In sum, funerals and mortuary rites could be said to comprise a "focal institution" (Adams 1981) that allows us to learn much about the contemporary social and cultural situations on the continent and how they have been shaped by various ideologies and forces: the stalwart traditions, the powerful world religions, and the incessant attractions of education, wealth, and mobility.[2] Funerals are part and parcel of the moral orders and "moral economies" of Africa, with the notions and powers of the living and the dead tightly connected to the social organization and hierarchy of a society, expressed in the reciprocities and consumption practices of everyday life. Indeed, the crucial link between the living and the dead should be part of the discussion of African political and economic change, as Chabal and Daloz (1999: 66) have argued.

Writing on mortuary rituals

This volume follows a long-standing anthropological preoccupation with mortuary ritual, which we can only briefly introduce. From the discussion of death rites by Tylor and Frazer to the classic studies by Hertz and Van Gennep, and more recently to Huntington and Metcalf (1979) and Bloch and Parry (1982), there is a considerable corpus of work on the practices, social functions, and meanings of death rites. This is not surprising given the centrality of the institution and the complexity and ambiguity of the practices and beliefs.

After the classic studies by Van Gennep and Hertz, a series of questions evolved from research on funeral rites. If both Van Gennep ([1909] 1981) and Hertz ([1907] 1970), for instance, consider mourning to be a social time corresponding to an assigned social position involving a series of prescriptions ("positive" and "negative" rites, to quote Durkheim's distinction), Hertz also develops an interest in the articulation of mortuary rites with the "mental work" (Hertz 1970:77) through which the deceased is progressively imagined "in a new world." In fact, Hertz introduces here the classic question of the relationship between funerals and the grieving or bereavement process. However, if attempts to connect mortuary rites and the psychic process of grieving are present in many classic works (Hertz 1970; Malinowski [1925] 1954; Radcliffe-Brown 1922; Durkheim 1912), the main line of thought in these classic texts is that "society" is shaken by death, and that it progressively rebuilds its unity and strength through mortuary rites that reinforce the group's integration and cohesion. Death is a crisis that requires a ritual treatment of the social body. These classic studies of mourning practices and mortuary rituals in anthropology understandably have the weaknesses of the conceptions of society on which they rely. In particular, funerals are scrutinized through the lens of a unified, harmonious conception of society that downplays the questions of domination, conflict, and change.

Working with a vision of society that takes political domination into consideration, Maurice Bloch and Jonathan Parry have probably produced the most influential text that reexamines the grand issues laid out by these classic works. Focusing on the symbolism of fertility in death rites, they underline that a fundamental dimension of mortuary rites in many societies was to express an ideology of "regeneration of life." From death are created regenerative powers, and mortuary rites essentially reaffirm a social (and political) order and work to perpetuate it beyond the death of individuals and the succession of generations (Bloch and Parry 1982: 15, 35).

Specifically, in the same way Geertz (1959) suggested that "classical" anthropological perspectives on ritual have contributed little to understanding the complex relations between "ritual and social change," Bloch and Parry's thesis does not really offer a completely satisfying picture of death rituals in differentiated societies where the sources of authority and legitimacy are multiple. Both the way authority is legitimized in contemporary African societies and the differentiation of the African religious landscape lead us to depict a more complex and more fragmented portrait of many current African ritual systems of regeneration of life. First, the political and religious differentiation of many African societies allows competing ritual systems and burial rites to develop. These differing ritual practices may then enter into a certain state of symbiosis, uneasy coexistence, or even conflict. What different ritual systems aim to regenerate and the kinds of regeneration that are at play may concern different social or religious groups: for example, when Catholic (or other Christian) rites are performed alongside (or simply replace) "traditional" lineage rites.

Second, in differentiated (and hence plural) societies, the ritual efficacy of the regeneration processes engaged by burial rites surely depends on the social or cultural legitimacy of the ritual system that is performed. When mortuary rituals engage regeneration processes, the efficacy of the latter inescapably depends on the social status of the ritual. As Katherine Snyder puts it in her critique of Bloch's theory of ritual, "rituals may lose their power to secure consent when the political-economic context provides actors with alternatives to the world view and ideology communicated through these rituals" (Snyder 1997: 562). In differentiated societies, the social conditions of the efficacy of rituals (see also Bourdieu [1975] 2001) are surely different than in societies where the sources of authority and power are less multiple. For instance, lineage mortuary rites have been increasingly challenged by Christian burials in many regions of the continent throughout the twentieth century. In central Kenya, when colonial authorities banned the practice of abandoning corpses to hyenas, people experienced a radical shift in the way they handled death (Droz, Lamont, this volume). In many other regions, more and more Christians have progressively, in the last decades, disregarded the "traditional" ways of regenerating life, while many others engaged in compromises between the path of lineage ritual and Christian or Muslim practices (Langewiesche 2003; de Witte 2001).

In the societies we discuss in this volume, the different ritual processes of the "regeneration of life" thus appear more fragmented, contested, and negotiated between different social and religious groups than in Bloch and Parry's picture. Thus we hope to offer a more complex picture of the structures of authority and power relations in which mortuary rites actually take place in contemporary Africa.

Mortuary rites and funerals on the continent

Beliefs and practices surrounding death get at the core of our critical sense of human destiny and purpose. In Africa, however, they go even further, being intimately involved with social structure, group identity, and even politics. Religious traditions, kin groups, and social relationships in general play a stronger role in funerals than in the West, where these events are generally handled in more intimate circles and are usually much smaller. In fact, the grand and spectacular bourgeois culture of death in nineteenth century Europe, epitomized in magnificent upper class tombstones (see Vovelle [1983] 2001: 532–650; Litten 1991; Ariès 1975), has since faded away. A very different dynamic has taken place in Africa, where important funerals proliferated throughout the twentieth century, as we see in this volume. In several Western countries, funerals are now regularly held *dans l'intimité familiale* (among only close family) as the French put it, a desire almost unheard of in Africa. As in Africa (though in contrasting ways), changes in both family dynamics and religion, such as the decline of Christianity in Europe, seem to have played a role here. The "individualization" and "repression" of death due to a number of factors, including longer life spans, are also important, all of which have combined to push death "behind the scenes" (Elias 1985: 12). Additionally, while family members in the West may find mortuary costs rather high on a personal level, there is no question of these costs having an impact on national development, as is the situation in Africa, where funeral expenses can play a major role in economies (Mazzucato et al. 2006; Monga 1995). Indeed, the central role funerals play contributes to the frustration of development experts and economists, who are regularly disappointed that humans are not *homo economicus* and that ordinary African rationales concerning funerals are not those of CEOs considering cost-cutting measures. Death may tear a hole in human hearts in the West as it does everywhere, but it does not rip the social fabric to the extent it does in Africa, with its stronger reliance on human relationships for subsistence.

Moreover, funerary events in Africa have often been seen to be a realm of social life that is more "traditional" than others. This is probably why anthropologists and ethnologists have tended to depict them in an ethnographic present with a focus on the complexities of their ritual logics, even in more recent collections (Liberski 1989, 1994; Henry and Liberski 1991). A discussion was often missing of how these rites evolved in the context of broader social changes in African rural and urban worlds. African mortuary rites can even be considered to be one of the key sites of the anthropological production of the image of "traditional" Africa.[3] The place they occupied in this image helps us understand why they have attracted the attention of historians, and of anthropologists more sensible to historical perspectives, only in the last decades. These events, however, have changed substantially. Answering questions on the evolution of the size of mortuary events, though, is not easy because of a lack of clear historical data about a number of areas, and because accounts of the changes in size of funerals are sometimes ambiguous. Historically, accounts of funerary rites indicate that the wealth of the slave trade enabled lavish funerals (which at the same time were deplored by observers) as early as the late seventeenth century in Angola, for instance (Vansina 2005: 24; see also Thornton 2002: 79). Just north along the Loango coast area, cloth (much of it imported) was wrapped extravagantly on corpses at "great man" funerals in the eighteenth century (Martin 1986: 3), and in the late nineteenth century in the Kinshasa and Brazzaville area due to the colonial and mission influx of wealth, which only intensified previously existing practices of conspicuous consumption at certain funerals (Vansina 1973: 211f).

In the Gold Coast area, accounts from the early eighteenth to the nineteenth centuries indicated that funerals have "always" been "the main social event in the Akan society of Ghana," evoking the "considerable sums" of money and goods that were spent, and even the phenomena of pawning and enslavement linked to the debts ensuing from funeral expenses (van der Geest 2000: 104–105).[4] Similarly, in nineteenth century Yorubaland, paying for funerary expenses was one of the "most common reasons why people went into debt," and unpaid debts often led to pawning or even slavery (Peel 2000: 60–62), as it also did in early nineteenth century Angola (Vansina 2005: 24n95). Moreover, funerals of important political figures were also major occasions for human sacrifice in nineteenth century Yorubaland (Peel 2000: 66–71), as was also the case during the final rituals of the funerals of the king in the neighboring Dahomean kingdom (Coquery-Vidrovitch 1964), a practice which of course came to an end by the colonial era. This historical evidence indicates that these events often changed with changes in religion and the political economy, and they also indicate the long-standing economic, social, and political significance of funerals, especially of major social figures along the Atlantic coast.[5]

However, in some regions of the continent, the great size and lavishness of funerals is relatively recent, as older early twentieth century accounts of funerals indicate they were rather small, except funerals given for social or political elites. For instance, many large "death celebrations" of the Grassfields in Cameroon look at first glance to be quite traditional, with the presence of Grassfields gowns, performances by dance groups using traditional instruments, specific foods and drinks, and the firing of old guns. Most observers, including Cameroonians themselves, take these celebrations to be so. But historical research reveals they have changed radically over the past century, not only in the elements of the event, but in their timing, their frequency, and for whom they're held. They are not quite so "traditional" as thought (Jindra 2005). Among the Kikuyu and Meru of central Kenya, for instance, only certain old men, and more rarely old women, were buried, the other dead being abandoned to hyenas and failing to become ancestors (Droz, Lamont, this volume). Dramatic long-term changes such as the shift, seen in a number of areas, from the fearful disposal of bodies to ritual and public burial in compounds or cemeteries, has gone largely unnoticed by scholars. In general, a survey of the Africanist literature on funerals[6] leaves us with evidence that funerary rites have significantly increased in number, size, and cost, even in areas where they had been rather large before.

In addition to its lack of sensibility to social change, another classical "bias" of colonial anthropology in Africa was its focus on elite burials, which had the richest symbolism and the most important political implications. This went hand in hand in most cases with a silencing of the voices of "subaltern" people, and with little attention paid to categories such as funerals for the young (see Honwana and De Boeck 2005). So it is common to find accounts of the deaths of "senior men" (Forde 1962), elites, and rulers, from which we learn much about the structure and ranking of society, but we often learn very little about the funerary rites of others, in particular women and children. As Vaughan (2008: 393) points out, anthropologist Audrey Richards included a discussion of the death and grand burial of a Bemba paramount chief in her monograph, but left out any mention of the "ignominious" death and burial of a woman who died in childbirth, even though it was recorded in her notes.

As the interest in social change developed and more dynamic conceptions of African societies gained space in the wake of the Manchester School, Georges Balandier in France, Marxist (mostly French) anthropology, and historically sensitive symbolic approaches (Fernandez 1978), a whole body of literature linking funerals and social change progressively emerged. The first chapter of this volume provides an extensive and analytical review of this corpus by examining how and why funerary practices extensively changed in many places across the continent, especially over the last century. Changes in social structures and hierarchies are tied to changes in funerary rituals and processes, while transformations involving the world religions are also highlighted. More contemporary evolutions, such as the use of mortuaries and the rise of AIDS, are also addressed.

The different chapters of this book build on this in various respects. The study of urban funerals is one example. Consistent with the already mentioned focus of classical anthropology on "traditional" death rites, they received little attention in African studies until recent decades, and a history of funerals in urban Africa is largely yet to be written. Engaging this issue in the impressively well documented second chapter, Terence Ranger shows how, in contrast to common views of townships as places of cultural alienation, crucial social dynamics shaped a new religious and political urban culture of death in colonial Bulawayo. Between the ritual relocations of deceased urban Ndebele to their rural places of origin and the performance of full funerary ceremonies in these rural Ndebele communities, Christian versions of "traditional" Ndebele funerary rites elaborated by "independent" African churches, and liturgies of the mission churches, various methods for dignified deaths and burials have coexisted in the different African populations and ethnic groups that have formed the colonial city of Bulawayo. The extensive development of burial societies also played a key role in this process, in providing various forms of assistance to bereaved families, and in making costly funeral feasts possible. Actually, it finally emerges that death is more difficult to dignify in today's Bulawayo than under colonial rule, since the progress of AIDS, the changes in relations between generations, and increased death rates among young people have led to more casual attitudes towards death in recent days.

Terence Ranger's text is undoubtedly a properly historical one. Nevertheless, most of the following chapters should be considered as "historically minded" anthropology rather than *stricto sensu* history, and their historical concerns differ, as does the historical depth of the issues they raise. Yvan Droz's chapter, however, charts significant evolutions in the disposal of corpses among the Kikuyu since the 1930s. Mobilizing oral histories and existing studies, Droz first shows how the system of disposal of corpses in the bush that existed prior to the implementation of burial was grounded in a system of distribution of social status that was tightly linked to age and righteousness: only old people with a certain high status in Kikuyu society were buried, while all the other dead were "thrown" to hyenas and other scavengers. Since the 1930s, however, under the double constraint of colonial administration and Christian missionary concerns, burial was made compulsory. In today's Kikuyu society, being buried on one's own plot of land has become the minimum criterion for a dignified burial, at least in rural areas, and a burial in public cemeteries is largely regarded as a sign of the poor management of a person's existence, or of a bad, untimely death. In that respect, the diverse forms of burial that exist today among the Kikuyu still reflect different degrees of personal achievement, as the distinction between the disposal and burial of corpses did at the beginning of twentieth century.

A very complementary chapter by Mark Lamont follows. In this text, Lamont examines the changing conceptions of death pollution among the Meru, a group geographically and linguistically close to the Kikuyu. Indeed, following the implementation of burial by the colonial administration in the central Kenya highlands in the 1930s, the Meru were confronted by the obligation to bury corpses, which were mostly abandoned to scavengers in the preceding decades, as in the Kikuyu case. However, while Droz focuses on the more or less dignifying forms of burials that emerged in the last two-thirds of the last century in the new culture of burial of the Kikuyu, Lamont focuses on how the Meru "pollution complex" was reworked since the 1930s under the triple effect of the enforced shift to burial ordered by colonial authorities, Christianization, and land reforms that increasingly led to a "secondary" use of burials as markers of possession of land in the central Kenyan Highlands in the 1960s. However, Lamont's vivid ethnography also stresses that death pollution is still an important issue among the Meru today, especially in the case of untimely or "bad" deaths.

A decline in death pollution and the generalization of burials are also at the heart of the cultural dynamics that have led to the multiplication of "death celebrations" in the Cameroon Grassfields, at the intersection point of West and Central Africa, as Michael Jindra shows in the next chapter. Here, along with a reduction of the fear surrounding death, changes in social structure (marked by a decline of "traditional" hierarchies) and transformations in the conceptions of the afterlife due to the impact of Christianity (and its promise of an afterlife for every human being) in particular have allowed more and more families and individuals to celebrate their dead through "death celebrations" which were celebrated only for a restricted male social elite in the first decades of the twentieth century. Today, diverse concerns and traditions often combine quite peacefully at these events, where ambiguities of the local religious context concerning the dead seem to be expressed through respective Christian ideas and ceremonies and the underlying desire for the much sought after benevolence of the ancestors. Combining, here as in many other places, with status concerns, these different motivations are all mixed and impossible to separate when examining the rise of death celebrations, and one should avoid the secular temptation to reduce religious motives to instrumental or functional ones.

Even before the systematic colonial enterprise that came out of the Berlin Conference, missionary encounters have largely played their part in framing the evolutions of death rites and funerals to come in the following decades and throughout the twentieth century. This became even more evident when encounters became more properly colonial. In the next chapter, Katrin Langewiesche continues to explore the patterns of interaction between religious traditions that research on funerals helps to chart. Through historical and ethnographic research on obsequies in the Yatenga Province of Burkina Faso, she shows how, in this region historically marked by religious pluralism, the issue is often the need for religious actors and institutions to reach compromises without compromising themselves. Langewiesche insists on the contextual and pragmatic nature of compromises or arrangements between religious traditions, which sometimes—as was the case for the Catholic Church—preceded the more theoretical developments and reflections on "inculturation." People's strategic interests play a key role here, as does the changing social status of the different religions. The current situation is characterized in particular by the fact that "traditional" religious practices are no longer considered as a sufficient, legitimate religious affiliation, and are now commonly performed by people claiming a simultaneous Christian or Muslim identity.

Drawing on fieldwork conducted in Benin's most popular prophetic church, the Celestial Church of Christ, Joël Noret's chapter engages more directly the debated issue of "syncretism." As several chapters of this book demonstrate, interactions between religious traditions are common in Africa, and funerals can be key sites of more or less diplomatic debates over proper religious procedures in order to ensure a dignifying burial. Depending on local situations and doctrinal positions, relations between religious groups can be either more or less supple and favorable to entanglement and close cohabitation, or violently "anti-syncretic" in their attitudes. In this range of possibilities, the Celestial Church of Christ has for several decades adopted a clear position of opposition to "traditional" lineage rites, which are emphatically proscribed when the church is in charge of the burial of one of its members, even if compromises with lineage authorities and family members often remain possible. Moreover, this "anti-syncretic" position combines with a sense of religious synthesis in the ritual framework that the church has established to manage the death of its members. Actually, despite their mostly confrontational discourses on "traditional" lineage rites, Celestials regularly hold conceptions of the figure of the dead that bear the mark of both Catholic Christianity and "traditional" ancestral cults.

The last two chapters, by Marleen de Witte and Jonathan Roberts, prolong this interest in the African conception of the dead in two differing ways. Indeed, de Witte evokes the ambiance of lavish display of Asante funerals, where huge sums of money are spent to organize memorable events whose richness will impress the attendees. In the Asante region, the disposal of the corpse acquires a more prominent status the longer it stays in a mortuary before burial, as does the use of various media to capture multiple images of the obsequies. In fact, contemporary funerals produce an idealized image of the deceased to be remembered. The dressing and preparation of the corpse is therefore subject to much attention: it must present an image of the good life. Additionally, Christian notions of personhood and of the afterlife continue to have a profound influence today on the modes of relationships people have with the departed. Current pictures of the dead draw in some respects on past uses of terra-cotta heads during elite burial rites, but also highlight important changes: for instance, photographs now help in remembering the dead after the funeral, while in the past terra-cotta figures were abandoned after the ceremonies. In this respect, as we see in other contributions, ancestors may in a sense be more present than in the past, even when they are no more worshipped as such.

Finally, in an ethnographically rich chapter, Jonathan Roberts accounts for current Ga death rites in the suburbs of Accra, showing both continuities and innovations in a set of funeral practices mostly thought of locally as inherited from the forebears. The treatment of the corpses and the eschatological stakes of the ceremonies here receive particular attention. Ritually ensuring a transition of the deceased toward the afterlife seems essential in these moments, and this is precisely the dimension of mortuary rituals that fetish interment practices (locally known as *agbalegba*) mirror at different and malevolent ends. Small coffins, wooden human figurines, and body parts are essential ingredients for these "shadow ceremonies," which are secretly held at night and imitate conventional burial rites in order to bring misfortune and death to a targeted person. In fact, such occult uses of mortuary symbolism reveal the expected outcomes of ordinary funerals: not only the peaceful transition of a soul to the afterlife, but also the possible ritual manipulations of this eschatological passage. Putting the spirits of dead people at work for malevolent ends, such widely feared rituals also highlight how serious the power of the dead is in contemporary Ghana.

In sum, these chapters cover a wide range of issues related to the current dynamics of African funerals, and we hope these texts help the reader understand essential dimensions of funerary rites in Africa. There are not many other topics through which one can not only get a sense of the deepest understandings of a people as expressed in such a visual and open way, but also see how these understandings have changed over time. With such a complex phenomenon on such a large, diverse continent, it is impossible to be comprehensive, but this volume should at least provide a framework to understand funerary rites and their histories. We also hope that it encourages future scholars to add further enlightenment to what we have presented here.

Notes

The volume editors would like to acknowledge Marleen de Witte, Jan Vansina, Benjamin Rubbers, and the anonymous reviewers of this volume for their input. Others who helped in various ways include Betty Videto and the interlibrary loan staff at Spring Arbor University.

Some of the major themes of this book were first presented in a paper by Michael Jindra, "Mortuary Ritual and Religious Change in Africa," delivered at the Baylor University conference "Global Christianity" in November 2005. A faculty scholarship grant from Spring Arbor University also provided assistance. Finally, the editors would both like to thank their families for their patience while this rather complex project was completed.

1. For instance, see Shipton (2007: 159), who describes the event as the "the biggest deal" among the Luo in Kenya. Similar comments about death rites are often found in other ethnographies.

2. This volume focuses less on the smaller, more isolated populations that are not as connected to wider networks, such as hunter-gatherers, nomadic groups, forest groups, and other small-scale populations, and more on the bulk of the African population that is more connected to the state and the wider economy, and that usually has at least some members who are teachers, civil servants, businessmen, and other members of the middle class.

3. This is particularly evident in the work of French anthropologist Louis-Vincent Thomas, who was still lamenting in the 1990s that the traditional wisdom of "ethnic" funerary rites was now confronted by the unprecedented "destructive attacks" of Islam, Christianity, and "Western Civilization" (Thomas 1995: 64), a perspective that actually offers little insight into current funerary changes.

4. Kwame Arhin, however, mentions a major change in scale during the first phase of colonial rule around the turn of the century, as the event became more secularized (1994: 313).

5. At the other end of the social hierarchy, the slave trade prompted a "spiritual cataclysm" when bodies along the trading routes were disposed without ritual treatment (Brown 2008: 43). And at the other end of the slave routes, their centrality to culture was revealed in how Africans in the Western hemispheric diaspora identified themselves according to differing funerary practices (Brown 2008: 64; Thornton 1998: 227).

6. See, for instance, on southern Africa (Palitza 2006; Ngubane 2004; Durham and Klaits 2002), Congo (Blakely and Blakely 1994: 410f; MacGaffey 1986), Kenya (Séraphin 2003a; Parkin 1991), Cameroon (Geschiere 2005; Jindra 2005; Séraphin 2003b), Nigeria (Smith 2004; Adamolekun 2001; Okaba 1997), Benin (Noret 2004a, 2004b), Togo (Cantrell 1992), Ghana (Greene 2002 , de Witte 2001; Arhin 1994), and Ivory Coast (Vidal 1986).

Bibliography

Adamolekun, Kemi. 2001. "Survivors' Motives for Extravagant Funerals Among the Yorubas of Western Nigeria." *Death Studies* 25: 609–619.

Adams, John. 1981. "Anthropology and History in the 1980s." *Journal of Interdisciplinary History* 12 (2): 253–265.

Arhin, Kwame. 1994. "The Economic Implications of Transformations in Akan Funeral Rites." *Africa* 64 (3): 307–322.

Ariès, Philippe. 1975. *Essais sur l'histoire de la mort en Occident du Moyen Age à nos jours.* Paris: Seuil.

Blakely, Pamela and Thomas Blakely. 1994. "Ancestors, Witchcraft, and Foregrounding the Poetic: Men's Oratory & Women's Song-Dance in Hemba Funerary Performance."

In *Religion in Africa: Experience and Expression,* eds. T. Blakely, W. van Beek and D. Thomson. London: James Currey.

Bloch, Maurice and Jonathan Parry. 1982. "Introduction: Death and the regeneration of life." In *Death and the Regeneration of Life,* eds. M. Bloch and J. Parry. Cambridge: Cambridge University Press.

Bourdieu, Pierre. [1975] 2001. "Le langage autorisé: les conditions sociales de l'efficacité du discours rituel." In *Langage et pouvoir symbolique.* Paris: Seuil.

Brown, Vincent. 2008. *The Reaper's Garden: Death and Power in the World of Atlantic Slavery.* Cambridge: Harvard University Press.

Cantrell, Brent. 1992. "Hosting Funerals in Dapaong, Togo." PhD diss., Indiana University.

Chabal, Patrick and Jean-Pascal Daloz. 1999. *Africa Works: Disorder as political instrument.* London: James Currey.

Coquery-Vidrovitch, Catherine. 1964. "La fête des coutumes au Dahomey: historique et essai d'interprétation." *Annales ESC* 4: 696–716.

de Witte, Marleen. 2001. *Long Live the Dead! Changing Funeral Celebrations in Asante (Ghana).* Amsterdam: Aksant Academic Publishers.

Durham, Deborah and Frederick Klaits. 2002. "Funerals and the Public Space of Sentiment in Botswana." *Journal of Southern African Studies* 28 (4): 777–795.

Durkheim, Emile. 1912. *Les formes élémentaires de la vie religieuse.* Paris: Felix Alcan.

Economist (US). 2007. "Bankruptcy and burials." 26 May: 49.

Elias, Norbert. 1985. *The Loneliness of the Dying.* Oxford: Basil Blackwell.

Fernandez, James. 1978. "African Religious Movements." *Annual Review of Anthropology* 7: 195–234.

Forde, Daryll. 1962. "Death and Succession: An analysis of Yako mortuary ceremonial." In *Essays on the Ritual of Social Relations,* ed. Max Gluckman. Manchester: Manchester University Press.

Geertz, Clifford. 1959. "Ritual and Social Change: A Javanese Example." *American Anthropologist* 61: 991–1012.

Geschiere, Peter. 2005. "Funerals and Belonging: Different Patterns in South Cameroon." *African Studies Review* 48 (2): 45–64.

Greene, Sandra. 2002. *Sacred Sites and the Colonial Encounter: A History of Meaning and Memory in Ghana.* Bloomington: Indiana University Press.

Henry, Christine and Danouta Liberski, eds. 1991. *Systèmes de Pensée en Afrique Noire* 11, Le deuil et ses rites II.

Hertz, Robert. [1907] 1970. "Contribution à une étude sur la représentation collective de la mort." In *Sociologie religieuse et folklore.* Paris: PUF.

Honwana, Alcinda and Filip De Boeck. 2005. "Introduction: Children and Youth in Africa. Agency, Identity and Place." In *Makers and Breakers: Children and Youth in Postcolonial Africa,* eds. Alcinda Honwana and Filip De Boeck. Oxford: James Currey.

Huntington, Richard and Peter Metcalf. 1979. *Celebrations of Death: The Anthropology of Mortuary Ritual.* Cambridge: Cambridge University Press.

Jindra, Michael. 2005. "Christianity and the Proliferation of Ancestors: Changes in hierarchy and mortuary ritual in the Cameroon Grassfields." *Africa* 75 (3): 356–377.

Langewiesche, Katrin. 2003. *Mobilité religieuse. Changements religieux au Burkina Faso.* Münster: LIT-Verlag.

Liberski, Danouta, ed. 1989. *Systèmes de Pensée en Afrique Noire* 9, le deuil et ses rites I.

———, ed. 1994. *Systèmes de Pensée en Afrique Noire* 13, le deuil et ses rites III.

Litten, Julian. 1991. *The English Way of Death: The Common Funeral Since 1450*. London: Hale.

MacGaffey, Wyatt. 1986. *Religion and Society in Central Africa*. Chicago: University of Chicago Press.

Malinowski, Bronislaw. [1925] 1954. *Magic, Science and Religion, and Other Essays*. New York: Anchor Books.

Martin, Phyllis M. 1986. "Power, Cloth and Currency on the Loango Coast." *African Economic History* 15: 1–12.

Mazzucato, Valentina, Mirjam Kabki and Lothar Smith. 2006. "Transnational Migration and the Economy of Funerals: Changing Practices in Ghana." *Development and Change* 37 (5): 1047–1072.

Monga, Célestin. 1995. "Cercueils, Orgies et Sublimation: Le Coût d'une Mauvaise Gestion de la Mort." *Afrique 2000* (21): 63–72.

Ngubane, Sihawukele. 2004. "Traditional Practices on Burial Systems With Special Reference to the Zulu People of South Africa." *Indilinga African Journal of Indigenous Knowledge Systems* 3 (2): 171–177.

Noret, Joël. 2004a. "Morgues et prise en charge de la mort au Sud-Bénin." *Cahiers d'Etudes africaines* 176: 745–767.

———. 2004b. "De la conversion au basculement de la place des morts. Les défunts, la personne et la famille dans les milieux pentecôtistes du Sud-Bénin." *Politique Africaine* 93: 143–155.

———. 2010. *Deuil et funérailles dans le Bénin méridional: Enterrer à tout prix*. Brussels: Editions de l'Université de Bruxelles.

Okaba, Benjamin. 1997. *Why Nigerians Bury Their Money*. Port Harcourt: Emhai Printing and Publishing Co.

Palitza, Kristin. 2006. "AIDS Puts Funeral Traditions Under Pressure." Inter Press Service (17 February). www.aegis.com/news/ips/2006/IP060203.html

Parkin, David. 1991. *Sacred Void*. Cambridge: University of Cambridge Press.

Peel, John D. Y. 2000. *Religious Encounter and the Making of the Yoruba*. Bloomington: Indiana University Press.

Posel, Deborah and Pamila Gupta. 2009. "The Life of the Corpse: Framing Reflections and Questions." *African Studies* 68 (3): 299–309.

Radcliffe-Brown, Alfred R. 1922. *The Andaman Islanders*. Cambridge: University Press.

Séraphin, Gilles 2003a. "Mourir en Chrétien à Nairobi: l'individuel dans l'interaction des collectifs." In *Les figures de la mort à Nairobi: Une capitale sans cimetières*, eds. Yvan Droz and H. Maupeu. Paris: L'Harmattan.

———. 2003b. "Mourir à Douala." In *La violence et les morts, Eclairage anthropologique sur la mort et les rites funéraires*, ed. Yvan Droz. Paris: Georg.

Shipton, Parker. 2007. *The Nature of Entrustment: Intimacy, Exchange and the Sacred in Africa*. New Haven: Yale University Press.

Smith, Daniel J. 2004. "Burials and Belonging in Nigeria: Rural-Urban Relations and Social Inequality in a Contemporary African Ritual." *American Anthropologist* 106 (3): 569–579.

Snyder, Katrin. 1997. "Elders' Authority and Women's Protest: the Masay Ritual and Social Change among the Iraqw of Tanzania." *Journal of the Royal Anthropological Institute* (n.s.) 3: 1–16.

Thomas, Louis-Vincent. 1995. "Leçon pour l'Occident: ritualité du chagrin et du deuil en Afrique noire." In *Rituels de deuil, travail du deuil*, eds. T. Nathan et al. Paris: La Pensée Sauvage.

Thornton, John K. 2002. "Religious and Ceremonial Life in the Kongo and Mbundu areas, 1500–1700." In *Central Africans and Cultural Transformations in the American Diaspora*, ed. Linda M. Heywood. Cambridge: Cambridge University Press.

———. 1998. *Africa and Africans in the Making of the Atlantic World*, 2nd ed. New York: Cambridge University Press.

van der Geest, Sjaak. 2000."Funerals for the living. Conversations with elderly people in Kwahu (Ghana)." *African Studies Review* 43 (3): 103–129.

van Gennep, Arnold. 1981 [1909]. *Les rites de passage*. Paris: Picard.

Vansina, Jan. 2005. "Ambaca Society and the Slave Trade *c.* 1760–1845." *Journal of African History* 46: 1– 27.

———. 1973. *The Tio Kingdom of the Middle Congo 1880–1892*. London: Oxford University Press.

Vaughan, Megan. 2008. "'Divine Kings': Sex, Death and Anthropology in Inter-War East/ Central Africa." *Journal of African History* 49 (3): 383–401.

Vidal, Claudine. 1986. "Funérailles et Conflit Social en Côte d'Ivoire." *Politique Africaine* 24: 9–19.

Vovelle, Michel. 2001 [1983]. *La mort et l'Occident de 1300 à nos jours*. Paris: Gallimard.

CHAPTER 1

African Funerals and Sociocultural Change

A Review of Momentous Transformations across a Continent

Michael Jindra and Joël Noret

Over the last centuries, sub-Saharan Africa has witnessed a series of broad and linked changes that have inescapably altered its funerary rites. These include alterations of outlook and practice caused both by colonialism and by the large scale adoption of world religions, an overturning of the system of hierarchy in favor of new processes of creating status, increased mobility and pluralism, and the different kinds of associations this mobility produced in the colonial and postcolonial context. The introduction of new technologies such as mortuaries and photography have had major effects on funerary rites, as have social turmoil and disease in some areas. In this chapter, we detail how these interrelated changes have significantly and in some cases radically transformed funerary practice across the continent.

Approximately the last twenty-five years have seen increased scholarly attention to changes in mortuary rites, after an earlier period that mostly examined unchanging "traditional" rites. Until now, however, no one has gone beyond regional case studies to examine the significant evolution of African funerals over the last century (and longer).[1] With the help of our scholarly forebears, it is to this task we now turn.

From colonial to postcolonial social change

The remolding of hierarchies and urban-rural relations

With the massive changes that have occurred in political economy, religion, and education over the last 150 years or so, social structures throughout Africa have been overturned and routes to higher social positions have been radically changed, resulting in social hierarchies that became progressively multifarious. When the traditional hierarchies (including chiefs, elders, and secret societies) who often controlled or regulated public events such as funerary rites lost power, and when new hierarchies based on connections with new institutions (whether colonial, religious, or nascent state institutions) and the modern economy began to rise, African death practices were significantly transformed, not only in form but in size.

As mentioned above, significant changes in funerary practices can be found going back centuries in some areas, for example, due to the upheavals in social hierarchy caused by slave trading (Vansina 2005: 25). The changes became even more intense within the colonial regimes and resulted from deliberate policies as well as from unexpected consequences. In colonial Kenya, for instance, colonial authorities worked hand in hand with mission churches to obtain a radical change to the common practice of quickly disposing bodies, some elders excepted, in the bush (Droz, Lamont, this volume). Sanitation concerns here were explicit, as they were across the continent (for Rwanda, see Spijker 1990: 91f). In Accra, in the first decades of the twentieth century, families were forced to abandon the practice of burying their dead inside the lineage compounds and instead to start building lineage cemeteries while missions and colonial authorities were establishing their own (Parker 2000).

Besides these deliberate attempts (only partially successful) to change African mortuary practices, the colonial encounter had effects in virtually every sphere of social activity, which can hardly be underestimated. As colonization stimulated increased urbanization in many areas of the continent, the subsistence activities of elites changed, rural-urban relations progressively evolved, and new social strata developed within the cities as a new "formal" system of education arose and economic opportunities and job markets diversified. The postcolonial regimes added still more to this "cultural complexity" (Hannerz 1992) with the end of colonial impediments on new African elites and the appearance of new African ruling castes.

The conversion of many Africans to world religions, discussed further below, also involved "conversions to modernities" (van der Veer 1996). In many regions, to convert to Christianity was at the same time to embrace a new lifestyle. Many converts—from those in the mission churches who were well disposed to internalize new "civilized" habits and values to those Christian cultural nationalists who turned to various "independent" churches (see Ranger 2004 and this volume)—were concerned about establishing their status. Kwame Arhin, for instance, suggested approximately fifteen years ago that Christianity had unexpected effects on the size of burials in southern Ghana by permitting the emergence of new elites who invested important sums in the burials they involved themselves in (Arhin 1994: 313). As these new elites emerged, particularly in urban contexts, rural-urban relationships were gradually remolded. For some decades now, they have been under pressure in different ways. Economic and identity issues in particular have often been at the heart of the dense and vital relations between urbanites and villagers. Issues of cultural identity also arose, as groups that did not have graves or that avoided them began to claim them as a part of their cultural heritage, as part of a process of increasing internal hierarchy, notably among some Khoisan groups (Widlok 1998), or as a part of ongoing land claims (Glazier 1984; Lamont, this volume).

Differences between rural and urban funerals still exist in many areas, but these contrasts may be minimal in other regions, and may vary depending on the mode of articulation between rural and urban areas (Geschiere and Gugler 1998). In his recent study of Igbo funerals in southeastern Nigeria, Daniel J. Smith mentioned the "continuing (and perhaps growing) strength of ties to place of origin" (Smith 2004: 569). This trend, however, is not found throughout the continent. In cities like Bulawayo since the colonial period (Ranger 2004) and in important cities of Central Africa like Brazzaville (Tonda 2000), Kinshasa (Grootaers 1998), or Lubumbashi (Noret and Petit 2011), the majority of corpses are no longer brought back to their region of origin, but buried in the quickly proliferating city cemeteries. The specific colonial and postcolonial histories of these cities help us understand funerary practices. In Haut-Katanga Province, the massive long distance migrations of workers engineered by Belgian colonial authorities helped establish the local working class (Higginson 1989; Fetter 1976) to the extent that an important part of the urban population today has only loose ties with their rural origins in Kasaï or Katanga, and certainly weaker ones than in many other regions of the continent. The historical importance of Haut-Katanga's large colonial and later national companies, which for much of the twentieth century followed a policy of "total" management of their employees' lives and deaths (Rubbers 2006; Dibwe 2001), remains relevant in contemporary burials. In Lubumbashi, two of the main city's mortuaries are the property of the national railway company and the formerly omnipotent national mining company, and big companies still regularly play a role in the organization of burials by providing a coffin or contributing money for other funeral expenses (Noret and Petit 2011; Mwilambwe and Osako 2005). On the West African coast as well, in Cotonou for instance, more and more people are not brought back to their town or village of origin, but are simply buried in the city to which they migrated (Noret 2010). Such burial practices most often involve a form of relocalization of the families, and the gradual emergence of new "places of origin" in African economic centers. New migrants of course still arrive and maintain strong ties with their places of origin, but there is also a growing number of urbanites in African cities whose ties with their rural places of origin are becoming weaker as the generation of those who migrated to the new colonial and postcolonial economic centers recedes.

With the rise of African international migration in the last decades, the issue of rural-urban connections took on another dimension: the connection between expatriates and people "at home," be they in cities or villages. Expatriates make significant use of telephone and Internet to maintain contact with their hometowns, as well as with other expatriates from the same region or ethnic group, and these technologies are often used to provide moral and financial support when an expatriate African resident in the West dies and needs the body sent "home" (Petit 2005; Mazzucato et al. 2006). Africans who live in the West are often expected to provide the required resources for large funerals or secondary rites, and thus new communications technologies also play an influential role in organizing these. Africans who live in the West may time their visits back to the continent for these kinds of events.

In areas where strong links between rural and urban contexts are maintained through burial events, the latter often offer key insights into crucial social dynamics of these societies. In many places, funeral rites, as well as succession rites after funerals, still serve their longstanding function of drawing people closer together and reproducing society, as well as forming part of an intentional reaction against the social changes that threaten to weaken clan solidarities and moral orders (Karlström 2004). At the same time, fissures erupt. Daniel J. Smith, for instance, has shown in his study of Igbo burials the "fundamental contradiction in the patron-client structure of Igbo society, highlighted and exacerbated in rural-urban relations, wherein people are both rewarded and resented for success, encouraged to show off their wealth, and jealously begrudged for their achievements" (Smith 2004: 571). In fact, while funerals are undoubtedly moments of expression of kin and group solidarities, they can also be moments when the failures and the deadlocks of kinship and family are experienced. Peter Geschiere, for instance, noted the profound ambivalence Cameroonian urban elites may have toward their place of origin. Being buried "at home" is still very important in southern Cameroon (as elsewhere), where autochthony is a dominant theme of national politics, but when returning home for funerals, urban elites often feel such intense pressure to share and to spend money that such occasions are apprehended with anxiety or even fear (Geschiere 2005: 52–55). The rhetoric of kinship in these contexts covers and conceals the differences between urbanites and villagers, but tensions and the limits of kin solidarities are of course experienced intensely and intimately by all participants in such occasions (Geschiere 2005).[2]

Genders and generations

Alongside the evolution of the criteria of a successful funeral and the changes in urban-rural relations, the fundamental social and cultural changes of the last decades also saw the reconfiguration of the relations between genders and generations, which inescapably affected funerals. While the social wars of status-making and the family competitions for prestige have dominated the profusion of research on southern Ghanaian funerals (see notably Gott 2007; Mazzucato et al 2006; de Witte 2001 and 2003; van der Geest 2000 and 2006; Arhin 1994), the transformation of relations between genders and generations has been at the heart of research on funerals in Central Africa. In Brazzaville, women are especially involved in mourning practices, and consider the ceremonies that end mourning periods as moments when their social identity and honor is very much at stake. Some women explicitly assert that they then "prove" to the other women "that they exist" through the successful organization of this ceremony in which women invest important sums of money, equivalent to several months' worth of their income (Tonda 2000: 11). Indeed, despite the persistence of practices that humiliate widows in both rural and urban settings in some areas of Africa (Strickland 2004; White 2002), some studies have also highlighted the agency of women (Ngwenya 2002; Tonda 2000).[3]

In Kinshasa, across the river from Brazzaville, for at least two decades funerals have been at the very heart of the remaking of relations between generations. Groups of young men of the neighborhood regularly take control of funerals and use the burial ceremony to put social relations on trial, especially when a child or young person dies and witchcraft accusations are most frequent (Vangu Ngimbi 1997), transforming the funeral into an "intergenerational battlefield" (De Boeck 2009: 54). Physically halting the bereaved family, whose elders they often hold responsible for the death, these groups of men block the street and extort money from people passing by, pretending that it will finance part of the cost of the wake. In fact, they buy alcohol and marijuana, shout at the family of the deceased, and sing obscene and politically subversive songs. As Vangu Ngimbi (1997) in particular shows in his vivid ethnography, funerals here turn into potentially violent protests especially directed against the social groups that these young men view as oppressive: the economic elites, but more broadly the older generation, whom they violently accuse of immoral, antisocial behavior (see also Dississa 2003 and 2009 on similar situations in Brazzaville).

In Kinshasa's context of an acute and general crisis of social reproduction, and in face of the subsequent remaking of the relations between genders and generations, it is of course worth noting that these subversions of funerals are organized by young men, whose social condition and masculinity is particularly put under pressure by the greater difficulties they have in finding the subsistence that would ensure them full recognition as adult men, able to support a family. In accusing economic elites and elders of killing the young people that they are about to bury, they undoubtedly express their own frustrations, and protest against their own social destitution as much as against the witch that, in their view, has killed the deceased. Not every funeral, however, generates this kind of social and political protest in Kinshasa, and even less so in other cities in the Democratic Republic of Congo (see Noret and Petit 2011).

Associations

When urbanization rates increased in several parts of colonial Africa in the middle third of the century, different forms and kinds of associations developed in African towns and cities. These diffused to rural areas, as villages tightly connected to towns quickly experienced the same burgeoning of associations. In the early 1950s, Kenneth Little pointed out that the new urban "social organization" of colonial cities was "based on" professional and ethnic "associations" (Little 1953: 277). While his sketch was somewhat rough, it nevertheless pointed to the quick development in African colonial cities of the diverse kinds of groups that partially replicated functions, mostly kinship functions, that other groups performed in rural areas. From the last decades of the colonial period forward, a series of new "associations" thus began to organize formal practices of solidarity among their members, in cities as well as in the neighboring and more or less closely tied rural areas. From the beginning, mutual help for the organization of funerals between members was an essential practice in these new solidarities (on Ghana, see Little 1953: 277–278; 1962; on southeastern Nigeria, see Ottenberg 1955). In late colonial southern Ghana, preparing a fitting funeral for oneself or ensuring support when one was faced with funeral expenses may have been at the heart of membership in some associations, in particular those based on professional activities (Little 1962).

In contemporary Africa, membership in associations is still often tightly associated with funerals and support for members facing death-related expenses. In urban contexts, the roles that associations of people from the same region play, notably in bringing corpses back "home" for burial, have been documented in various regions, including West, East and southern Africa.[4]

Associational life in African societies involves things other than funerals, but concern for the ability to arrange decent burials for one's close relatives (or even for oneself) is a major part of many associational practices in African cities and villages, as numerous studies have now demonstrated. From trader associations in Ghana (Lyon 2003: 16), Malawian "home villagers' associations" (Englund 2001) or Cameroonian *mutuelles* organized in Yaoundé between people who share a common village origin (Atim 1999) to specific "funeral associations" or "group-based funeral insurances" in Ethiopia or Tanzania (Dercon et al. 2006; Mariam 2003), as well as in southern Africa (Dennie 2009; Bähre 2007; Verhoef 2002), the social and economic support for funerals that associations provide constitutes a key part of what social actors expect from their membership. Different associations exhibit different degrees of formalization, however, regarding the forms of mutual support their members can expect: from conventional contributions to the members' funeral-related expenses to very precise and codified payments in the case of burial societies or "group-based funeral insurances," the forms of trust and obligation are not the same everywhere. Associations that offer their members forms of insurance for funerals seem, however, to constitute popular financial services—or an "insurance for the poor," as Philippe Lemay-Boucher (2007) calls similar associations in southern Benin—rather than new bonds between disinterested solidarities: it is the calculated, strategic aspects of these reciprocities and exchanges of support that are most often central, and codified, precisely defined contributions are the norm in the overwhelming majority of cases. Economic and social or moral support often entwine, however, since members of "burial societies" and other associations often take part in funerals through performing specific tasks and activities.

Technological changes and the material culture of death

Technological changes readily adapted by entire populations played key roles in the evolution of African funerals in most regions of the continent throughout the twentieth century. First, the gradual diffusion of schools throughout the population, from missionary and colonial to post-colonial, had by the second part of the twentieth century encouraged the propagation of writing practices and their appropriation for popular use. In the 1970s in northern Ghana, Jack Goody noticed that written lists of contributions at funerals were kept, a practice already popular in southern Ghana. These records allowed for a more calculated mode of reciprocity (Goody 1987: 144–147; see also Vidal 1986 on Ivory Coast). Additionally, written records were and are necessary to the functioning of the above-mentioned associations, essential to the politics of death in contemporary Africa.

Second, announcements of deaths were also progressively transformed by developments in public media, from printed obituaries in newspapers (restricted to a literate elite, see Lawuyi 1991 on Nigeria) to posters publicizing funerals in towns, as well as the growing prevalence of obituaries on radio and even on television in several African countries (Noret 2010 on Benin; *East African Standard* 2004; de Witte 2003 on Ghana). In parallel with the development of African diasporas in the last decades (and the growing movements for corpses to be brought "back home" from the West to Africa), electronic obituaries now appear on the websites of immigrant associations or churches. Anyone familiar with European neighborhoods that have large African populations will have noticed the regular appearance of obituaries on the façades of "African food" shops or bars that publicize deaths and funerals in Africa, or will have noticed mortuary night vigils being held in the neighborhood.

Today, printing facilities, mass media, mobile phones, and Internet announcements enable funerals to be advertised far and wide.

In recent decades, the development of printing capacities and technologies also actively stimulated a new material culture of death, one that involved the distribution to funeral or postburial ceremony attendees of pieces of clothing ("wax") and T-shirts printed with images of important dead (or, more recently, similarly printed plastic bowls and fans.) Less directly personalized, for a few decades now families and the social networks of the deceased have worn uniforms during the funeral or at later events (such as the "death celebration" in the Cameroon Grassfields; see Jindra, this volume), which offers a novel way of marking group affiliations as well as a new, material way to evoke memories of the dead.

Important changes to the material culture of death have been in continuous development throughout the colonial and postcolonial decades. The colonial period saw—and saw first in urban settings—a more extensive use of coffins, European-inspired black clothes for survivors, and written obituaries or "faire-parts," among other innovations. More recently, an entire "funeral industry" has developed. In regions like southern Ghana or southern Benin, funeral entrepreneurs are now to be found in every little town, renting all or part of the material needed to organize a successful funeral (Noret 2010; de Witte 2003). Additionally, many other professions obtain a significant part of their income from funeral occasions: from the masons and painters active in repairing houses before funerals to the photographers and cameramen hired to cover the event, funerals certainly increase the circulation of money in African economies.

Finally, another major technological change profoundly influenced African ways of death when mortuaries were gradually adopted in various regions of the continent. For the last few decades, mortuaries, where used, have enabled kin to modify the time structure of funerals and to delay burials for weeks or even months (Page 2007; Durham and Klaits 2002; Noret 2004; de Witte 2001; van der Geest 2000, 2006). The extra time allows people to gather resources, communicate the news to distant parties, and organize a grand affair for the burial of the corpse itself. This new time structure of funerals has of course had consequences for the whole cycle of "traditional" rites, at least in the regions where it was maintained. However, it has been unequally appropriated throughout Africa, and the existence of mortuaries does not necessarily imply delayed burials (Noret 2004). The interplay or entanglement of different factors must always be taken into account when understanding the different social uses of mortuaries. In many Muslim regions and countries, for instance, delayed burials are still avoided, since burying the deceased as soon as possible is a fundamental Islamic duty, but in Lubumbashi (southern Democratic Republic of Congo), the main motivation to avoid delaying burials seems to be economic destitution, since the huge majority of households have neither the resources to gather and organize grand events, nor enough to pay expensive mortuary fees in the city's "economy of precariousness" (Petit 2003; Noret and Petit 2011).

In fact, about twenty years ago, scholars began to discuss funerals as events that also play a structuring role in ongoing processes of social change (e.g. Gilbert 1988; Vidal 1986). Funerals today regularly appear in the literature as crucial social moments where diverse solidarities and patronage relationships are (un)made, and communities as well as social differences are (re)produced. Similarly, the grand size of funerals in many regions of sub-Saharan Africa is widely acknowledged, as well as the ostentatious and lavish nature of these expensive events. Indeed, in many regions, the internalized norms and social pressures of today often convince the vast majority of social actors to organize obsequies beyond their means. The quest for family prestige and status is certainly a major cause of the extravagance observed at many funerals in contemporary Africa (van der Geest 2000; Arhin 1994). However, to assume this extravagance is mostly about ostentatious and strategic status seeking does not really do justice to the multiple tensions and frustrations that characterize the everyday life of a vast majority of Africans today. In fact, the potential expenses of mortuary events may be seriously debated in both nuclear and extended families. Writing about Malawi, Harri Englund writes that "the existential and material burden of funerals" may even be "particularly distressing for both moral and material reasons" in urban townships (2001: 99–100). In southern Africa, Erik Bähre (2007) similarly points out the difficulties and social and psychic tensions that arise from the difficulties in facing both the demand for solidarity that comes from burial societies and the obligation one has toward close kin within the household or family. Similar conflicts between competing social commitments exist in West Africa also (Noret, Jindra, this volume), and one could consider this general dimension of African funerals to be the all-too-common hidden face of the lavishness that is more regularly reported.

The AIDS pandemic and its aftermath

The AIDS pandemic has affected large areas of the continent, including funerary practices (Dilger and Luig 2010). The rise of mortality rates in some areas due to AIDS and other diseases creates space issues that make it challenging to find proper burial places in a number of areas (Ngubane 2004). In Tanzania, human resource managers complain that increased mortality from AIDS imposes additional costs on organizations because of the days their members spend attending funerals and the funerary costs which they help provide (Baruch and Clancy 2000). The increase in health care and funerary costs in

HIV affected households also means that people may fail to have enough money for other basic expenses as food, education, or housing, a situation that causes debts that can affect entire household and family networks (on South Africa, see Booysen and Bachmann 2002). The proliferation of orphans constitutes another dramatic generational effect, one that tends to increase the number of children who lack proper support for food, education, and health care. In western Kenya, funerals are sometimes organized without much thought about the orphans, and the assets of AIDS victims may be used to cover the victims' own funeral expenses, leaving any orphans even more deprived (Nyambedha, Wandibba, and Aagaard-Hansen 2003). In Uganda, however, some funerals seem to have been reduced in scale in order to limit expenses related to deaths from AIDS (Schoepf 2003: 565). In a recent report from Malawi (Kiš 2007), the entire "funeral culture" is affected. Individuals have so many funeral events to attend because of AIDS deaths that they must pick and choose among them based on considerations of reciprocity. This changed cultural context means that burial places no longer have the significance they used to, and the sheer numbers of dead in places where AIDS is prevalent have in a few places caused radical changes in social practices (Ngubane 2004).

In areas such as the Congo, AIDS, endemic warfare, and economic turmoil have ravaged the population. Filip de Boeck (2005, 2009) has written on how death has become a "banal reality" in Kinshasa, where corpses may be abandoned anonymously (see also Grootaers 1998), cemeteries are used for squatting, markets or drinking places, and coffins and grave goods are dug and resold. Even funerals themselves are raided by youth who demand payment as a form of appeasement. With death and cemeteries violated and made trivial in these various ways, respect for elders is lost in unprecedented proportions, and the social breakdown in Kinshasa seems almost complete. It is also interesting to note how this indicates that the fear of the pollution of death, traditionally as strong a notion here as elsewhere, is all but eliminated, though the fear of sorcery and the power of the dead that sorcerers utilize remains. This instability has also sparked some of the religious change discussed above, as De Boeck (2009) juxtaposes the strong growth and omnipresence both of death and of the new Pentecostal and other independent churches in Congo.

In some areas of South Africa, because of AIDS, lack of space for burials, complications with transportation, and other issues, cremation is becoming more common among blacks (Ngubane 2004). Cremation in Africa has always been extremely rare (Lee and Vaughan 2008: 355), regarded as an "insult to the past" that "threatens the future with discontinuity" (Jua 2005: 346; Ngubane 2004: 175), and also expressed when fire or some other destructive method was used for disposal of a corpse to prevent someone, such as a witch, from returning (Einarsdóttir 2004: 120; Schoffeleers 2000: 120; Noret and Petit 2011).

The transformation of African religious worlds

The impact of religious changes on death rites in Africa has been ongoing for centuries, but in recent periods has become even more dramatic. Religious changes had multiple consequences, including the transformation of world views and of notions of personhood, death, and afterlife, as well as the transformation of social structures that allowed for the development of new associations and organizations based on a shared religious affiliation. The specifics of these changes in funeral culture depended on the epoch and the region involved. The Christian and Muslim influence on mortuary processes has been extensive, and also played a role in conversions to the respective religions, with the two faiths sometimes influencing the rites of the other as well.[5] Also important is the aesthetic appeal of rites, those involving choirs, symbols, and an officiant—a visual representative of a higher authority, whether a priest or a mallam—to conduct the service. Both religions had the broad effect of making rites across the various ranks of society more equal, since in many societies ancestorhood (the condition that warranted a performance of the full cycle of mortuary rites) was previously restricted to a small male elite. Along with changes in the disposal of the body and the rites associated with this, the most significant changes were in attitudes towards the corpse and the pollution of death, as well as interconnected beliefs about the presence and power of ancestors.

The declining fear of pollution

As the colonial era began, and at different times in different places, one can see a major transition from unmarked graves, or sometimes disposal of the corpses in the bush, to marked graves and cemeteries. Along with this often came a shift in the shape of graves, where burial was the practice, from round to square, and with the use of coffins. Before this shift, graves were left unmarked and allowed to grow over, whereas today they are often permanently marked, especially when in cemeteries.[6] Compound burial, probably the most common form of burial outside of cities, is now normally (but not always) marked.

This shift to marked graves also meant a decline in the sense of danger that surrounded death and bodies. Fear associated with death, stemming from either the contagion/pollution of death or the possibly dangerous spirit of the deceased, was a common theme historically in many (but not necessarily all) areas.[7] Where this attitude was prevalent, it was also often connected with hurried burials. In Kenya, the quick disposal of bodies in the bush was common among the various ethnic groups of the Central Highlands, along with strong notions of fear of the corpse and pollution (see Droz 2003; Glazier 1984; Lamont, Droz, this volume). In Nigeria among the Rukuba, Jean-Claude

Muller noted in the 1970s that "when a commoner dies he is interred immediately and the fear of the dead and the hurry to put him away may stem from the fact that the Rukuba do not do anything more for a dead person except hope that he will not come back as a ghost" (Muller 1976: 270).

In fact, where historical literature on death rites exists, it generally highlights notions such as the pollution of death and fear associated with it. The importance of keeping death at a distance was (and still is, in some areas) also reflected in the language used surrounding death, characterized by avoidance, restraint and euphemisms (Barreteau 1995). However, the fear surrounding death pollution has not necessarily been equally strong everywhere, and there may have been early changes in notions about death in areas where religious cosmologies have been influenced for centuries by contacts with the broader "Atlantic world."

The fear surrounding death, however, is much less common now than earlier in the twentieth century (Jindra 2005; MacGaffey 1986: 70; McKenzie 1982: 9; Sepeng 1969; Wilson 1957: 23f). Where children previously could not see a corpse, now such cautions are much more rare—though again still found among more traditionalist groups (Gottlieb 2004: 94). Where burials used to take place at night, they are now done normally in the day. Delayed burial (along with mortuaries, as discussed above) also indirectly indicates that corpses are not surrounded with as much fear as has historically been the case in many regions. This decline is also manifested in the decline of purification rituals, which in previous times most often involved a ritual sweeping, washing, or shaving (Thomas 1982: 166f; Noret and Petit 2011), and which today have generally changed their focus from eliminating the presence of death to other concerns, such as sociality (Karlström 2004: 599).

Connected with the decline of beliefs about pollution, the last century also witnessed the reduced length and severity of mourning periods and rituals, a reduction which of course varies quite a bit by region. In some cases, as among the Efik in Nigeria (Offiong 1987: 53), the reduction in length is from five years to just a few days. These changes have particularly lessened the burden on women, who in the case of the death of husbands frequently had severe restrictions placed up on their bodily care, mobility, and relations with others.

Though witchcraft is still regarded as a factor in both untimely and "normal" deaths, the most institutionalized ways of dealing with such an etiology (as in "questioning the corpse" rituals) have progressively declined due to religious change, even if witchcraft-related deaths can still provoke intense and violent reactions in contexts of major family crises (on Ghana, see van der Geest 2004) or broader social turmoil (on Brazzaville, see Dississa 2003, 2009; on Kinshasa, see De Boeck 2009; Vangu Ngimbi 1997).

Some of these changes are of course due to the impact of the world religions. Death is especially fraught with danger for the living if the deceased does not depart normally, or if the deceased has special powers or feels anger towards the living. Christianity and Islam, on the other hand, at least in their official doctrinal forms, conceive of it as a passage that is harmless to the living. The decline of fear surrounding the potential for contagion related to death, in the many areas of the continent where these religions have taken hold, is rather remarkable. In general, one sees this shift in the mortuary cycle, where the initial fear of the dead has declined, while the hoped for benevolence of ancestors remains, which may also involve a stronger focus on celebration.[8] This marks a significant change, as many societies and cultures worldwide have long held (and some still do) strong fear of the spirits of the recent dead (Taylor 2002: 27–8).

World religions and the changing meanings of funerals

In precolonial Africa, the social ranking of an ancestor was most often based on age, gender, marital status, and especially the existence of children. This was reflected in beliefs about the immortality of the dead, and thus also in funeral rites. Commoners, the unmarried, children, women (especially those without children), and those defined as "bad deaths" were often denied immortality as ancestors. This often meant minimal or nonexistent burial rites and no secondary rites.[9] In general, the influence of the world religions has caused a certain universalization of the afterlife.[10] With Islam and Christianity, individuals could be sure on the one hand that their religious community would arrange their burial, as Droz (this volume) describes in Kenya. On the other hand, the Christian promise of an afterlife was attractive to women and to others who were not offered any afterlife under the traditional cosmology (Jindra 2005: 369; Hamer 2002: 608; Peel 2000: 176). Part of the attraction of the world religions, particularly for people of lower status, has been in these world religions' funerary rites, the final statement of a person's life.

World religions have profoundly remolded both institutional and communal forms of life, including death rites, world views, and religious schemes of thought. In areas of West Africa and along the East African coast, burial practices had already changed with the early spread of Islam. In Muslim areas, one common practice consists of a relatively simple burial soon after death with low-key visitations in the days after, followed by a memorial ceremony forty days later (Roberts, this volume; van Santen 1995). Many variations on this, however, occur in different areas and depending on the different Islamic sects (Langewiesche, this volume; Lee and Vaughan 2008: 353f). The more sober Islamic rites in some areas stand, for instance, in sharp contrast to the elaborate ones among the traditionalist populations of the southern Chad basin (Baroin 1995: 187). In fact, Islam is more decentralized than many major Christian denominations, with little direction from Hadith or the Qu'ran applying to burials. This leaves significant room for local variations. In the last decades, for instance, even in regions where the Islamic presence has been longstanding and where the religious influences between Islam and local "traditional" cults were for centuries reciprocal[11] more recent and radical evolutions have taken place. In the Minyanka region of Mali, for instance, reformist Muslims have since the 1990s refused to attend funerals performed according to the local "traditional" *bamana* rites (Jonckers 1998: 42). This, however, does not prevent funerals from being grand, expensive affairs in both Muslim and non-Muslim areas of Mali, with quick Muslim burials followed by important post-burial ceremonies that mobilize extended social networks and receive multitudes of guests, ceremonies similar to those found in many other regions of Africa.

In general, at the same time that funerary practices changed, control over these ceremonies also changed, with compromises and conflicts emerging among the different parties, both religious and otherwise. In fact, there is a considerable degree of diversity in religious practice in Africa today, and burial rites surely reflect this pluralism, with a spectrum of practices that range from an exclusive commitment to the practice of one religion (even then with much diversity, depending on the specific denomination or tradition) to the common situation of both Christian and traditional rites being performed in parallel, sometimes with tension, sometimes with mutual respect (Langewiesche, Noret, this volume; see also Okite 1999; Offiong 1987: 52).

Actually, being buried "the right way" can be a key motivation for many significant life decisions in contemporary Africa, from religious conversion to choice of residence and even marriage (Langewiesche, Ranger, this volume). Moreover, tensions regarding funeral options are regularly found at the very heart of relations between the generations, as when the desire to convert conflicts with the desire to respect one's filial duty or parents. In places such as Mali (Jonckers 1998), Burkina Faso (Langewiesche 2003), and Benin (de Surgy 2001), conversions can be delayed after one has taken part in the "traditional" mortuary rituals at one's parents' (particularly father's) death, or after the prohibition to conversion has ended with a parents' death.

Not only did "traditional" conceptions of death and customary funerary rites change with religious transformations, however, but the religions, particularly the Christian churches, also changed by adapting to local beliefs. At first, nearly all mission-founded churches "insisted that their converts abandon all contact with African traditional religions and cultures" (Kirby 1994: 61; see also Spijker 1990: 131f; see Karlström 2004: 601 specifically on funerary rites).[12] But in the second half of the twentieth century, more churches began to adopt elements of local traditions, from rites to musical styles. The Catholic Church led some of the opening to local tradition with Vatican II from 1962 to 1965, when it underwent a wholesale reevaluation of the relationship between liturgical and local cultural practices, including a beginning of the "inculturation" of some traditional rites into Church practice (Lado 2009). Catholic priests in Togo may conduct séances to find the cause of death, a process which involves ritual queries answered by Biblical quotations (Pawlik 2008). The *kurova guva* ritual among the Shona in Zimbabwe, which integrates the deceased's spirit into the family as an ancestor, was adapted and reinterpreted within a Catholic framework that incorporated the concept of purgatory (Gundani 1998; for inculturated death rites in other areas, see Noret 2010; Shiino 1997; Mbuy 1994). Indeed, in several places, "a new form of Christianity is emerging, shaped by the configurations of African life, bound to take account of the ancestors" (Walls 2002: 128; see also Ajayi 1993). Even within churches, however, changes are unpredictable, as in Cameroon where an archbishop in the early 1990s had been allowing burial in compounds if the body was first taken to church. Prompted by reports of "pagan practices" at funerals, however, he then allowed compound burial with a church mass to take place only in situations where no church cemetery was available (Jindra 1997: 160).[13] In effect, he reacted against this aspect of the compromise between Christianity and "culture" by promoting a stronger differentiation between the two.

Explicit breaks from "traditional" lineage rites and from ancestor veneration in general are often stronger in Protestant and "African Independent Churches" (AICs), where an "anti-syncretism" discourse regularly dominates, although situations vary across the continent and although some churches take doctrinal positions that lean toward compromise (Noret, this volume; Engelke 2010; Anderson 2001: 202f). In the last three decades, Pentecostal churches, which are largely confrontational toward traditional funerary rites and ancestor veneration, have somewhat overtaken other AICs in growth and have shaken up the mainline mission-founded churches (Meyer 2004).

Another source of tension and ambiguity occurs within the secondary funerary rites that can be held weeks, months, or years after a death in various locations.[14] In fact, calling them "secondary" is often a misnomer, as they can be larger and more important than the "primary" burial rites. These events can mark the end of mourning, the transition of the deceased to the world of the ancestors, the succession of a new family head or ruler, the dedication of a tombstone, or a simple Christian commemoration or memorial. In some cases—even in Christian areas—they are necessary to please the deceased, lest "bad luck" occur. Given the different beliefs and opinions that Africans hold over the presence and power of ancestors, and given the tensions over religious synthesis, these secondary events can carry a multitude of possible meanings (Noret, this volume). While Christian converts were sometimes pressured to forego some of these practices (Smith 2004: 573; Hutchinson 1996: 324), the desire or need to have postburial rites means that in some places, new forms of delayed commemoration are popping up that involve Christian memorial services (Spijker 2005: 164), sometimes combining these services with traditional rites (Jindra 2005; Häselbarth 1969). As discussed above, these rites may also be combined with the delayed burials allowed by the use of mortuaries.

A symbolic separation between burial and secondary events may, however, endure in both terminology and practice. Thus in some places secondary rites are actually declining or disappearing because of the increased focus on the delayed burial (Roberts, this volume). The exhumation and reburial of remains, as found famously in Madagascar (Bloch 1971), are not common, but practices such as exhumation of skulls in the context of ancestralization processes do exist in parts of West Africa (Jamous 1994; Pradelles de Latour 1991: 87; Dumas-Champion 1989).

Ancestors remain a "vigorous element" of most African societies despite their neglect by scholars (McCall 1995), and it is at mortuary rites where ancestors may be the most "visible," and where processes of forgetting and remembering are often framed. As Richard Werbner (2004: 139) writes on Botswana: "Having found a way to forget the dead, the living eventually become concerned to remember them, when feeling weighed down by affliction and by the intractables of social life," a theme found in many places on the continent. The recent dead need to be safely forgotten because of the disruption and pollution death brings, but the need to remember and call upon them for help often becomes crucial at a later point. In some of the essays in this volume, the ancestors become key players that influence the living, while in others, ancestors are merely "remembered," their power is muted, and other, more secular concerns come to the fore.

Conclusion

The changes in funerary rites on the continent have been considerable and complex, and we hope this volume gives the reader a sense of these changes as well as an account of how and why they have occurred. The complex literature on the topic, which we have attempted to summarize but of course can only sample, reveals the varying perspectives on the meaning of these rites. One may think of the ancestors first of all, and the reality in most situations indicates a continued role for ancestors, but a more indirect one than in the past. As de Witte mentions in her chapter, changes in funeral celebrations often "involve a partial shift from communication with to commemoration of the dead," with a stress on the partial, as photos and other mementos often still include at least an implicit form of communication with the dead. Religious, social, economic, and technological changes have combined in contrasting ways to offer a type of immortality to a broader swath of people. In the meantime, one witnesses an ongoing creativity in the organization of funerals as people adjust to various upheavals while also taking advantage of technological changes and various new networks of mobile kin and contacts. One can see processes of "globalization" occurring in African funerary practice, but here as in other domains of social life, the complexities of local social and religious conditions, family dynamics, and aesthetic sensibilities surely continue to play key roles.

Notes

1. Archaeological evidence of prehistoric burials in Africa is not extensive, but see de Maret (1994) or Meister (2010).
2. Tensions at funerals may exist for other reasons, of course, such as in Rwanda where survivors of the 1994 genocide continue to look for the bodies of relatives, and burials and commemorations continue to occur. Rival segments of the population, however, may not participate for a variety of reasons, including political reasons, but also notions of shame or fear of attack by ancestral spirits (Spijker 2008).
3. For an overview of the role of widows in African societies, see Potash 1986. Also see van Santen and Rasing (in press).
4. See Vidal 1986 on Ivory Coast, Smith 2004 on southeast Nigeria, Geschiere 2005 on Cameroon; Droz (this volume) on Kenya, and Durham and Klaits 2002 on Botswana.
5. See Pawlik 2008; de Witte 2001; Hastings 1994: 331; Gray 1990: 67f; Droz, Langewiesche, this volume. For a recent survey on religion across sub-Saharan Africa, see "Tolerance and Tension: Islam and Christianity in sub-Saharan Africa" at http://pewforum.org/executive-summary-islam-and-christianity-in-sub-saharan-africa.aspx.
6. For examples, see Werbner 2004: 139; Langer 2004; Vivian 1992; Lamont, Jindra, this volume. The following passage, from research in northern Togo, also nicely sums up the transition: "The use of a coffin, the position of the body inside the grave, the decoration of the body—bring about the disintegration of the link between the funeral rituals and other aspects of culture. For instance, the dead are no longer perceived as returning to the mother-earth in the way they entered the world: naked, in embryonic position, put into a grave that is shaped like the womb. The disapproval of this situation is best expressed in the words of an old one of the old Bassari: 'Is a man brought into this world in a box to bury him in a coffin?'" (Pawlik 2008).
7. Examples include areas within these countries: South Africa (Hirst 1985; Schapera [1937] 1950; Gluckman 1937), Rwanda (Spijker 2005), Congo (Douglas 1963: 226; Manker 1932), Zimbabwe (Ranger, this volume), Tanzania (Wilson 1957), Sudan (Evans-Pritchard 1949), Cameroon (Jindra 2005, Bureau 2002), Ghana (Vollbrecht 1978), Ivory Coast (Etienne 1986: 253). For West Africa in general see Thomas 1982:166. For other areas of Nigeria, see Ogbuagu 1991; Forde 1962: 119; Meek 1931, and for other areas of Kenya, see Morovich 2003; Parkin 1991; Leakey 1977. This is of course only a partial list.
8. For mentions of these changes, see for instance Jindra 2005; Blakely and Blakely 1994: 410; MacGaffey 1986: 71; Vansina 1973: 220; Wilson 1957; Gluckman 1937 .
9. See Ranger, this volume; Bernault 2006: 213; Jindra 2005: 364; Einarsdóttir 2004: 35; Awolalu 1996; van Santen 1995: 170; Parkin 1991; Spijker 1990: 92f.; Offiong 1987; Onunwa 1987: 42; Hirst 1985: 108; McKenzie 1982: 15; Thomas 1982: 136f; 1968: 120f; Glaze 1981: 150–2; Vollbrecht 1978: 310; Vansina 1973: 210; Bradbury 1965; Goody 1962: 149 .

10. In Africa, personhood has generally developed over time out of social interactions and accomplishments (Peatrik 1991; Vansina 1973: 210, 220; Middleton 1971; Fortes 1971; Goody 1962: 149), and not from an inherent or ascribed status or rights, as in the Western tradition (Sahlins 2008: 101). (A reincarnated baby believed to be an ancestor is an exception.) It culminated in marriage(s), children, and any ranks or titles that may have been attained, all of these reflecting a person's social interaction and inter-dependency with family and community. Not having children meant not becoming an ancestor (where ancestor worship existed), with a major impact on the size of funeral and any secondary rites. "Strangers and friendless people, having no social relationship with the community, are buried without ceremony" (Gluckman 1937: 125).

11. Jean-Loup Amselle suggested, for instance, interpreting the local "traditional" cults of the Bamana region under the label "white paganism" because of the ancient and profound Islamic influences that the "local" cosmologies and ritual systems have integrated, a category that would mirror that of "black Islam," which has been in use for some decades to describe West African reinterpretations of Islam (Amselle 1991).

12. One still sees wholesale resistance to local traditions more recently among some churches (not necessarily those connected to missions) and in some areas, such as among the Nuer, where Christian converts in the 1980s turned to adopting the Muslim mortuary feast because their own church practices left them without postburial mourning rites (Hutchinson 1996: 324).

13. In a 1992 pastoral letter that encouraged church cemetery burial, the archbishop admitted that "Deep down in our hearts, we all know fully well that the reasons for insisting to bury a departed Christian at home, and not in the Christian cemetery, are reasons which we are not ready to admit publicly" (Verdzekov 1992: 2).

14. There are of course many examples from around the continent, including De Boeck 2009; Degorce in press; Spijker 2005: 168; Jindra 2005; Karlström 2004: 598f; Morris 2000: 171f; Gundani 1998; Blakely and Blakely 1994; Katesi 1994; Cantrell 1992; Vollbrecht 1978: 331; Vansina 1973: 219; Häselbarth 1969; Evans-Pritchard 1949: 58.

Bibliography

Ajayi, Ade J. F. 1993. "On the Politics of Being Mortal." *Transition* 59: 32–44.

Amselle, Jean-Loup. 1991. *Logiques métisses.* Paris: Payot.

Anderson, Allan. 2001. *African Reformation: African Initiated Christianity in the 20ᵗʰ Century.* Trenton, NJ: Africa World Press.

Arhin, Kwame. 1994. "The Economic Implications of Transformations in Akan Funeral Rites." *Africa* 64, no. 3: 307–322.

Atim, Chris. 1999. "Social Movements and Health Insurance: a critical evaluation of voluntary, non-profit insurance schemes with case studies from Ghana and Cameroon." *Social Science and Medicine* 48: 881–896.

Awolalu, J. Omosade. 1996. *Yoruba Beliefs and Sacrificial Rites.* Brooklyn, NY: Athelia Henrietta Press.

Bähre, Erik. 2007. "Reluctant solidarity: Death, urban poverty and neighbourly assistance in South Africa." *Ethnography* 8, no. 1: 33–59.

Baroin, Catherine. 1995. "La Mort Chez les Daza du Niger." In *Mort et Rites Funéraires dans le bassin du Lac Tchad,* eds. C. Baroin, D. Barreteau, and C. von Graffenried. Paris: Orstom.

Barreteau, Daniel. 1995. "La Mort et la Parole Chez les Mofu-Gudur." In *Mort et Rites Funé-raires dans le bassin du Lac Tchad*, eds. C. Baroin, D. Barreteau, and C. von Graffenried. Paris: Orstom.

Baruch, Yehuda and Patricia Clancy 2000. "Managing AIDS in Africa. HRM challenges in Tanzania." *International Journal of Human Resource Management* 11, no. 4: 789–806.

Bernault, Florence. 2006. "Body, Power and Sacrifice in Equatorial Africa." *Journal of African History* 47, no. 2: 207–239.

Blakely, Pamela and Thomas Blakely. 1994. "Ancestors, Witchcraft, and Foregrounding the Poetic: Men's Oratory & Women's Song-Dance in Hemba Funerary Performance." In *Religion in Africa: Experience and Expression*, eds. T. Blakely, W. van Beek and D. Thomson. London: James Currey.

Bloch, Maurice. 1971. *Placing the Dead: Tombs, Ancestral Villages and Kinship Organisation in Madagascar*. London: Seminar Press.

Booysen, F. and M. Bachmann. 2002. "HIV/AIDS, Poverty and Growth: Evidence of a Household Impact Study conducted in the Free State Province, South Africa." Paper presented at the Annual Conference of the Centre for Study of African Economies (CSAE), St Catherine's College, Oxford, March 18–19.

Bradbury, R. E. 1965. "Father and Senior Son in Edo Mortuary Ritual." *African Systems of Thought*, ed. G. Dieterlen. London: Oxford University Press.

Bureau, René. 2002. *Anthropologie, religions africaines et christianisme*. Paris: Karthala.

Cantrell, Brent. 1992. "Hosting Funerals in Dapaong, Togo." PhD diss., Indiana University.

De Boeck, Filip. 2005. "The Apocalyptic Interlude: Revealing Death in Kinshasa." *African Studies Review* 48, no. 2: 11–32.

———. 2009. "Death Matters: Intimacy, Violence and the Production of Social Knowledge by Urban Youth in the Democratic Republic of Congo." In *Can There be Life Without Others?* ed. António Pinto Ribeiro. Manchester: Carcanet Press.

Degorce, Alice. In press. "Young women's ritual roles and redefinition of gender relationship in Moose's funerals (Burkina-Faso)." In *Gender and Death in Africa*, eds. José van Santen and Thera Rasing. Münster: Lit Verlag.

de Maret, Pierre. 1994. "Archaeological and Other Prehistoric Evidence of Traditional African Religious Expression." In *Religion in Africa: Experience and Expression*, eds. T. Blakely, W. van Beek and D. Thomson. London: James Currey.

Dennie, Garrey. 2009. "The Standard of Dying: Race, indigence, and the disposal of the dead body in Johannesburg, 1886-1960." *African Studies* 68, no. 3: 310–330.

Dercon, Stefan, Joachim De Weerdt, Tessa Bold and Alula Pankhurst. 2006. "Group-based Funeral Insurance in Ethiopia and Tanzania." *World Development* 34, no. 4: 685–703.

de Surgy, Albert. 2001. *Le phénomène pentecôtiste en Afrique noire. Le cas béninois*. Paris: L'Harmattan.

de Witte, Marleen. 2001. *Long Live the Dead! Changing Funeral Celebrations in Asante (Ghana)*. Amsterdam: Aksant Academic Publishers.

———. 2003. "Money and Death: Funeral Business in Asante, Ghana." *Africa* 73, no. 4: 531–559.

Dibwe Dia Mwembu, Donatien. 2001. *Bana Shaba abandonnés par leur père: Structures de l'autorité et histoire social de la famille ouvrière au Katanga 1910-1997*. Paris: L'Harmattan.

Dilger, Hansjörg and Ute Luig, eds. 2010. *Morality, Hope and Grief: Anthropologies of AIDS in Africa*. New York and Oxford: Berghahn Books.

Dississa, Vincent. 2003. "Violence et funérailles au Congo-Brazzaville." *Bulletin de l'APAD* 25: 89–97.

———. 2009. "Pouvoir et chansons populaires au Congo-Brazzaville. Les funérailles comme lieu de la dénonciation politique." *Civilisations* 58, no. 2: 81–95.

Douglas, Mary. 1963. *The Lele of the Kasai*. London: Oxford University Press.

Droz, Yvan. 2003. "Des hyènes aux tombes: Moderniser la mort au Kenya central." In *Les figures de la mort à Nairobi: Une capitale sans cimetière*, eds. Y. Droz and H. Maupeu, 17–54. Paris: L'Harmattan.

Dumas-Champion, Françoise. 1989. "Le Mort Circoncis: Le Culte des Crânes dans les populations de la Haute Bénoué." *Systèmes de Pensée en Afrique Noire* 9: 33–74.

Durham, Deborah and Frederick Klaits. 2002. "Funerals and the Public Space of Sentiment in Botswana." *Journal of Southern African Studies* 28, no. 4: 777–795.

East African Standard. 2004. "Pricey Vehicles to Darkness." (November 29).

Einarsdóttir, Jónína. 2004. *Tired of Weeping: Mother Love, Child Death, and Poverty in Guinea-Bissau*. Madison: University of Wisconsin Press.

Engelke, Matthew. 2010. "Past Pentecostalism: Notes on Rupture, Realignment, and Everyday Life in Pentecostal and African Independent Churches." *Africa* 80 (2): 177–199.

Englund, Harri. 2001. "The Politics of Multiple Identities: the Making of a Home Villagers' Association in Lilongwe, Malawi." In *Associational Life in African Cities: Popular Responses to the Urban Crisis*, eds. A. Tostensen, I. Tvedten and M. Vaa. Uppsala: The Nordic Africa Institute.

Etienne, Mona. 1986. "Contradictions, Constraints, and Choices: Widow Remarriage among the Baule of Ivory Coast." In *Widows in African Societies*, ed. Betty Potash. Stanford: Stanford University Press.

Evans-Pritchard, E. E. 1949. "Burial and Mortuary Rites of the Nuer." *African Affairs* 48, no. 190: 56–63.

Fetter, Bruce. 1976. *The Creation of Elisabethville 1910–1940*. Stanford: Hoover Institution Press.

Forde, Daryll. 1962. "Death and Succession: An analysis of Yako mortuary ceremonial." In *Essays on the Ritual of Social Relations*, ed. Max Gluckman. Manchester: Manchester University Press.

Fortes, Meyer. 1971. "On the Concept of the Person Among the Tallensi." In *La Notion de Personne en Afrique Noire*, ed. G. Dieterlen. Paris: Centre National de la Recherche Scientifique.

Geschiere, Peter. 2005. "Funerals and Belonging: Different Patterns in South Cameroon." *African Studies Review* 48, no. 2: 45–64.

Geschiere, Peter, and Josef Gugler. 1998. "The Urban-Rural Connection: Changing Issues of Belonging and Identification." *Africa* 68, no. 3: 309–320.

Gilbert, Michelle. 1988. "The Sudden Death of a Millionaire: Conversion and Consensus in a Ghanaian Kingdom." *Africa* 58, no. 3: 291–314.

Glaze, Anita. 1981. *Art and Death in a Senufo Village*. Bloomington: Indiana University Press.

Glazier, Jack. 1984. "Mbeere Ancestors and the Domestication of Death." *Man* 19: 133–48.

Gluckman, Max. 1937. "Mortuary Customs and the Belief in Survival after Death Among the Southeastern Bantu." *Bantu Studies* 11: 117–136.

Goody, Jack. 1962. *Death, Property and the Ancestors*. Stanford: Stanford University Press.

———. 1987. *The Interface between the Written and the Oral.* New York: Cambridge University Press.

Gott, Suzanne. 2007. "'Onetouch' Quality and 'Marriage Silver Cup': Performative Display, Cosmopolitanism, and Marital *Poatwa* in Kumasi Funerals." *Africa Today* 54, no. 2: 79–106.

Gottlieb, Alma. 2004. *The Afterlife is Where We Come From.* Chicago: University of Chicago Press.

Gray, Richard. 1990. *Black Christians and White Missionaries.* New Haven: Yale University Press.

Grootaers, Jan-Lodewijk, ed. 1998. "Mort et maladie au Zaïre." *Cahiers africains* 31–32.

Gundani, Paul. 1998. "The Roman Catholic Church and the *Kurova Guva* Ritual in Zimbabwe." In *Rites of Passage in Contemporary Africa,* ed. James L. Cox. Cardiff: Cardiff Academic Press.

Hamer, John H. 2002. "The Religious Conversion Process Among the Sidāma of North-east Africa." *Africa* 72, no. 4: 598–627.

Hannerz, Ulf. 1992. *Cultural Complexity.* New York: Columbia University Press.

Häselbarth, H. 1969. "A Christian Approach to the Bringing Home of the Dead." In *Report on the Missiological Institute, Umpumulo on Concepts of Death and Funeral Rites.* Lutheran Theological College: Natal, South Africa.

Hastings, Adrian. 1994. *The Church in Africa 1450–1950.* Oxford: Clarendon Press.

Higginson, John, 1989. *A Working Class in the Making: Belgian Colonial Labor Policy, Private Enterprise, and the African Mineworker, 1907–1951.* Madison: University of Wisconsin Press.

Hirst, Manton M. 1985. "Some Ideas about Dying and Death among the Western Xhosa." *Curare* 8: 103–106.

Hutchinson, Sharon. 1996. *Nuer Dilemmas: Coping with Money, War and the State.* Berkeley: University of California Press.

Jamous, Marie-Josée. 1994. "Fixer le nom de l'ancêtre (Porto-Novo, Bénin)." *Systèmes de Pensée en Afrique Noire* 13: 121–157.

Jindra, Michael. 1997. "The Proliferation of Ancestors: Death Celebrations in the Cameroon Grassfields." PhD diss., University of Wisconsin-Madison.

———. 2005. "Christianity and the proliferation of ancestors: changes in hierarchy and mortuary ritual in the Cameroon Grassfields." *Africa* 75, no. 3: 356–377.

Jonckers, Danielle. 1998. "'Le temps de prier est venu' : Islamisation et pluralité religieuse dans le sud du Mali." *Journal des Africanistes* 68 (1–2): 21–45.

Jua, Nantang. 2005. "The Mortuary Sphere, Privilege and the Politics of Belonging in Contemporary Cameroon." *Africa* 75, no. 3: 325–355.

Karlström, Mikael. 2004. "Modernity and its Aspirants: Moral Community and Developmental Eutopianism in Buganda." *Current Anthropology* 45, no. 5: 595–619.

Katesi, Yime-Yime. 1994. "Notes on Some Customary Beliefs and Practices of the Angwi-Angye." *Annales Aequatoria* 15: 23–32.

Kirby, Jon P. 1994. "Cultural Change & Religion Conversion in West Africa." In *Religion in Africa: Experience and Expression,* eds. T. Blakely, W. van Beek and D. Thomson. London: James Currey.

Kiš, Adam D. 2007. "An Analysis of the Impact of AIDS on Funeral Culture in Malawi." *NAPA Bulletin* 27: 129–140.

Lado, Ludovic. 2009. "The Politics of Religious Essentialism." In *Encounter, Transformation, Identity,* eds. I. Fowler and V. Fanso, 199–211. New York: Bergahn.

Langer, Christoph. 2004. *Die Leiter des Todes: Bestattungen in Süd-Ghana seit Mitte des 19. Jahrhunderts.* University of Leipzig Papers on Africa, Leipziger Arbeiten zur Geschichte und Kultur in Afrika Nr. 6.

Langewiesche, Katrin. 2003. *Mobilité religieuse. Changements religieux au Burkina Faso.* Münster: LIT-Verlag.

Lawuyi, Olatunde B. 1991. "The Social Marketing of Elites: The advertised self in obituaries and congratulations in some Nigerian dailies." *Africa* 61: 247–263.

Leakey, Louis. 1977. *The Southern Kikuyu before 1903.* New York: Academic Press.

Lee, Rebekah and Megan Vaughan. 2008. "Death and Dying in the History of Africa since 1800." *Journal of African History* 49, no. 3: 341–359.

Lemay-Boucher, Philippe. 2007. "Insurance for the Poor: the Case of Informal Insurance Groups in Benin." Discussion paper of the *Centre for Economic Reform and Transformation,* Heriot-Watt University.

Little, Kenneth. 1953. "The Study of 'Social Change' in British West Africa." *Africa* 23, no. 4: 274–284.

———. 1962. "Some Traditionally Based Forms of Mutual Aid in West African Urbanization." *Ethnology* 1, no. 2: 197–211.

Lyon, Fergus. 2003. "Trader Associations and Urban Food System in Ghana: Institutionalist Approaches to Understanding Urban Collective Action." *Journal of Urban and Regional Research* 27, no. 1: 11–23.

MacGaffey, Wyatt. 1986. *Religion and Society in Central Africa.* Chicago: University of Chicago Press.

Manker, Ernst. 1932. "Niombo: Die Totenbestattung der Babwende." *Zeitschrift für Ethologie* 64, no. 2: 159–172.

Mariam, Damen H. 2003. "Indigenous social insurance as an alternative financing mechanism for health care in Ethiopia (the case of *eders*)." *Social Science and Medicine* 56: 1719–1726.

Mazzucato, Valentina, Mirjam Kabki and Lothar Smith. 2006. "Transnational Migration and the Economy of Funerals: Changing Practices in Ghana." *Development and Change* 37, no. 5: 1047–1072.

Mbuy, Tatah Humphrey. 1994. *African Traditional Religion as Anonymous Christianity.* Bamenda, Cameroon: Unique Printers.

McCall, John C. 1995. "Rethinking Ancestors in Africa." *Africa* 65, no. 2: 256–270.

McKenzie, Peter R. 1982. "Death in Early Nigerian Christianity." *Africana Marburgensia* 15, no. 2: 3–16.

Meek, C. 1931. *Tribal Studies in Northern Nigeria.* Vols. 1 and 2. London: K. Paul, Trench, Trubner & Co.

Meister, Conny. 2010. "Remarks on Early Iron Age Burial Sites from Southern Cameroon." *African Archaeological Review* 27: 237–249.

Meyer, Birgit. 2004. "Christianity in Africa: From African Independent to Pentecostal-Charismatic Churches." *Annual Review of Anthropology* 33: 447–474.

Middleton, John. 1971. "The Concept of the Person among the Lugbara of Uganda." In *La Notion de Personne en Afrique Noire,* ed. G. Dieterlen. Paris: Centre National de la Recherche Scientifique.

Morovich, Barbara. 2003. "Pollution ou Libération? Le dilemme de la mort dans les Eglises *akûrino.*" In *Les figures de la mort à Nairobi: Une capitale sans cimetières,* eds. Y. Droz and H. Maupeu. Paris: L'Harmattan.

Morris, Brian. 2000. *Animals and Ancestors: An Ethnography.* Oxford: Berg.

Muller, Jean-Claude. 1976. "Of Souls and Bones: The Living and the Dead among the Rukuba." *Africa* 46, no. 3: 258–273.

Mwilambwe, Claude and Angèle Osako. 2005. "Départs et succession: rites funéraires." *Cahiers Africains* 71: 191–216.

Ngubane, Sihawukele. 2004. "Traditional Practices on Burial Systems with Special Reference to the Zulu People of South Africa." *Indilinga African Journal of Indigenous Knowledge Systems* 3, no. 2: 171–177.

Ngwenya, Barbara Ntombi. 2002. "Gender, Dress and Self-Empowerment: Women and Burial Societies in Botswana." *African Sociological Review* 6, no. 2: 1–27.

Noret, Joël. 2004. "Morgues et prise en charge de la mort au Sud-Bénin." *Cahiers d'Etudes africaines* 176: 745–767.

———. 2010. *Deuil et funérailles dans le Bénin méridional. Enterrer à tout prix.* Brussels: Editions de l'Université de Bruxelles.

Noret, Joël and Pierre Petit. 2011. *Mort et dynamiques sociales au Katanga (République Démocratique du Congo).* Tervuren and Paris: MRAC-L'Harmattan.

Nyambedha, Erik O., Simiyu Wandibba and Jens Aagaard-Hansen. 2003. "Changing patterns of orphan care due to the HIV epidemic in western Kenya." *Social Science and Medicine* 57: 301–311.

Offiong, Essien A. 1987. "Efik Traditional Concepts of Death and the Hereafter." *Africana Marburgensia* 12: 45–54.

Ogbuagu, Stella C. 1991. "Changing Burial Practices in Nigeria: Some evidence from the obituaries." *Savanna* 12, no. 1: 21–33.

Okite, Odhiambo. 1999. "Toppling Tradition?" *Christianity Today* 43, no. 10: 30–31.

Onunwa, Udobata. 1987. "A re-examination of the meaning and significance of the mask among the Ibibio." *Africana Marburgensia* 12: 36–44.

Ottenberg, Simon. 1955. "Improvement Associations among the Afikpo Ibo." *Africa* 25, no. 1: 1–28.

Page, Ben. 2007. "Slow-Going: The mortuary, modernity, and the hometown association in Bali-Nyonga." *Africa* 77, no. 3: 419–441.

Parker, John. 2000. "The Cultural Politics of Death and Burial in Early Colonial Accra." In *Africa's Urban Past,* eds. D. Anderson and R. Rathbone. Portsmouth, NH: Heinemann.

Parkin, David. 1991. *Sacred Void.* Cambridge: University of Cambridge Press.

Pawlik, Jacek. 2008. "Funeral Practices in the Context of Sociocultural Change in Northern Togo." Unpublished manuscript.

Peatrik, Anne-Marie. 1991. "Le Chant des Hyènes Tristes: Essai sur les rites Funéraires des Meru du Kenya et des Peuples Apparentés." *Systèmes de Pensée en Afrique Noire* 11: 103–130.

Peel, John D. Y. 2000. *Religious Encounter and the Making of the Yoruba.* Bloomington: Indiana University Press.

Petit, Agathe. 2005. "Des funérailles de l'entre-deux rituels funéraires des migrants Manjak en France." *Archives de Sciences Sociales des Religions* 131–132: 87–99.

Petit, Pierre, ed. 2003. *Ménages de Lubumbashi entre précarité et recomposition.* Paris: L'Harmattan.

Potash, Betty. 1986. *Widows in African Societies: Choices and Constraints*. Stanford: Stanford University Press.

Pradelles de Latour, Charles-Henry. 1991. *Ethnopsychanalyse en Pays Bamileke*. Paris: EPEL.

Ranger, Terence. 2004. *"Dignifying Death*: the Politics of Burial in Bulawayo." *Journal of Religion in Africa* 34, nos. 1–2: 110–144.

Rubbers, Benjamin. 2006. "L'effondrement de la Générale des Carrières et des Mines. Chronique d'un processus de privatisation informelle." *Cahiers d'Etudes Africaines* 181: 115–133.

Sahlins, Marshall. 2008. *The Western Illusion of Human Nature*. Chicago: Prickly Paradigm.

Schapera, Isaac. [1937] 1950. *The Bantu-Speaking Tribes of South Africa*. New York: Humanities Press.

Schoepf, Brooke G. 2003. "Uganda: Lessons for AIDS control in Africa." *Review of African Political Economy* 30, no. 98: 553–572.

Schoffeleers, Matthew. 2000. *Religion and the Dramatisation of Life: Spirit Beliefs and Rituals in Southern and Central Malawi*. Blantyre: CLAIM.

Sepeng, J. P. 1969. "Ukubuyisa and contemporary funeral rites." *Report of (Lutheran) Missiological Institute Umpumulo on Concepts of Death and Funeral Rites*. Lutheran Theological College, Natal, South Africa.

Shiino, Wakano. 1997. "Death and Rituals among the Luo in South Nyanza." *African Study Monographs* 18, nos. 3–4: 213–228.

Smith, Daniel J. 2004. "Burials and Belonging in Nigeria: Rural-Urban Relations and Social Inequality in a Contemporary African Ritual." *American Anthropologist* 106, no. 3: 569–579.

Spijker, Gerard Van't. 1990. *Les Usages Funéraires et la Mission de L'Eglise: Une étude anthropologique et théologique des rites funéraires au Rwanda*. Uitgeversmij j.j. Kok-Kampen.

———. 2005. "The Role of Social Anthropology in the Debate on Funeral Rites in Africa." *Exchange* 34, no. 3: 156–176.

———. 2008. "Funeral Customs in Rwanda: Change and Continuity." Unpublished paper.

Strickland, Richard S. 2004. *To Have and to Hold: Women's Property and Inheritance Rights in the Context of HIV/AIDS in Sub-Saharan Africa*. Washington: International Center for Research on Women.

Taylor, Timothy. 2002. *The Buried Soul: How Humans Invented Death*. Boston: Beacon.

Thomas, Louis-Vincent. 1982. *La Mort Africaine: idéologie funéraire en Afrique Noire*. Paris: Payot.

Tonda, Joseph. 2000. "Enjeux du deuil et rapports sociaux de sexe au Congo." *Cahiers d'Etudes Africaines* 157: 5–24.

van der Geest, Sjaak. 2000. "Funerals for the living. Conversations with elderly people in Kwahu (Ghana)." *African Studies Review* 43, no. 3: 103–129.

———. 2004. "Dying peacefully: Considering good death and bad death in Kwahu-Tafo, Ghana." *Social Science and Medicine* 58, no. 5: 899–911.

———. 2006. "Between Death and Funeral: Mortuaries and the Exploitation of Liminality in Kwahu, Ghana." *Africa* 76, no. 4: 485–501.

van der Veer, Peter, ed. 1996. *Conversion to Modernities: The Globalization of Christianity*. New York: Routledge.

Vangu Ngimbi, Ivan. 1997. *Jeunesse, funérailles et contestation socio-politique en Afrique*. Paris: L'Harmattan.

van Santen, José. 1995. "We attend but no longer dance: Changes in Mafa funeral practices due to Islamization." In *Mort et rites funéraires dans le bassin du Lac Tchad,* eds. C. Baroin, D. Barreteau, C. von Graffenried. Paris: ORSTOM.

van Santen, José and Thera Rasing, eds. In press. *Gender and Death in Africa.* Münster: Lit Verlag.

Vansina, Jan. 1973. *The Tio Kingdom of the Middle Congo 1880-1892.* London: Oxford University Press.

———. 2005. "Ambaca Society and the Slave Trade *c.* 1760–1845." *Journal of African History* 46: 1–27.

Verdzekov, Paul (Archbishop). 1992. "Message to the Christian People on the Rite of Funerals." Archdiocese of Bamenda, Cameroon. February 29.

Verhoef, Grietjie. 2002. "Money, Credit and Trust: Voluntary Savings Organisations in South Africa in historical perspective." Paper presented to the International Economic History Association Congress, Buenos Aires, July 22–26 2002.

Vidal, Claudine. 1986. "Funérailles et Conflit Social en Côte d'Ivoire." *Politique Africaine* 24: 9–19.

Vivian, Brian C. 1992. "Sacred to Secular: Transitions in Akan Funerary Customs." In *An African Commitment,* eds. Judy Sterner and Nicholas David. Calgary: University of Calgary Press.

Vollbrecht, Judith A. 1978. "Structure and Communitas in an Ashanti Village: The Role of Funerals." PhD diss., University of Pittsburgh.

Walls, Andrew. 2002. *The Cross Cultural Process in Christian History.* Maryknoll, NY: Orbis.

Werbner, Richard. 2004. *Reasonable Radicals and Citizenship in Botswana.* Bloomington: Indiana University Press.

White, Seodi Venekai-Rudo. 2002. *Dispossessing the Widow: Gender based violence in Malawi.* Blantyre: Christian Literature Association in Malawi.

Widlok, Thomas. 1998. "Unearthing Culture: Khoisan Funerals and Social Change." *Anthropos* 93: 115–126.

Wilson, Monica. 1957. *Rituals of Kinship Among the Nyakyusa.* Oxford: Oxford University Press.

CHAPTER 2

A Decent Death

Changes in Funerary Rites in Bulawayo

Terence Ranger

Africanist scholars have often made a distinction between a countryside full of "culture" and townships full of traditional anomie. Indeed, academics and some politicians still assume that Africans in towns are unable to create their own culture.[1] The history of funerary rites in Bulawayo, and in particular the crucial *umbuyiso* ceremony a year or so after death, however, reveal the creativity of cultural agents in the urban environment. Elites, migrants, Christians: all played a role in making new arrangements, revising rituals, and forming associations to take care of their own, thus dignifying death in their own way, something that has become much more difficult to do today with AIDS and more casual attitudes towards death.

Though southern African urban social history has flourished in the last decade (e.g., Maylam and Edwards 1996), when I began to research the social history of African Bulawayo, I assumed that I would be dealing with a story of the colonial creation of a town, with white repression and with African resistance. This is certainly a widely shared view. When I talked about my Bulawayo research at the University of Pennsylvania, a member of the University of Zimbabwe's literature department told me: "If your book is entertaining, it will be of no interest to us." All that one needed to know about the history of Africans in Bulawayo up to 1980, he said, was that they had been "crushed under the boot of colonialism." They had been denied citizenship, had been unable to exercise agency, and had been unable to create culture. Given such a perspective, all that could be said about the politics of death for Bulawayo Africans was that they were forced to be buried in soulless Municipal cemeteries. If they were "paupers" or kinless, they were wheeled naked in barrows to be piled up in a common grave.

It seemed that the social, cultural, and religious history of African Bulawayo was bound to be very different from the fascinating essays in Anderson and Rathbone's collection about precolonial African cities and the twentieth century history of long established towns like Tunis and Kumasi. In these essays, there was a great deal of African agency and cultural politics. There was certainly what John Parker in his chapter on early colonial Accra calls "the cultural politics of death and burial" (Parker 2005: 205–221). As I read Parker, I was of course struck by the great differences between Accra and Bulawayo.

But I realized that these differences arose at least as much from differences in African perceptions as they did from differences between imperial and white settler societies. There had never been among Africans in Zimbabwe what Parker calls "intramural sepulture"—the interment of people in the floors of their houses. Nor did there develop in Bulawayo itself "a new form of social action—mausoleum politics."[2] However, having read Parker, I began to look at the Bulawayo data with fresh eyes. I found there abundant evidence—in oral interviews, in African newspapers, in the minutes and correspondence of burial societies—of urban African cultures and politics of death.[3] This was as different from what happened in Accra as it was different from what happened in the Zimbabwean countryside. But these urban practices seemed to constitute an important dimension of black Bulawayo's social and cultural history. As a recent study of "funerals and the public space of sentiment" in urban Botswana insists: "Funerals are key to the exercise of civil conduct." People at funeral ceremonies are "managing the social impact of sentiments of sorrow, love, jealousy, anger, and resignation … preventing recognized differences from causing permanent disruptions in social relations. In the context of death, people shape forms of community and difference—along lines of ethnicity, class, religion, gender, and kinship—through the mutuality of their emotions. Funerals thus give rise to a public space and a civil discourse." As in contemporary Gaborone, so in Bulawayo between 1903 and 1960 (Durham and Klaits 2002: 777).

This urban culture of death also seemed to constitute an important element in the Christian history of Bulawayo. It was by no means only Christians who engaged in the struggle to achieve dignified deaths in the townships—many African traditionalists and Muslims were also involved. But there were distinct positions taken by missionaries, by African members of the mission churches, by "Ethiopian" churches, and by "Zionist" and "Apostolic" churches. Certainly from the 1930s onward the politics of death in black Bulawayo were essentially Christian politics, though very divisive and contested ones. They were also increasingly nationalist in character, related to but nevertheless distinct from the secular program of nationalism. By exploring the debates and differences over burial in Bulawayo, we can throw new light on African urban Christianity.

In what follows, I will first discuss to what extent one can talk about a "traditional" culture of death relevant to the black residents of Bulawayo. Then I will seek to argue that Bulawayo was not just another town created entirely by whites, but that from the beginning there was an African "town" within white Bulawayo that developed its own complex, composite urban culture, some part of which was Christian. I will go on to show that in the 1920s and 1930s, the Bulawayo Municipality attempted to break African autonomy and to impose its own model of an African location. At the same time, Christianity became the dominant ideology of black residents. Overall, I will explore the implications of this for the politics of burial throughout the industrializing years of the 1940s and 1950s, during which the Bulawayo African population grew so rapidly.

Death and burial among the Ndebele

Modern Bulawayo was never a purely Ndebele town. Nevertheless, it was from the beginning very different from colonial Salisbury. Salisbury grew up more or less in isolation from the surrounding Shona-speaking countryside, and for decades its African population overwhelmingly consisted of northern migrants (Yoshikuni 1999). By contrast, both black and white Bulawayo were built adjacent to Lobengula's town. From the beginning, both the black and white sectors were constructed of the same wooden and thatched materials, and for many years Africans in the "Location" were more or less left to manage themselves. Africans built and rented their own houses. They buried their dead themselves—at first mainly children—in ground just to the north of the Location, where Mzilikazi township later developed.[4] There were many connections with the Ndebele past. Several of Lobengula's queens lived in the Location and offered hospitality there to visiting members of the Ndebele royal family. Other Ndebele aristocrats were among the black "pioneers" who established the African urban society of the new Bulwayo. These Ndebele Location dwellers maintained close connection with the countryside and its funerary practices.

Ndebele rites of death were very different from those found in Anlo or among the Fante of Ghana. No one was buried in a house. Men were buried in oxskins near the cattle pen; women were buried near the granary. The first king, Mzilikazi, was buried in a cave in the eastern Matopos Hills; no one knew where his son, Lobengula, was buried. For commoners, a grave was dug and the body was placed lying on its side in a recess—*ingoxo*—made in the side. The body was surrounded by space rather than covered by earth, the *ingoxo* was closed up with logs, and then the main grave was filled with soil and covered with stones. The body had to be buried with its face looking to the direction from which the person's ancestors had come. Those who carried out the burial had to be purified with herbs and the digging tools had to be ritually cleansed.

All this was important, but much more crucial was the *umbuyiso* ceremony carried out at the grave a year or so after the burial. Pathisa Nyathi (2001: 133–34), the leading historian of the Ndebele, asserts that the *umbuyiso* "forms the basis of Ndebele religion":

If the dead are not brought back, the living man will not communicate with them. The dead need to be elevated from the status of the dead to that of the living dead. The dead live only when they are part of the community that embraces them and the living . . . If the living do not take steps to bring the dead to life, the living dead cannot exist. If the living do not attribute events to spiritual influence, the communications system will collapse.

The performance of an *umbuyiso*—accompanied by the brewing of special beer, the sacrifice of a beast, invocation of the dead—was the key testimony of a dignified death. The ritual was not performed for the childless, for witches, or for suicides. It turned the dead into ancestors: it ended the period of mourning for a widow and it allowed for the distribution of property.

It became increasingly difficult to carry out this kind of burial, and particularly to perform *umbuyiso* ceremonies, in the Bulawayo Location. The Municipal authorities, when they established cemeteries, dug graves that lacked recesses and that all pointed in the same direction. They did not allow animal sacrifice. Missionaries prohibited the *umbuyiso* ceremony. But it was still possible to carry out "traditional" ceremonies during the first two decades of the Location's history, and in the 1950s cultural nationalists supported the "Ethiopian" churches that performed *umbuyiso* rites. By that time, Ndebele tradition had, for nationalists, become a symbol of African heritage as a whole and *umbuyiso* rites were carried out for well known men, whether "Ndebele" or not.

Rites of death for the pioneers of early black Bulawayo

In the years before the Bulawayo Municipality began to assert control over the Location, black urban culture was led by three different groups. There was an elite Ndebele group, consisting of the queens and those members of aristocratic or royal families who had acquired mission education and who had entered the colonial economy as truck drivers, clerks, interpreters, etc. These men established urban dynasties and their sons emerged as social, athletic, and political leaders in the 1940s. There was a group of educated Christian immigrants from Bechuanaland and South Africa. And there were Africans who built houses, lived in some of them, and rented the rest out to tenants. The majority of these builders were women of very varied ethnicity, some Ndebele, but also Sotho, Xhosa, "Colored," and Shona. These powerful landladies are remembered even today as great characters. They were later remembered as the first permanent occupants of the Location, enjoying what amounted to complete ownership of the land and property, until from the late 1920s onwards the Municipality forced them to hand over their holdings.

These three different urban elites had different strategies of death and different concepts of dignity. Some of the Ndebele elite, including some of the queens, were staunch Christians. Nevertheless, they desired Ndebele traditional rituals as well as Christian ceremonies in order to give meaning to their deaths and to renew their links with their rural clans. The educated South African immigrants, on the other hand, asserted an entirely nontraditional Christian identity. They aspired to dignified church funerals, with Christian graveside ceremonies in the cemetery. But many of the female house builders—especially those who had used prostitution to raise the capital needed to lease stands and build houses—were not in good standing with the churches. They could not enjoy lavish Christian burials, and many of them were not Ndebele. Yet black urban society itself insisted that they were dignified as pioneers.

Old Prince Gumede recalls the death politics of the Ndebele residents of the Bulawayo Location (or Makokoba, as it came to be called):

> If a person who died had a homestead in rural areas, the *umbuyiso* ceremony for him/her was conducted in the rural area. But if that person's body was buried in the township his/her relatives would come from the rural areas and then go to the grave . . . They would start performing various traditional rituals there, talking to the grave, saying "We have today come to take you (your spirit) so that you could go and protect your children." After that they would then take some soil from the grave and go with that to the dead person's homestead. When in the rural area these relatives would then sprinkle that soil around the place which used to be the deceased's favorite resting place at home ... They would then perform other rituals there to complete the ceremony amid great feasting on beer and meat.

Gumede went on to contrast these urban-rural interactions with the death rituals held for "those people who had their roots in the township." In their case, there could also be *umbuyiso* ceremonies, but:

> For each and every one of them [it] was always conducted in the township. I used to attend a lot of these ceremonies and even nowadays there are a lot of these ceremonies conducted here in Makokoba. Right now I can still remember that a number of popular township women who earlier on had their own stands, like Mazonde, Masuku, Sipambaniso's mother, and many more had *umbuyiso* ceremonies conducted here in the township after their death.[5]

N. Moyo also recalls:

> Permanent township dwellers like those who owned stands had their *umbuyiso* ceremonies conducted in the township. Second and Third

street areas in Makokoba were earlier on occupied by women who owned stands and these were the people we always referred to as the real true citizens of Makokoba.[6]

The holding of an urban *umbuyiso* was certainly not a means of avoiding the expense of elite Christian death rites. A "traditional" burial in itself might be simpler and cheaper than a Christian interment. But the ceremony held a year later was an elaborate and expensive affair. The whole point was that the later ceremony was collective and communal, involving kin and neighbors. It ran for three days, commencing with the rituals at the grave on a Friday night and continuing with feasting in the township on a Saturday.

A cow and a goat were purchased in the countryside; the cow was slaughtered there and its meat ferried "to the township, where it was then cooked in preparation for the feasting part of the *umbuyiso* ceremony." The goat was taken to the Location alive. On Friday night, it was led to the grave. "The relatives would start performing the rituals … declaring that 'we have come to take your spirit with this goat so that you can protect your children.'" The goat was sacrificed and its meat "eaten during the night of that Friday." On Saturday, the feast took place. Beer had been brewed in preparation "just behind the house," using grain contributed freely by relatives and neighbors. "On a Saturday again the relatives would choose the deceased's older son or daughter as the family's new leading spirit-incarnate or *ukamba*."[7]

Such ceremonies ran into difficulties during the 1930s and 1940s when the Municipality was asserting its control of the Location, its housing, and its cemetery. All beer drinking was supposed to take place in the Municipal Beer Hall so that people brewing ritual beer for an *umbuyiso* behind a Location house could be arrested by Municipal police. Animal sacrifice was banned in the cemetery, which was patrolled by watchmen, so the Friday night ceremonies at the grave had to be attenuated or abandoned. Nevertheless, the idea that the "owners of the Location" should be buried with special honors persisted even after the Municipality had bought out all the plot holders and knocked down most of their houses. In the 1950s, the Bulawayo Townships Advisory Board, which represented Makokoba and Mzilikazi, kept "a very few graves specially reserved" in the old cemetery "for people who are in the opinion of the BATAB fit to be buried there" because of their contributions to the community. A special place had replaced a special ceremony as a marker of dignified death.[8]

Dignifying migrant deaths: sending the dead back home

From the earliest days of the Bulawayo Location, and increasingly with the Municipal policy in the 1940s of replacing family houses with accommodation for "single" men, migrant workers came to live in Makokoba. (Many of the tenants who rented huts around the houses of the powerful landladies were men of this sort.) The Location was a place of many cultures, even if Ndebele and Christian cultures were the most prestigious:

> You know [says the septuagenarian Mrs. Bhelamina Ndlovu] this Township, small as it may appear, is a vast place, I tell you. It has many people of different ethnicities, of different cultures and beliefs, and it is very possible for one to stay in Makokoba for many years without knowing that something like funeral ceremonies are being held.[9]

Mzongelwayizayizizwe Khumalo was born in 1910 and came to Bulawayo with his parents in 1918. He was brought up in the Location, *ezitendini*, "in the stands of pole and dagga huts." He remembers the period of relatively unfettered African practices of burial before the Municipal takeover:

> In the 1920s and 1930s, Africans were not buried in coffins in the townships. Their bodies were just wrapped in blankets and then carried in *ithala*, a stretcherlike thing, for burial … Africans used to dig their own graves where they buried their deceased relatives and friends.[10]

As we have seen, this allowed *umbuyiso* ceremonies to be performed by long term Ndebele Location residents and for famous women stand holders. But it also allowed the expression of many different "traditional" practices. "During that time," recalls Khumalo, "people were buried according to their traditional customs":

> Not all people were buried facing upwards as we see now. The typical Ndebele families used to bury the body of their deceased placed sideways, facing the south where they originated from. The AmaNyasaranda (Nyasas) would also bury their dead according to that custom, not facing upwards.

Some Nyasa migrants enjoyed a good deal of prestige in the colonial economy of Bulawayo. They provided many of the waiters and chefs for the town's hotels. When advisory boards were established in Makokoba in the 1940s, they were dominated for a time by Nyasas, led by the head waiter at the Bulawayo Club. But Nyasas expressed their urban identity not only in terms of modern politics. They also maintained an important fiction about their traditional rural affiliations, which they expressed through the politics of death:

> We always believed [says Khumalo] that the AmaNyasaranda took their dead back to their country for burials … We wondered how they did that but we later realized that they performed rituals which con-

vinced them that they had sent their dead back home, whilst in fact they had buried him/her in Bulawayo.[11]

Madliwayo, a Ndebele woman married to a Mozambican migrant, told us that she was "not well versed in the Christian religion." But she clearly remembers "the traditional religion which was mostly practiced by foreigners in towns." Migrants from Northern Rhodesia and Mozambique would "meet according to their place of origin and hold private sessions, singing their traditional songs. They would meet at a certain place behind doors … honouring their ancestors and asking for protection in a foreign land." These rituals extended to burials. Tonga migrant workers danced and drummed at funerals, and other people kept well away from these often violent occasions. People of all nationalities were careful to confine as well as to express the power of their dead. As Madliwayo explains, "from the cemetery people would wash their feet at the gate with water mixed with some traditional medicines meant to chase the spirit of death and protect those remaining alive."[12]

In Bulwayo, as in all the towns of southern Africa, migrant workers banded together voluntarily in self help contributory associations. These existed for all sorts of purposes—to help in the purchase of clothes or property, to assist at times of illness or unemployment, to assert a certain standard of conduct—but above all, to ensure a dignified funeral. The first burial societies were established by Nyasa migrants, like the West Nyasa Burial Society, whose constitution set down that the society had "nothing to do with outside persons who do not belong to your family."[13] Soon other northern migrants were founding their own, like the Achewa North Rhodesia East Province Helping Society, which was headed by Manjoni, kitchen boy at the Grand Hotel, who lived in Makokoba with his wife and children.

There are passing references to these burial associations in the African press.[14] But the great source for their history are the files on African associations compiled by Bulawayo's director of native administration, Hugh Ashton, in the late 1950s.[15] The extraordinary variety of societies recorded in these files reveals that the politics of death underlie every kind of association in black Bulawayo.

Some of them have an "ethnic" character, though large "ethnicities"—like the Chewa—were often broken down into smaller regional groupings. These ethnic associations often stated as a major objective their desire to preserve "traditional" burial customs. The Lunda Unity Association declared that its purpose was "to see that Lunda customs, manners, and culture are preserved in death." Other associations claimed a territorial rather than an ethnic base. One was the Bechuanaland Cultural Society, which aimed to provide for "the burial of their kind … with necessary modifications to suit the environment."[16] The Northern Rhodesian Chiefs Unity Association consisted of "tribal representatives" who were "anxious to deal with family squabbles according to their tribal customs." They sought to relax the Municipal ban on funeral beer by asking that "when one of their people dies they would like a permit to buy £1 of beer to be consumed by the relatives in the house of the tribal representative."[17] Other associations were pan-African like the African Unity Burial Society, which aspired to run its own funeral parlor. Some were explicitly religious—like the Nyasaland Muslim Association, which existed to ensure Islamic burial rites and which was headed by Issa, night watchman at the Bulawayo Mosque.

Others were occupational, bringing together hawkers, carpenters, or industrial workers, and operating to protect their interests, but also offering sickness and death benefits. A dignified death had become by the 1950s not only a death properly marked by traditional, Christian, or Muslim ritual, but also a death marked by decency—a proper coffin, properly conveyed to the cemetery, and attended by properly dressed mourners. This was an aspiration of the most "modern" and least "traditional" inhabitants of black Bulawayo. The African section of the Native Welfare Society ran a burial fund for its progressive members; the Bulawayo African Townships Women's Association, made up solely of respectable married women, collected money to hire a bus to travel "to the graveyards and back only for women of the Association who crammed themselves in all the available space."[18] Young modernizers were no exception. The splendidly named African Jiving Society, formed in January 1957 in Mabutweni township, aimed to "create mutual understanding and to advance a high standard of jiving among the African people of Southern Rhodesia." It would organize lectures and competitions, assist members when they were sick or arrested, and "bury any deceased member of the Society by providing coffin and transportation."[19]

By the late 1950s, many people in black Bulawayo belonged to more than one such association—ethnic, regional, occupational, recreational—each offering assistance towards a dignified death. The associational form had become so dominant that one was created specifically to remember the original elites of the black town, who once had controlled their own burials—the Bulawayo and District African Pioneer Society, which aimed "to bury pioneers and to erect memorial stones to commemorate the NAMES of those who have served the public."

The Christianization of death in Bulawayo

We tend to take for granted that ethnic burial associations were established in order to preserve—or to reinvent—"traditional" culture. They connected urban migrants to their rural homes. But by the 1950s, the mark of many southern African rural societies had become their specific style of Christianity. In Southern Rhodesia itself, with the allocation of different districts to different missionary societies, migrants arrived in town already equipped with a Methodist or an Anglican or a Catholic culture.

But the most striking example among the associations in Bulawayo was the Nyasa Moyenda Nanga Titani Burial Society. Its constitution laid down that every meeting should begin with a hymn, proceed with prayer, continue with Proverbs 3:6, and conclude with benediction. The Society provided that "if the deceased person is a Christian or was a Christian, a Minister or Evangelist of the very church is liable to direct the funeral accordingly." The verses from Proverbs, however, were equally appropriate to members of any church, making as they did a direct application of biblical wisdom to the facts of urban life:

> Wisdom calls aloud in the streets
> She raises her voice in the public squares
> She calls out at street corners
> She delivers the message at the city gates …
>
> Keep you from the alien woman
> From the stranger with her wheedling words …
> Towards death her house is declining
> Down to the Shades her paths go
>
> My son, do not forget my teaching
> Let your heart keep my principles
> Fear Yahweh and turn your back on evil
> … [else] strangers will batten on your property
> Your labors going to some alien house [20]

But however wary these virtuous migrants were of the snares of the city, long before the late 1950s the culture of black Bulawayo had itself been profoundly Christianized. Indeed, there was a specific Ndebele urban Christian culture which gradually overlaid an earlier insistence on traditional rites of death. Above, I quoted Mzongelwayizayizizwe Khumalo and his account of how in his youth in the 1910s, 1920s, and early 1930s "people were buried according to their traditional customs." But Khumalo also described how "Christian church customs were slowly infiltrating the township."

Khumalo himself was baptized as a Catholic in the name of Petros. He associates Ndebele Christianity with the more austere forms of the mainline mission churches: Catholicism, Anglicanism, Congregationalism, Presbyterianism. Churches like the Jehovah's Witnesses, he says, were known as *ichurchi yamanyasaranda* because they were "brought from Nyasaland." Zionist and Apostolic churches, when they came in the 1950s, were thought of as Shona.

Ndebele Christianity was dour and Ndebele Christian rites of death were sober:

> In the funeral gatherings we were not seeing these singing and danc-
> ing *pungwes* (all night Shona services) during that time. You know,
> typical Ndebele funeral gatherings mourners could sing one Chris-
> tian song and then spend the whole night just quiet on that very sor-
> rowful occasion. If we heard people in a funeral gathering singing
> and playing some traditional drums we could tell that these were not
> Ndebele people.[21]

From the 1930s, Ndebele cultural associations developed in Bulawayo, and in the late 1940s and 1950s, Ndebele-speakers increasingly took over the ad-visory boards from Nyasas. Ndebele identity came to be seen as formed by a combination of royal traditions and mission Christianity. This somber Nde-bele religion combined with Municipal regulations to restrict the ritual oppor-tunities of the old days. The mission churches did not possess their own burial grounds, but interred their dead in the sections of the Municipal cemetery reserved for them. A Ndebele Christian idea of dignity and decency was en-forced on all burial ceremonies. It was no longer possible to take a goat into the Municipal cemetery for sacrifice, nor to engage in competitive Tonga dancing and drumming.

Nduna Tafa, born in 1935, did not attend mission school and was never part of the dominant Christian culture of the Location. He remembers that in the 1950s:

> People complained that burials in town meant following the rules of
> the City Council as it was the Council's burial ground. Some declared
> that according to their custom the heads of their beloved ones had
> to face north in the grave but they had to follow the plan of the City
> Council, which might mean that the head faced east, west or south.
> As they could not follow these customary practices they preferred go-
> ing to the rural areas to bury their beloved ones where they could
> perform all the rituals.[22]

Paradoxically, as urbanization intensified more people—including long term residents of the Location—chose to bury their dead outside Bulawayo.[23]

Nevertheless, black urban Christianity, even Ndebele mission Christianity, offered possibilities of its own for the politics of death in Bulawayo. In fact, those politics developed as contests essentially *between* and *within* different kinds of Christians rather than between Christians and traditionalists. To ex-plore this, we need to move from oral interviews to the African press of the 1940s and 1950s.[24]

By 1940, the Makokoba Location was surrounded by churches and church schools. The Municipality did not allow any formal religious activity inside Makokoba, and churches had to obtain special permission to hold a procession or a march inside the Location. But there were many plots for church buildings immediately adjacent to it. An Anglican church lay to the north; along the eastern flank came the Methodist Episcopal, the Presbyterian, the Dutch Reformed, the Seventh Day Adventists, the Wesleyan Methodists, and the Salvation Army; along the southern side came the main Anglican mission, St. Columba's, the Jesuits, the Churches of Christ, and the Christian Missions in Many Lands. The churches formed a sort of *cordon sanitaire* between the Location and the city.

Adults were drawn to these churches partly because they had been baptized in the various denominations in their home districts. (Thus people from Manicaland went to the American Methodists while people from central Mashonaland went to the Wesleyan Methodists). They went to the churches for weddings. Their children went to the church schools. And though no church possessed a cemetery or burial plot of its own, people went to the churches for funerals. The coffin would be carried from the mortuary to the church and after the service carried to the Municipal cemetery.[25]

By the early 1940s, evangelical activity in Bulawayo was booming. The *Bantu Mirror* of April 22, 1944, described Easter in the Location:

> The Bulawayo African Township inhabitants had the opportunity of listening to religious teaching of all dogmas during the Easter holidays, as many of the local churches conducted services in the streets. Various kinds of religious uniforms, badges, and ribbons, according to the various religious faiths, were worn; these seemed to attract the curiosity of onlookers more than the preaching and teaching ... The climax of this religious activity came on Sunday morning—Resurrection Sunday—when blissful sleepers were awakened by the strains of select religious tunes by worshippers parading the streets.

The *Mirror's* correspondent noted that "some preachers, through excess of zeal or ecstatic hatred of evil," made a point of warning elderly unbelievers "of the awful time they shall have in hell." According to the paper, these warnings were met by younger listeners with indifference or resentment, but they had their effect on the old.

A couple of months earlier, indeed, young Solomon Dizwittie had won a *Mirror* essay prize with thoughts on the generation gap in Makokoba's churches. Because they seemed to condemn pleasure, the churches were shunned by "the young, the gay, the ardent." They attracted only "the sick in their tossing to and fro; the bereaved whose hope is the grave; the aged who front the sunset; and the dying." So far as Dizwittie was concerned, the Christian culture of black

Bulawayo was much too much a culture of death.[26] But however "quiet and sorrowful" Bulawayo's churches seemed to be, they had certainly come to provide a service for the bereaved and dying of the Location.

As we have already seen in discussing the Burial Societies, a constant anxiety in Bulawayo was the prospect of dying either kinless or as a pauper. Bodies unclaimed at the mortuary were flung together, naked, into "a covered handcart" and dumped by African prisoners into mass graves over which no religious service nor ritual of any kind was performed. This was the quintessential undignified death, severing the dead person from their ancestors, their kin, their community, and their religious group.[27]

There were various strategies for avoiding such a fate. One, of course, was to join a burial society. Another and sometimes supplementary strategy was for a migrant to marry a Ndebele woman. Mr. Mowena, who was born in Mozambique in 1928, came to Bulawayo in 1947. He told Hloniphani Ndlovu:

> As a Mozambican, it was obvious that I could not go and be buried in Mozambique if and when I died. As a result, we foreigners had to find some means of burial. Times of death were difficult for us foreigners because it was in such times that one thought of home and became homesick. We were few in a foreign country … It was easier when someone was married to a Ndebele wife. If such a foreigner died, his in-laws usually took the burial and funeral arrangements in their hands … It has been said some foreigners were eager to marry local women to ensure a decent burial.

Mowena himself married an Ndebele girl, though he insists it was not for this reason![28] But another increasingly applied strategy was to join a local church and to trust in the solidarity of its members. Mowena and his wife married in the Roman Catholic church in Makokoba and both later joined Catholic sodalities. As we have seen, many of the Makokoba denominations had connections with migrants from particular districts or countries. (Predictably, the Dutch Reformed Church took this principle the furthest, dividing up seating in the church—and associational life—among the various African ethnic groups represented in its congregation. These DRC ethnic associations acted as burial societies). Other denominations were particularly closely linked to the Ndebele. But as the expenses of a dignified funeral increased, and as the performance of Christian ceremonies and the participation of fellow Christians became more and more essential to a respectable death, long term Ndebele residents of the Location needed the help of churches as much as migrants.

Moreover, there was an additional, gendered dimension. Ndebele wives and mothers had always been included in the traditional culture of death. Nevertheless, even the most honored women had received less dignified burials than men, and unmarried or childless women could not have the *umbuyiso* cer-

emony performed for them. Now the Bulawayo churches offered really elaborate and dignified burials for women.

A long letter to the *Mirror* from a young Presbyterian schoolteacher, Mercy
Sinyoka, illustrates all this well. Mercy's parents lived at Hyde Park Farm,
an area twelve miles from Bulawayo where almost as many people lived as
in Makokoba. Her father was a Northern migrant who worked in the city;
her mother was Ndebele. They were members of the Hyde Park Presbyterian
church. When Mercy's Ndebele mother died in January 1942, it was neither
her own kin nor those of her migrant husband who bestowed dignity.

Mercy received a message that her mother had died and she hurried home:

> Upon my arrival, I realized that people were eagerly waiting for me,
> for I saw them lined up patrolling about the hole, comforting and
> cheering the old man, my father … As the old man did not have any
> of his own people to encourage him, his church members who are so
> very kind stood beside him.

A leading role was taken by the chairwomen of the Presbyterian associations of Makokoba and Hyde Park. But in addition to "my mother church,"
comfort was offered by "every denomination of Hyde Park Farm." As Mercy
testified, Reverend Tshiminya, the Hyde Park Presbyterian minister, took "no
rest day and night in such disasters. I lack a thousand tongues to thank him."
Mercy was deeply comforted: "The grave is closed upon the dead and opened
for the living."[29] Oral informants speak equally positively about church burials
of women. As the septuagenarian Mrs. S. Nkomo told Busani Mpofu about
funerals in the 1940s and 1950s:

> In the funeral gatherings of that time all women used to wear some-
> thing on their heads as a sign of respecting the dead. In a funeral gath-
> ering you could find people there in a very sorrowful state, I tell you,
> with most of them crying and sobbing. Those singing church songs
> did so at their lowest, controlled voices to show that they were sing-
> ing on a very sorrowful occasion. The relatives and church members
> used to contribute towards meeting funeral expenses. If the deceased
> had been a full church member, especially in our Methodist Church,
> only women members carried the coffin of the deceased if the de-
> ceased was a woman. If the deceased was a male church member male
> church members were responsible for carrying the coffin.[30]

These are touching testimonies of the comfort which could be offered by
the black Bulawayo Christian culture of death. But it became increasingly clear
that there were also serious flaws in it. It was a culture whose rhetoric was
unity. But in several ways it divided. It divided Christians from traditionalists.
It divided "respectable" women from others. It divided rich and poor. And it
divided "mission boys" from "independent Africans."[31]

In the early 1950s, black Christian ministers persuaded the Makokoba advisory board to divide the African cemetery into two parts—one for *Makolwa* (Christians) and the other for *Maqaba* (heathens). This spatial division "even in the grave" was bitterly opposed by Makokoba's rising cultural nationalists, who claimed to speak in the name of the general township population. When a new cemetery was opened in July 1957, and was divided on the same lines as the old, Ngcebetsha's *Home News* described the people of Makokoba as "wild with anger and resentment … the so-called non-Christians are part and parcel of them, being bone of their bone, blood of their blood, and flesh of their flesh."[32] An editorial a month later complained that "members of one family have to buried at different sections of one graveyard, the psychological effect being that one whose body is placed in a Christian grave his soul goes to God, while the one buried in a non-Christian grave his soul goes to hell." Peter Lesabe of the "Ethiopian" African Methodist Episcopal Church, which had become increasingly influential among Bulawayo's cultural nationalists, wrote that "some have taken up the task of judging the living and the dead—treading where angels fear to tread."[33]

The uniformed women's associations of the mainline churches organized splendid funerals for women—but only for some women. To receive the full burial ritual, the dead woman had to be a "full member" of the church, and she had to be a monogamously married wife. So far as men were concerned, the difference between a truly dignified funeral and an ordinary one was less the result of differential piety and more the result of differential reputation and wealth. By the end of the 1950s, the mark of an outstanding funeral was its size, its opulence, and the number of "leading men" who attended it. Prestige funerals became leading features of the elite social calendar.

In a single month—September 1956—Ngcebetsha's *Home News* reported no less than four "dignified" funerals, each attended by the editor himself. One was the "biggest funeral at Luveve"—the government-built village north of Makokoba. The dead man was a famous young footballer and community leader, Stephen Chigumira. Fifty-three cars brought mourners. There were speeches by representatives of the advisory board, the African Chamber of Commerce, the Mashonaland Cultural Society, and by Ngcebetsha himself. African ministers of several different churches attended.[34]

Another was the funeral of Reverend Thompson Samkange, the Methodist pioneer and ex-African National Congress president, who was based at the time of his death at the Makokoba Wesleyan church. His memorial service there was "suffocatingly overcrowded." The most expensive type of coffin was donated by the leading firm of undertakers. The Bulawayo associations met all the expenses of sending the coffin and the Samkange family back to Thompson's Native Purchase farm in Makwiro. Full reports appeared in the Bulawayo African press. Thompson's brother, Zacharia, declared that "the funeral at Makwiro was the largest he had ever seen," with "scores of cars and lorries."

There were dozens of white and black clergy and a crowd of two thousand. Afterward, Zacharia came to Bulawayo to thank the Wesleyan Methodist congregation, with tears in his eyes:

> I am the voice and eyes of the elders who have sent me to you to give expression of their feelings for the marvellous work you did in raising such a lot of money for the burial at such very short notice ... My brother was dearly loved by you all.[35]

Such funerals were regarded as the finest fruit of Bulawayo's Christian culture of death. But they contrasted all the more painfully with the interment of "deceased Africans, [who] because they have neither relatives or friends to attend to their burial, are buried by the Government in the most shameful manner, in that prisoners just put them into the grave anyhow without that respect and dignity that is naturally due to the dead." To do him justice, while he gloried in the lavish funerals, Ngcebetsha lamented that the Christian culture did not extend to paupers. No prayers were said over *their* graves. He demanded that the Bulawayo Municipality engage an African minister to conduct a service instead of "them being buried as though they were dead dogs."[36]

The practice of Bulawayo's Christian culture of death, then, divided "heathens" from believers, "respectable" women from ordinary women, wealthy and well known men from impoverished and unknown ones. It also increasingly created tensions between white missionaries and their loyal converts on the one hand and critical black Christians on the other. The most spectacular example of this was the "Sign of the Cross" scandal of November 1956. This was given extensive coverage in Ngcebetsha's *Home News*. The scandal took place in the "Fingo Location" outside Bulawayo, and Ngcebetsha was a "Fingo" who had come up from South Africa in the 1920s. The scandal involved the Free Presbyterian church, the dominant mission among the Fingo. Ngcebetsha came in the 1920s to teach in the Presbyterian mission school. By 1956, however, he had ceased to be a teacher and was running a shop and a newspaper in Mzilikazi township. He had also ceased to be a mainline Presbyterian and instead supported the breakaway African Presbyterian Church. The "Sign of the Cross" scandal was meat and drink to him.

In November 1956, a Fingo resident of Makokoba, Mvuleni Mzamo, died. His body was escorted back to the Fingo Location on the next morning by several of Bulawayo's big men. Mzamo was a member of the Free Presbyterian church and his widow, a staunch member of the Presbyterian Women's Association, wanted him buried with the rites of the church. But by four in the afternoon, no missionary had arrived to perform the service, nor had permission been sent for one to be conducted by Cecil Sobantu, the Presbyterian deacon. The big men from Bulawayo and Mzamo's male relatives overruled his widow, whom they declared to have no rights in the matter by "Fingo custom." Instead, they asked a local Methodist preacher, Skapeyi Ndatyana, to conduct the service, according to "Christian rites and Fingo customs." The widow looked on, stonefaced.

The service was almost concluded when a white Free Presbyterian deacon, Norman Miller, arrived. In the view of the big men from Bulawayo, Miller was improperly dressed in his shirt sleeves. Miller was furious to discover a Methodist funeral going on in his church. (It is not recorded whether he noticed the "Fingo customs"). In the middle of prayers and ignoring the male elders, he went over to Mrs. Nzamo and asked her what was going on, "in defiance of Fingo codes and customs." She told him "that she was not consulted about the funeral service ... sufficient [declared the Fingo Council] to warrant a charge against her. For this she is likely to lose her rights as wife." And then Miller really saw red—or rather, black and white. On Mzamo's coffin was a cloth bearing a white cross on a back background. Miller rushed to the coffin "and tore off the cross sign saying that his church was not the Roman Catholic church which did this sort of thing and that he would not tolerate that being done with members of his church."

There was a furious reaction. Young men wanted to assault Miller; "the womenfolk burst into a loud cry." The Bulwayo delegation returned to Makokoba and Mzilikazi where they spread news of this "disgrace." The Fingo Council declared that Miller must never enter the area again. "Our moral feelings," they declared in a memorandum to the provincial native commissioner, "have been unparalleledly wounded"; in the days "when the government of the Africans was still wholly in their hands, the penalty would have been obvious—capital punishment."

Ngcebetsha himself took full opportunity of this chance to express his Ethiopian feelings: "We think it is not right for European missionaries to fight about our African people, dead or alive." Africans possessed a fundamental moral code and a culture of death which must be respected. Missionaries must "allow the work of God among Africans to be carried on by Africans themselves." Africans must act to prevent their "mortal remains being played with."[37]

Challenging and learning from mission Christianity: memorializing kings

There were few missionary provocations as flagrant as Miller's. But missionary control of black urban Christianity was widely resented because of the white prohibition on expressions of veneration of the African dead. As always, it was Ngcebetsha who expressed this most frequently and strongly. As well as carrying Makokoba news and commentary in his newspaper, he wrote a serialized story about two Ndebele Christians called Mary and Tshuma. The couple could not have a baby because, writes Ngcebetsha, "like parrots they follow the ways of the white people and even go so far as to worship the Gods of other races." When Tshuma consults a prophetess in Makokoba, she tells him that "the cause of the whole trouble" is that his "father's spirit is angry" because Tshuma no longer makes offerings to it. In a later episode, Tshuma's uncle Sikalele tells him: "These Christian churches of yours could not possibly be right if their doctrines compel you to do away with the fundamental customs of our race." After all, says Sikalele, white missionaries are just hypocritical when they condemn veneration of the African dead. They themselves "worship" Cecil Rhodes![38] The whites have a culture of the dead, but they deny it to Africans.

This was a constant theme in the African press in the 1940s and 1950s. Every year white missionaries took part in the annual service at Rhodes's statue in Main Street in the center of Bulawayo. Bishops and moderators led pilgrimages to Rhodes's grave in the Matopos Hills.[39] In 1953 Joshua Nkomo, black Bulawayo's leading trade unionist and nationalist—in cultural matters a close ally of Ngcebetsha—visited London. He went to Westminister Abbey and to the Chapel Royal in Windsor "and walked on the grave of kings":

> I began to think [wrote Nkomo later] about Christianity and power. At home becoming a Christian meant giving up all our old ways to follow white clergymen and a white Christ. Our religion, in which we approached God through our ancestors, and the history of our people, was said to be primitive and backward. But here in England the ancestral tombs in the churches signified the community of the nation (Nkomo 1984: 52).

Of course, the white Christian culture of the famous dead was different from African traditions. Africans were—and remain—horrified at the idea of burying the dead in the floors of churches. Their kings were not on public display, to be visited by any man, woman, or child. But as well as using it as proof of white hypocrisy, Bulawayo's cultural nationalists were impressed by the prestige of white memorial culture. They wanted monuments and pilgrimages for dead African chiefs and kings. For more than a decade before Ngcebetsha's call for African action, indeed, some of Bulawayo's Christian young men had been playing their own mind games with African "mortal remains."

In the early 1940s, two Christian young men, one a Ndebele and the other a Manyika, became close friends. Together they represented the new elite culture of black Bulawayo. They both worked at Stanley Hall, the social hub of Makokoba. One was Arthur Sipambaniso Manyoba Kumalo, the quintessence of the township's Ndebele tradition. Sipambaniso's father, a member of the royal clan, had been involved in transportation; his mother was one of the famous pioneer landowners. In the early 1940s, he was the assistant welfare officer. The other was W. L. Makubalo, an educated migrant to Bulawayo from eastern

Zimbabwe. Makubalo was assistant sports organizer and librarian. Both had studied and played football in mission schools. Both conducted church choirs in which their wives sang; both took a leading part in the dances and concerts which entertained Makokoba; both put their literacy and self-confidence in the service of the many township associations.

Their Christianity was certainly not dour. When Makubalo married in the Presbyterian church in Makokoba in June 1943, for instance, Sipambaniso's choir performed; during the wedding "an air of sanguine serenity pervaded," but at the reception after it there was "jollification and pompous festivity" which reached its climax when the band played the tsaba-tsaba. Makubalo struck a jovial note in his speech, saying that "unlike Gandhi, who starves himself, he believed in feasting for 365 days!"[40]

One might not have expected two young men who had achieved such a successful balance between Christianity and pleasure to worry themselves too much about death and burial. But in fact the topic fascinated them. They wanted to achieve a balance between Christianity and tradition as well. Makubalo wanted to organize a proper commemoration for a dead Manyika chief; Sipambaniso wanted to organize a proper commemoration for a dead Ndebele king. Makubalo collected money for a monument to be erected to the late Chief Mutasa in 1943. In 1944, Sipambaniso organized the burial of Lobengula's son, Nguboyena, at the foot of his grandfather Mzilkazi's tomb at Entumbane, making it the grandest African funeral since Mzilkazi's own death.

Challenging Christianity: bringing back *umbuyiso*

The climax of the cultural nationalist politics of death came with Joshua Nkomo's and Charlton Ngcebetsha's campaign to develop a Christian version of the *umbuyiso* ceremony. In Ngcebetsha's story of Tshuma and Mary above, Mary's infertility is in the end cured by a return to the ways of the ancestors. Rebuked by the Bulawayo prophetess—"When your father died did you bring his spirit back? That is the cause of the whole trouble"—Tshuma organizes an *umbuyiso* for his father. Tshuma is excommunicated by the missionaries. But Mary becomes pregnant.[41] But why, asked Ngcebetsha, did Africans have to choose between Christianity and *umbuyiso*? Why could there not be an African church which brought the two together?

Sipambaniso had used Ndebele royal deaths to make his points about monuments and memorials. Now Ngcebetsha used Sipambaniso's death to make his own points. He choreographed a splendid funeral for Sipambaniso and ensured that it was conducted by Revered Lesabe, bishop of the "Ethopian" African Methodist Episcopal Church, even though Sipambaniso had not been a member of it.[42] A year later came an ideal opportunity for an *umbuyiso*. In the months before the planned ceremony, Ngcebetsha had persuaded Sipambaniso's old soccer team, the Highlanders, to play a series of fundraising matches. With the proceeds, "a beautiful tombstone" was purchased. The stone was erected over the grave by the players. In August 1953, Ngcebetsha organized a ceremony for the unveiling of the stone. As he explained in the *Home News:*

> Actually, it was originally hoped that there would be an *Umbuyiso* ceremony on the day of the unveiling but the [Municipal] African Administration Department has refused permission to brew "in the traditional manner," suggesting the use of the Beer-Hall which is quite unacceptable (Nkomo 1984: 8–11).[43]

In 1955, however, Christian *umbuyiso* ceremonies were achieved. Joshua Nkomo's father, Nyongolo, had been a teacher and preacher at the London Missionary Society Bango mission. His own upbringing "was strictly Christian. There were Bible-readings, hymns, and prayers every night before bed. We were taught not to eat any food prepared for our neighbours' 'traditional worship.'"[44] Nevertheless, when Nyongolo died in 1954, his son prepared an *umbuyiso* ceremony for him. This was carried out in July 1955 and enthusiastically announced in the *Home News*. "Some educated Africans," rejoiced Ngcebetsha, "are convinced that African ancestral spirits ought not to be discarded."[45]

Finally, in December 1955, Ngcebetsha was able to announce the performance of a Christian *umbuyiso* in Bulawayo itself. Fittingly, it was performed by the African Presbyterian Church, which had broken away from the Free Presbyterian missionaries. The *umbuyiso* was for Elizabeth Miti, a pioneer both of the mission church and of its African-initiated successor. Ngcebetsha described the occasion in his most dramatic style:

> When the Israelites moved out of the house of bondage in Egypt, under the leadership of Moses, Moses carried away to the land of promise the dead bones of Joseph [inviting] Joseph's spirit, Joseph's soul, to accompany the large crowds of Israelites on their pilgrimage.

Miti had "in God's appropriate time" acted like a second Moses, leaving "the Presbyterian which is under the control of the white missionaries, and very largely assisting in the formation of a pure African church."

Reverend Poya, together with the black and white uniformed *Manyano* women of the new church, knelt at Miti's grave. Poya addressed it: "Mother, we have come to take your spirit, in accordance with the custom of our people. We humbly beseech you to return to the house where your husband, children, and grandchildren live and give them all the protection they need as well as your continual blessings. We humbly beseech you to consent to go back in spirit to guide the African Presbyterian Church." Ngcebetsha concluded: "More and more Christians seem to be convinced that the spirits and souls of our departed people cannot belong to the Devil but to God their Creator."[46]

For the rest of the 1950s, Ngcebetsha campaigned for the various "Ethiopian" churches, seeking to bring them together in a united "Home Church" and an "All African Missionary Conference." But there was an ironic paradox. By the end of the 1950s, there were many more members in Bulawayo of a quite different type of African-initiated church, the Zionist and Apostolic churches of the spirit. Ngcebetsha detested them. In his eyes, they were alien, "Shona"; they were noisy and irrational; they scorned tradition. Zionists, he wrote in November 1956, did not worship God "in accordance with African customs, i.e. through their ancestral spirits." Zionists and Apostolics were even less likely than enculturating mission churches to organize *umbuyiso* ceremonies.[47] Indeed, in the eyes of the Christian progressive elite which dominated the African press, the spirit churches had no culture of death at all. It was reported in June 1960 that residents in Pelandaba Township in Bulawayo were asking about the Apostolics: "Where and when do they bury their dead? No-one has seen them attending a funeral nor a gathering of mourners."[48] In death-obsessed Bulawayo it was the worst thing that could be said about anybody.[49]

Conclusion

Even without bringing in all the material available, this chapter abundantly demonstrates that there *was* a politics of death in black Bulawayo.[50] But it does not merely demonstrate that there was an "African agency" in the making of black urban culture and that a key issue in that culture was the question of death. What it reveals is the existence of multiple and competing agencies. The social and cultural history of black Bulawayo is much more complex than the story of helpless submission to the colonial boot, but it is also much more complex than one of resistance to missionaries and municipalities. There was a struggle in black Bulawayo over which Africans should be the shapers of urban culture.

It was this issue which underlay at least two of the great explosions of violence which marked the colonial history of Bulawayo: the so-called ethnic faction fighting in December 1929; the general strike of April 1948; and above all, the *zhii* riots of July 1960. All three have been construed as anticolonial or as anticapital. In a classic of political economy, Ian Phimister and Charles Van Onselen (1979) reinterpreted the 1929 faction fights as a struggle of the established workers against the cheap migrant labor that undercut them. The general strike of 1948 has been interpreted variously as marking the beginning of nationalist or proletarian resistance. The *zhii* riots of 1960 have been seen as the beginning of the mass nationalist turn to violence. But these are not total explanations. In at least two of the three upheavals, debates over black urban culture and who should dominate it were at stake.

The 1929 faction fights allied the "Ndebele" residents of the Location together with southern African migrants—the two groups who had constructed and contested Location culture in its first decades—against the brash, young, and educated "Manyika" dandies who loudly proclaimed their own ownership of "Buruwayo Style" (Ranger 2000a). The *zhii* riots of July 1960 demonstrated not so much the radical unity of African nationalism as its sharp division along lines of class and culture. The stores and houses of the rising African middle class—who had been the articulators of cultural nationalism—were torched and stoned by the unemployed and nationalist street youth. Charlton Ngcebetsha published an eloquent lament for the losses of his class (Ranger 2000b).[51]

In some senses, 1929 and 1960 *were* landmarks in the history of death in black Bulawayo—men died violently in both. But during these brief, intense, and direct confrontations there was no time, and no need, for cultural differences and conflicts to be expressed symbolically through the culture of mortality. It was during those long periods when open violence was repressed that cultural struggle took this form. It was inevitable that it did so. As a black undertaker lamented when taxed with lateness: "We Africans take funerals seriously and it is not always possible to keep to the time agreed."[52]

There are some obvious continuities between the period I have been discussing and the politics of death in the Zimbabwean present. The cultural nationalist obsession with monuments—and the conflicts between that obsession and tradition—has reached its height with the debates over Heroes' Acre (Werbner 1998), and surfaces too in the demands made in Bulawayo in April 2002 that National Monuments stop maintaining Rhodes's grave and concentrate instead on developing Mzilikazi's.[53] The mainline churches are still obsessively discussing whether there can be such a thing as a Christian *umbuyiso*. But I wish to end with one of the main perceived differences between the past and the present.

Much of the literature on southern African towns has commented on the extreme unhealthiness of colonial locations and compounds. But in the oral memory of men and women in the Bulawayo townships, the years before 1960 were a time when hardly anybody died! This comes as a surprise at the end of a paper which has emphasized that urban Africans were preoccupied with death and burial. But our informants are unanimous.

"You know," says Mrs. Bhelimina Ndlovu, "death was a rare thing in the township and many people used to be very much afraid of it."[54] "Generally what is notable," says Mrs. Madlela, "is that a few people died in those days."[55] The Mozambican migrant, Mowena, says:

Important to note is that there were few funerals in those early days. People did not just die like nowadays. Long back people were much stronger and healthier and there were no funny diseases infecting people … Hospitals were not death's doom like how it is in these days. Months would go by without seeing a funeral and it was difficult for some people to know where people were buried.[56]

"Death was not common," says MaMlalazi. "It was something sacred which even young children did not know about. Few people died in those days."[57]

These statements are obviously a reaction to the age of AIDS. They also reflect a time when the African population of Bulawayo was overwhelmingly young, when a sick or dying migrant would make every effort to go home, and when there were few epidemic diseases. But they are also statements of a moral position. In a period when death was rare, and therefore terrible and significant, when it was a secret kept from children, and therefore a business for adults, and when few young people went to funerals which were therefore controlled by elders—it was easier to dignify death. "Nowadays it is different," says MaMlalazi. "A lot of people are dying, every child knows about death, and funerals are sometimes held like ceremonies and not sacred moments." Other voices chime in—today, people shake hands at funerals, feast at funerals and attend them just for the food, don't take funerals seriously. Today, it has become much more difficult to dignify death.

Notes

This article is a revised and abbreviated version of "Dignifying Death: The Politics of Burial in Bulawayo." *Journal of Religion in Africa* 34 (1): 110–144.

1. A valuable survey is Sapire and Beall (1995). As for politicians, one example is President Mugabe's description of black townsmen as "people without totems," without cousins, and without culture. Less partisan observers—churchmen, for example—may deplore such antiurban prejudice. Yet in Zimbabwe, for instance, there has been a great deal of sophisticated theological debate about how to "inculturate" key African rituals, among them the rituals of death. But all the research carried out by participants in this debate have focused on the "traditional" cultures of rural societies.

2. Another treatment of the politics of death in Ghana is Greene (2002). Here the differences with Zimbabwe are even more striking. Not only does Greene expand on "'intramural sepulture,'" but she insists that the Bremen missionaries were quite indifferent to how or where their converts were buried. This contrasts strongly with the determined attempts by missionaries in Zimbabwe to replace burial among the rocks with Christian village cemeteries (Ranger 1987).

3. There have been a number of recent attempts in southern African studies to make use of this kind of evidence and of participant observation of funeral ceremonies (Dennie 1997 and 2003; Durham and Klaits 2002; Englund 2002).

4. S. Msebele, whom Busani Mpofu interviewed in Mzilikazi in June 2000, remembers "an area full of graves" where Mzilkazi now stands. When Mzilkazi was being developed in the late 1940s, some of the children's bones were unearthed, causing much consternation.

5. Interview between Busani Mpofu and Prince Gumede, June 14, 2000, Makokoba. Busani Mpofu, then a final year student at the University of Zimbabwe, conducted oral interviews for me in January, February, June, and July 2000. Sipambaniso was Arthur Sipambaniso Manyoba Kumalo, "Mr. Bulawayo" in the 1940s: socialite, soccer player, trade unionist, politician. He appears several times in this article both as an entrepreneur in the politics of death and as the object of a cultural nationalist ceremony of death.

6. Interview between Busani Mpofu and N. Moyo, Makokoba, July 24, 2000.

7. Interview with Prince Gumede.

8. *Home News,* October 11, 1958. On July 16, 1960, the *Home News* wrote of the "few unused graves in the old graveyard on the Old Falls Road [which] are solely reserved for certain old and much respected Africans of very long residence in Bulawayo." The *Home News* was edited by the Chairman of the BATAB, Charlton Ngcebetsha, who figures largely in this article.

9. Interview between Busani Mpofu and Mrs. Bhelamina Ndlovu, Makokoba, July 24, 2000.

10. Khumalo says that the use of African prisoners to dig graves in the Municipal cemetery began in the 1940s and that the first car to carry bodies there was used in the 1950s.

11. Interview between Busani Mpofu and Msongelwayizizwe Khumalo, Makokoba, July 26, 2000. Harri Englund emphasizes that for most Nyasa "permanent urbanization is not widely desired … Migrants envisage a definite return to the village only when they die. Burial should always take place in the village of origin … Burial in town indicates, therefore, failure among township dwellers" (Englund 2002: 153).

12. Interview between Hloniphani Ndlovu and Madliwayo, Pelendaba, June 2000. Hloniphani Ndlovu, at that time a final year student at the University of Zimbabwe, carried out interviews for me in the Bulawayo townships.

13. Eighty-year-old K. Banda told us that he came to Bulawayo because he had heard so much about it in Nyasaland. It was his "dream town." He worked and lived in the Railway Compound. "We Malawians were the first to have a burial society. We never neglected each other." Interview between Busani Mpofu and K. Banda, Nguuboyenja, June 12, 2000.

14. *Bantu Mirror,* January 17 and October 17, 1942; June 26, 1943; February 12 and 19, 1944.

15. When in the 1980s the offices of the old Municipal departments closed down in order to move into the glass tower near the city hall, many of them dumped or destroyed their files. J. S. Ncube, who had been involved with the township advisory boards since the 1960s, preserved many of the Native Administration Department files and held them for safe keeping in the Bulawayo Housing Department. With his permission, I have worked on the African Association files between 1957 and 1960 in the S. O. 8 series. All citations from burial society constitutions come from this source.

16. Some "national" associations did not in fact mention burial as an objective. The Belgian Congolese Joint National Society, for instance, stressed "the spirit of brotherhood

amongst ourselves as foreigners in this country … to find out how we can know and obey the rules of this country in which we now stay."

17. The Northern Rhodesia government labor officer, who forwarded this request to Ashton, said he had "told them that if such permits were granted I hoped it would not encourage too many funerals."

18. *Home News,* June 6, 1959.

19. The African Jiving Society, largely composed of "single" migrants, was very concerned with respectability. It offered to collaborate with the police in excluding "gangs of law-breaking Africans" from dance halls. Its own members would "come to the dance smartly dressed and if possible competitors should look respectable."

20. File S. O. 8 Vol. 1 T Box 100, Housing Department, Bulawayo.

21. Interview with M. P. Khumalo, July 26, 2000.

22. Interview between Hloniphani Ndlovu and Nduna Tafa, Bulawayo, June 2000.

23. In 1959 "Karanga" migrants to Bulawayo from Gutu in south-central Southern Rhodesia formed the Munyaradzi Club, which was to "be responsible for carrying his dead body home so that his parents will bury him at home. Many Africans want to be buried at their homes."

24. In what follows, I will draw mainly on the *Bantu Mirror* and the *Home News.* The former was initiated in 1934 as a paper for Christian Africans and took a Christian "progressive" line from its founding to 1960. The latter emerged in the early 1950s and was owned and edited by the maverick Charlton Ngcebetsha, an outspoken critic of mission Christianity.

25. As of this date, I have not been able to identify the small mosque that was erected at the southern end of Makokoba, near the market square. This was attended by the Location's Muslims who came almost entirely from the Islamic areas of Nyasaland. Many Muslim residents of Makokoba married Christian wives and allowed their children to attend church schools. But they themselves were buried in Bulawayo's Islamic cemetery together with Asian Muslims. Interview between Terence Ranger and Virginia Phiri, Harare, August 6, 2000.

26. *Bantu Mirror,* January 16, 1943. Dizwittie urged the churches to find a way to combine Christianity and pleasure. In fact, Bulawayo Christianity was neither as gloomy nor as aged as Dziwittie made out. Every church school had its youth choirs which competed with each other not only in singing spirituals but in tap dancing. Bulawayo popular urban music had its roots in these choirs. See *Bantu Mirror,* April 4, 1943 and March 11, 1944.

27. Interview between Busani Mpofu and Machingauta Sibanda, Mzilikazi, June 23, 2000. Sibanda was born in 1922. He remembers that mass burials by prisoners always took place on Wednesdays.

28. Interview between Hloniphani Ndlovu and Mr. Mowena, Emakadeni, June 16, 2000.

29. *Bantu Mirror,* January 24, 1942.

30. Interview between Busani Mpofu and Mrs. S. Nkomo, Mzilikazi, June 19, 2000.

31. There is, of course, a large literature on women's church associations, particularly in South Africa. The most interesting recent discussion can be found in Rebekah Lee's Oxford doctoral thesis on African women in Cape Town (2002). In chapter five, "Associational Life in Town," Lee draws on the huge unpublished report compiled in 1955 by Mia Brandel, "The Needs of African Women," which lists and discusses church associations, savings groups, welfare societies, and burial associations. Lee herself draws

on rich oral evidence to show how crucial burial societies were to black women in Cape Town and how they often belonged to many overlapping associations. In a fascinating article, Lee (2001) discusses women's disillusionment with the expense, hierarchies, and "maternalism" of the Christian associations. She cites a former Anglican whose funeral was attended by women wearing black rather than the more prestigious whites. "I thought I would love to be buried in a church by people who are wearing white"—but her husband had not paid his dues and only got "cruel" black.

32. *Home News,* July 20, 1957.
33. *Home News,* August 31, September 21, and November 2, 1957.
34. *Home News,* September 20, 1956.
35. *Home News,* September 1 and 13, 1956. For the life and death of Thompson Samkange, see Ranger 1995. As I explain in the introduction to this book, the idea of it was conceived in the Samkange family graveyard on Tambaram farm.
36. *Home News,* January 24, 1956. To do them justice, the Location advisory board and other elite bodies had also long protested against this sort of undignified death. In February 1944, the Advisory Board objected to "the present undignified mode of conveying African corpses from the mortuary to the cemetery, crowding several corpses into a covered hand-cart." In July 1944, the Council of African Delegates protested against the practice of "Africans who die in hospital having no relatives being buried naked." Worse still, there were constant suspicions that the city council intended to erect a crematorium "to burn the bodies of dead Africans because the African cemetery is full." *Bantu Mirror,* February 19 and July 22, 1944; *Home News,* March 3, 1956.
37. *Home News,* November 3 and 24, 1956. There was plenty of politics in this scandal. The unpopular Fingo Chief, Kona, had not attended the funeral and did not condemn Miller: Ngcebetsha and the Fingo Council demanded that Kona be deposed. He was not—and Miller did not suffer capital punishment—but the provincial commissioner held an inquiry and called upon missionaries to be more discreet.
38. *Home News,* November 5 and December 10, 1955.
39. For discussion and photographs of such pilgrimages, see Ranger 1999.
40. *Bantu Mirror,* June 5, 1943.
41. *Home News,* November 5 and 19, 1955.
42. *Home News,* January 8, 1955.
43. *Home News,* August 29, 1953.
44. Ironically, many people in Matabeleland today say that the region's current problems of underdevelopment, violence, and hunger are due to the fact that no *umbuyiso* has been carried out for Joshua Nkomo.
45. *Home News,* July 16, 1955.
46. *Home News,* December 17, 1955.
47. *Home News,* November 23, 1956. Oral informants, when asked about Ngcebetsha today, always recall how much he disliked Zionists and Apostles.
48. *Daily News,* June 16, 1960.
49. Unfortunately the Apostolics and Zionists had no press of their own. However, academics have subsequently explored their ideas about death in detail (Mukonyora 1998). One of the two case studies in Durham and Klaits's study of funerals in Botswana (2002) is of death rituals in the Baitshepi spirit church. A pioneering study of an African prophetic church as an expression of *urban* culture is Scarnecchia 1997.

50. I have left out two main topics much discussed in oral memory, in the African press, in advisory board minutes and elsewhere. One of these concerns complaints against undertakers. In the 1950s the competing firms were accused of touting for custom. Their touts would prowl hospital corridors marking down the dying or lie in wait for relatives outside the mortuary. Particular firms claimed to deal with particular 'tribes' and there were sometimes fights over a dying man by touts disputing his ethnic identity. Dirty hearses and shoddy coffins were provided; Christian dead were delivered late to church and relatives were left waiting there after the service while the hearse went off to pick up another corpse. All this denied dignity to the dying. It violated 'the honour and respect of the African race.' *Home News*, 16 August 1958. The other much discussed topic was the extravagant eulogies delivered at funerals. Writers in the *Bantu Mirror* thought these were going too far. You could not recognise your old friend in the picture painted!

51. These assertions about 1929 and 1960 are controversial and I argue them fully in Ranger (2010).

52. *Home News*, March 16, 1957.

53. In an editorial entitled "Respect our National Shrines" and published on April 25, 2002, the *Chronicle* wrote: "We are disappointed that nothing has been done to spruce up King Mzilikazi's shrine at the Matopos. We are not amused at the conduct of officials of the Department of Museums and National Monuments, who have shown no respect for our heritage, but continue to spend national resources in the upkeep of Cecil Rhodes's grave. We are surprised that our own people think that that crook, who stole our land and cattle, is worth the State resources expended on his grave at the expense of our ancestors."

54. Interview between Busani Mpofu and Bhelimina Ndlovu, Mzikazi, July 27, 2000. Mrs. Ndlovu was born in 1929.

55. Interview between Hloniphani Ndlovu and Mrs. Mandlela, Entumbane, June 14, 2000.

56. Interview between Hloniphani Ndlovu and Mr. Mowena, Emakhandeni, June 16, 2000.

57. Interview between Hloniphani Ndlovu and MaMhlalazi, Nkulumane, June 19, 2000.

Bibliography

Dennie, G. M. 1997. "The Politics of Burial in South Africa, 1886–1990." PhD. diss., Johns Hopkins University.

———. 2003. "Flames of Race, Ashes of Death: Re-inventing Cremation in Johannesburg, 1910-1945." *Journal of Southern African Studies* 29, no. 1: 177–192.

Durham, Deborah and Frederick Klaits. 2002. "Funerals and the Public Space of Sentiment in Botswana." *Journal of Southern African Studies* 28, no. 4: 777–795.

Englund, Harri. 2002. "The Village in the City, the City in the Village." *Journal of Southern African Studies* 28, no. 1: 137–154.

Greene, Sandra. 2002. *Sacred Sites and the Colonial Encounter: A History of Meaning and Memory in Ghana*. Bloomington: Indiana University Press.

Lee, Rebekah. 2001. "Conversion or Continuum? The Spread of Islam among African Women in the Cape Town." *Social Dynamics* 27, no. 2: 62–85.

———. 2002. "Locating Home: Strategies of Settlement, Identity-formation and Social Change among African Women in Cape Town, 1948-2000." PhD thesis, University of Oxford.

Maylam, Paul and Iain Edwards, eds. 1996. *The People's City. African Life in Twentieth Century Durban.* Pietermaritzburg: University of Natal Press.

Mukonyora, I. 1998. "The dramatization of life and death by Johane Masowe." *Zambezia* 23, no. ii.

Nkomo, Joshua. 1984. *Nkomo: The Story of My Life.* London: Methuen.

Nyathi, Pathisa. 2001. *Traditional Ceremonies of AmaNdebele.* Mambo, Gweru.

Parker, John. 2005. "The Cultural Politics of Death and Burial in Early Colonial Accra." In *Africa's Urban Past,* eds. D. Anderson and R. Rathbone. Portsmouth, NH: Heinemann.

Phimister, I. and C. Van Onselen. 1979. "The Political Economy of Tribe; Animosity: A Case Study of the 1929 Bulawayo Location 'Faction Fight.'" *Journal of Southern African Studies* 6, no. 1: 1–43

Ranger, Terence. 1987. "Taking Hold of the Land: Holy Places and Pilgrimages in Twentieth Century Zimbabwe." *Past and Present* 117: 158–94.

———. 1995. *Are We Not Also Men? The Samkange Family and African Politics in Zimbabwe, 1920–1964.* London: James Currey.

———. 1999. *Voices From the Rocks: Nature, Culture and History in the Matopos Hills in Zimbabwe.* Oxford: James Currey.

———. 2000a. "The Meaning of Urban Violence: the 1929 Bulawayo Faction Fight." Economic History Department seminar, University of Zimbabwe, April.

———. 2000b. "The Meaning of Urban Violence: Zhii in Bulawayo, July 1960." Economic History Department seminar, University of Zimbabwe, March.

———. 2010. *Bulawayo Burning: The social history of a Southern African city.* Oxford: James Currey and Harare: Weaver Press.

Sapire, Hilary and Je Beall. 1995. "Urban Change and Urban Studies in Southern Africa." *Journal of Southern African Studies* 21, no. 1: 3–18.

Scarnecchia, Timothy. 1997. "Mai Chaza's Guta re Jehova (City of God): Gender, Healing and Urban Identity in an Independent Church." *Journal of Southern African Studies* 23, no. 1: 87–105.

Werbner, Richard. 1998. "Smoke from the Barrel of a Gun: Postwars of the Dead, Memory and Re-inscription in Zimbabwe." In *Memory and the Postcolony,* ed. R. Werbner. London: Zed.

Yoshikuni, Tsuneo. 1999. "Notes on the Influence of Town-Country Relations on African Urban History before 1957: Experiences of Salisbury and Bulawayo." In *Sites of Struggle,* eds. B. Raftopolous and T. Yoshikuni. Avondale, Zimbabwe: Weaver Press.

CHAPTER 3

Transformations of Death among the Kikuyu of Kenya

From Hyenas to Tombs

Yvan Droz

The funeral practices of the Kikuyu were quite shocking to their first visitors because Kikuyu people very rarely buried their dead, but instead exposed their bodies to scavengers.[1] Today, however, all the dead are buried without distinction of sex, age, or status. Burial has become the only way of disposing of the dead, and the hyenas—important animals in Kikuyu tradition—no longer feed on exposed bodies. Being buried instead of being exposed to scavengers no longer classifies individuals according to their own social achievements in a ritualized and hierarchical society.[2] The final rite of passage for the successful man who formerly saw the end of his life crowned by burial disappeared. Those funeral rites, just like the second birth and even circumcision, are "traditional" rites of passage that now only take place, at best, in a modified form and that have lost most of their symbolic value. This chapter presents the history of funeral rituals, their changing meanings, and the ongoing differences in their practice, such as the differences between rural areas and the Kikuyu area of Nairobi. We will also see that behind the Christian discourse of the urban Kikuyu, one can discover the persistence of funeral practices that have only a remote relationship to Christianity.

What to do with the corpse?

In precolonial times, what we generally call the Kikuyu society was relatively egalitarian but at the same time strongly hierarchical.[3] Although young people formed a single age group, a hierarchy existed based on the prestige of their extended family, their lineage, and their personal qualities (bravery, zeal in work, stoicism in the face of sorrow, etc.). Several positions awaited the men who were leaving the ranks of young warriors and embarking on their individual paths in the hope of ending their lives with a burial. In fact, only people who died after a long life—and especially those who had met certain requirements—received a status called *ahomori,* conferring the honor of burial. This was reserved for older men or their spouses: anyone whose sons were old enough to carry the bodies.

The bodies of children and adults who died before fulfilling what the Kikuyu ethos considered to be an accomplished life did not receive such favored treatment. Generally the body was abandoned in the area where relatives had watched over the dying person. To avoid having death pollute the homes of the living, sick people—once they were dying—were led into the bush that encircled the homes. There was a place there set aside for the dying called the *kĩbĩrĩra.* One of the informants remembers when asked about funeral practices during his youth:

> So what happened was that … irrespective of whether it was a baby or an adult, if they found that the person was going to die, but he had not died, he would be taken beyond the gate to the entrance. Then they would light some fire. That fire was meant to scare away wild animals, to prevent them from coming to eat the person. … So they … he was saying it was like a present ICU, Intensive Care Unit.[4]

If a person's death had occurred unexpectedly inside the home, family members made a breach in the back wall. Hyenas then carried off the person and ate the body. The same informant added, "So at the back, there was *mĩhĩrĩgo,* some enclosures. OK, the door would be shut, and then at the back, they would remove some wood, some pieces of wood. And that would be an entrance for the animals to get into and find the body and to collect it." This brief summary of funeral practices[5] requires an important qualification: the exposition of the body was not an issue of neglecting or of rejecting the deceased person, but one of avoiding the ritual uncleanness *(thahu)* that surrounded all dead bodies: "A dead body was an unclean thing, and in this sense death was contagious. Therefore, if any person touched a dead body, he or she had at once to be purified, as otherwise the contagion of death would be transferred" (Leakey 1977: 938). Derek Peterson confirms this as well: "Dead bodies were supremely dangerous: dying men and women were taken from their homes and left in the bush by their relatives. Who feared that death would extend its reach on the living" (Peterson 2000: 47). As we shall see, any kind of physical contact with the dead required complex and costly purification rituals.[6]

The burial was also reserved for wives who, like their husbands, had fulfilled their destinies, the exception being the sole wives of elders. "A woman who was the only wife of a Kikuyu elder was never buried no matter how old she might be, but her body was carried out and placed in the *kĩbĩrĩra*" (Leakey 1977: 960). This particularity was the expression of the esteem that polygamy had in Kikuyu society. It placed a heavy burden on the precolonial woman who refused to accept co-wives; her refusal would remove any hope for her to be buried.[7] This condition spurred the first wife on to manage domestic matters very well because her own personal achievement depended on, among other things, the second marriage of her husband. Efficient management of the household by the first wife allowed her husband to graciously receive acquaintances and members of his family, and this was the first step in mobilizing his resources to achieve a second wedding. The husband relied on the work of the first wife to wed a second spouse, and the first wife saw her achievements completed by the arrival of a new wife.

Louis Leakey—the son of Canon Leakey, who was brought up at the beginning of the twentieth century among a Kikuyu age set[8]—sees death as the last rite of passage, one that demonstrated a person's final achievement. An individual was supposed to die "in his own time," which meant that the natural course of the person's life had not been disrupted by a violent death—if it had been, the person could not completely participate in the final ritual of burial. The retrieval of the deceased's personal effects (or "ornaments") was part of the preparation for the ceremonies that occurred in the ritual, just as occurred in earlier rites of passage:

> If a Kikuyu were asked why all ornaments had to be removed from a dead person who died in a normal way, the answer was always that when he was born he had no ornaments, when he went through the second birth ceremony he had no ornaments, when he was actually operated upon at initiation he had no ornaments, and at death, therefore, when he went to become a spirit, he had none (Leakey 1977: 990).

Louis Leakey's informants—some of whom were from Kabete, nearly ten miles north of Nairobi, where I conducted part of this research[9]—explicitly linked death to other important rites of passage. In addition, only a "normal" death allowed for the complete ceremonial performance—including burial—of this last ritual[10]. It was, therefore, necessary for a person to die well so that his status as *mūthamaki* could be sanctified by a complete burial.

The *mūthamaki* represents the self-ideal of the precolonial Kikuyu. We should note that the ideal of the *mūthamaki* applies only to men. However, in the precolonial era, the wife gained a similar status through the social success of her husband. Reciprocally, the husband acquired his status thanks to his wife's talent for managing the household. Moreover, it was not enough to be a married man and a father to obtain this status. At least one of his children needed to be circumcized, and he was also required to have managed a plot of land successfully and to have conducted himself well throughout his life (participation in rituals, respect for elders, respect for prohibitions, etc.). We can consider the status of *mūthamaki* as a step towards the complete achievement that burial as a high status *ahomori* represented. Thus death and funeral were conceived as a stage in one's overall journey through life. In Leakey's ethnography, death was not an irreparable break with life, but simply a passage—between being alive and being a spirit—that confirmed the social status of the deceased.

The meaning of death

Four categories of deceased persons existed in precolonial time. First, the men (or women) who had completely finished the course of their lives were called *mūhomori* (singular). These were honored with the complete funeral ritual. The extended family was informed and had to be present; the ceremony of *hukūra*—literally, "disinterment"—was fully performed,[11,] and the body was buried. Second, people with at least one child, or older people who had died a violent death, had the right to all the rituals, but they could not be buried, a restriction that expressed the unfinished state of their lives. Third, the *thaka*, were people who were fundamentally incomplete because they had achieved "nothing" during their lives (i.e., they had not begotten children) and became undifferentiated spirits prone to haunting the living.[12] Their names were not reused by the family, and only a simplified ritual of "disinterment" took place. Finally, we can mention the children who did not go through the ritual of the second birth: "Until he or she had been through the second birth ceremony, a child was still regarded as a part of its mother" (Leakey 1977: 964). In this case, only the child's mother and father underwent the simplified ritual of "disinterment," and the patrimonial family did not concern itself with this death.[13]

Greet Kershaw affirms that Kikuyu people assigned a different meaning to the death of a person according to the deceased's age or, by extension, according to the stages in life the deceased had reached, which corresponded to the person's social status:

> Any death is mourned, but the younger the child, the fewer the people involved who will feel personal grief, although the child's death will be deeply felt by its immediate kin. However, as death is not an end, but a point within a cyclical time-reckoning, consolation is found in the thought that death is a decision made by the ancestors who, when they are ready, will return to the living. Man has the right to do whatever he can to keep death at bay, though he would violate the beliefs of the people and be engaged in futile action if he opposed death in principle. Death is necessary for the living as the ancestors take care of the living; the living are necessary to the dead as they provide for them. Small children die more easily as they are close to the ancestors and their memories are still with the past. In the same way old

[people] die as their thoughts are already with the ancestors (Kershaw 1973: 58).

She is speaking here only of "normal" death and does not distinguish it from violent death. Death, then, was not thought as the end but rather a *final* passage into the world of spirits who, with the living, constitute a balanced universe.

Today, the death of very young children is still an event that essentially concerns only the parents and their close circle of relatives. However, the death of young people—often considered to be children—is a kind of death that grieves both neighbors and the entire family. The death of a young man or woman who has begun his or her journey through life is a mishap that seems more serious than the death of an older person. Older people have already "lived" and accomplished what they were meant to do on earth, while the young adult had a destiny that will now remain unfulfilled:

> For the old people who have accomplished things, who have lived their lives, they have children … they are called seeds in the world. Unlike these others, for the young people who have not left any seed, any quote. For a young person, he has a lot in front of him, he can have his very productive use, he is strong. So that kind of death is sad and it affects people a lot.[14]

Usually, the deceased's age determined both the social meaning of this death and the range of its effective implications. The category of *thaka* confirms this interpretation because the death of an individual without descendants—*a fortiori* a child—did not allow for a complete metamorphosis of the spirit, which then became undifferentiated. Thus to be circumcised, to get married, to have children, to gain the prestige that led to social respect, and to die peacefully: these were the conditions *sine qua non* for the achievement of a "self." If one of these stages did not occur, the individual could not be considered as having completed his life's journey; this is the rationale for the importance of dying "well."

Why bury the body?

Burial became widespread fairly quickly at the beginning of colonization,[15] but not without stipulations.[16] The British had urged the Kikuyu to bury all their dead, without much initial success. One event accelerated the transformation of their funeral practices. In February 1933, Chief Koinange had the remains of his grandfather disinterred to prove that the land occupied by an English settler belonged to his family. He was thus able to assert to the members of the Carter land commission his lineage right to property that colonists had claimed to have found as virgin territory.[17]

It seems that this event struck the Kikuyu imagination. Despite the fact that lost land had been recovered only through the powerful violation of a *thahu*, the ritual uncleanness, that resulted from physical contact with the dead body, burial was transformed into a means of ascertaining control of property (Lonsdale 1992: 377–378). The current "landowners" immediately tried to control the burial of the dead, and only the landowner or his descendants were allowed to be buried in the lineage land. The landless Kikuyu were forbidden to bury anyone on the lands of their patrons, since such burial would have provided them with an argument for reclaiming titles to property through the remains of their ancestors. John Lonsdale emphasizes this point when he describes the alliance between chiefs and the Kikuyu Central Association:[18] "Chiefs could not otherwise have cooperated with KCA councilors to compel burial; only if right holders controlled the graveyard would *ahoi* stay submissive even underground" (Lonsdale 1992: 378). The dynastic concerns of the chiefs combined with the hygienic considerations of the KCA catalyze the modification of funeral practices. Burial became a way to affirm one's modernity and to mark out inherited property: a new concept of land ownership was born.[19] Previously, it had been controlling people, not owning land, that meant wealth.

A young Kikuyu from the Laikipia Plateau summarizes the current concept of burial, telling us in plain terms:

> I wish to be buried on my shamba [plot]. Because if I will not be buried where I buy then there was no need of buying the land. It is not like the one who has the plot can be buried at the cemetery, no. If you have a shamba, it means that you have been thrown away by your family when buried at cemetery.

Today, the question of land property is at the center of concerns about the fate of the body. Since the 1930s, land and death have been indissolubly linked.

After the first third of the twentieth century, burial was intended for everyone and no longer constituted the culminating point of an individual's life: "I found that the practices [of disposing the bodies in the bush], those early practices had almost disappeared [by 1937 in Kabete]." and our informant added these details:

> Those who were not baptized were buried in the Kikuyu manner. Even the prayers were conducted in a Kikuyu version, unlike those who were Christians, whose ceremonies now were Christian. The Kikuyu manner was conducted mostly by *mūndo mūgo* [ritual healer] and what happened is that they did not have so many things during that particular day of the burial. Except that when he was buried he

would be told whether he was a good person, his relationship with the people, he has so many children and things like that.[20]

In one of the cradles of Kenyan Christianity, Kabete (today one of Nairobi's suburbs), only a few older people remember the "traditional" funeral practices, and they recall them with some discomfort. One of them said:

> During those early times, if for example one got sick, he got seriously sick, he would be removed from the main house and would be taken later away from the houses and that is where he would be fed from. So that every now and then, somebody would be going to check you there. During those early times, dead were not buried. What happens if such a person died, he would only be taken away and thrown into the bushes and the hyenas and other animals would come and eat the body.[21]

Our informant acknowledged that he never saw such practices personally. His eldest sister, however, was the last person in Kabete to be "thrown" to the hyenas. She had the measles and was fully expected to die. Some time after her abandonment, however, she reappeared. This "mistake" seems to have sounded the death knell of this former funeral practice, and we can understand the ridicule cast on this family who abandoned their living child to wild beasts by the villagers who had converted to Christianity.

This same informant remembers the purification ceremonies that followed the death of a family member, conducted by a *mũndo mũgo*. It had been necessary to gather the whole household, including animals and the family's goods, and to sprinkle everything with fluid from the foot of a ram sacrificed for the occasion. The ritual healer dipped the foot in the stomach of the strangled ram and went around the group to chase away the spirits (*ngoma*). He touched everyone's tongue with the ram's foot and deposited some traces of the stomach contents, which the "unclean" people had to swallow to chase away the ritual uncleanness *(thahu)*. Some informants still remember the pleasant taste of the substance.

Even though the custom of placing the dying in the bushes that encircled the dwellings rapidly disappeared, the purification ritual survived in Kabete: dead bodies were buried, but the family was purified. Men born in the thirties remember those burials:

> He buried his grandfather by wrapping his body in with *ndarua,* that is, dry skin. And perhaps a little while before the body was being thrown in the forest; it's because there were four forests. Later, the forests were cleared and it would not be very good to go throwing people around. That's why, perhaps, the concept of burying ... brought a new sense of doing things. (Man, ~60, Kabete, 2001)

Another informant adds more detail:

> Yes, people used to fear the death very much even when you were growing-up. So that even our people from the surroundings would not be left to know that somebody had died. What happened when somebody died, the immediate family would wrap the dead body with a *shuka* or a blanket, because they do not prepare coffin and they would just go and buried him. And those people who buried that person were feared a lot and they would not be ... other feared them so that they could not come closer to them and they had to be shaved, cleaned. (Man, ~75, Kabete, 2001)

It was the fear of ritual uncleanness (*thahu*) that led the inhabitants of Kabete to participate in these purification rituals. At the time of the first interments, villagers hired Muslims to dig the grave and lay the body in it in order to avoid uncleanness.[22] The Muslims were paid for their role as gravediggers and received, over and above that, the tools they had used: no Kikuyu would be permitted to touch them, as they had become unclean.

The ritual, however, was not complete without an act of intercourse to finish purifying the close relatives of the deceased. If a child died, the parents had intercourse; widows or widowers had to purge themselves with the help of one of the dead person's close relatives. One of our informants links this practice to the widow's inheritance:

> It was something that was there and it was considered to be a practice. So that even the people knew that in the event of a husband dying it was the younger brother who had to sleep with ... to have sexual intercourse with the lady. And even in the ceremony that was conducted by the *mũndo mũgo*, it was incorporated there, that cleansing by the younger brother to the husband ... the younger man would kind of marry [*gũthabia*] now the widow. So that even in the event of them getting a baby boy, they would name the boy after the deceased man.

However, he added:

> The Kikuyu left that practice a long time ago.[23] But what happened, especially when it took shift, when I was a child. It was if a person who was widowed, what happened is that the brother to the husband would just build a house for this widow. But she would not have any sexual relationship with him, she would even get some other children from other people outside, but not with the brother.[24]

Men born in the thirties do not recall this particular practice, even though they clearly recall the purification ritual. In making burial widespread, the Kikuyu stopped placing bodies on the outskirts of the village and progressively modified the purification ritual. The funeral practices which had shocked the Europeans so much now quickly disappeared in the areas around Nairobi. Kikuyu people in Kabete found themselves caught between Doctor Arthur of the Church Missionary Society (CMS) and Canon Leakey of the Anglican Church, the father of the Kikuyu ethnographer Louis Leakey. We can thus reasonably suppose that the evolution of funeral practices occurred much more quickly in the Nairobi area.

Funeral practices therefore progressively lost their functions of hierarchical affirmation (the four categories of the dead) and of reproducing the Kikuyu ethos (by the consecration of the *mūhomori*). These complex and differentiated funeral practices had played an essential role in producing different regulations at the heart of "Kikuyu society," as well as in the ideal of maintaining the ethos of the accomplished man. The disappearance of former practices was followed by the vanishing of the ritual uncleanness (*thahu*) that offered a powerful means of social control.[25] This evolution laid a heavy burden on Kikuyu social reproduction, which was undergoing simultaneous attacks by missionaries, administrators, and settlers.

> Christianity and public health changed Kikuyu burial practice more than any other aspect of life. … Converts took some persuading that all dead should be interred, not just the wealthy old; deaths in mission hospital then loaded a growing grave-digging burden on them. One of the LNC's [Local Native Council, composed of elders] first public health enactments required all dead to be buried by their relatives. … each *mbarī* then had to set aside a graveyard; this meant breaking another taboo [*thahu*], on the carriage of bodies (Lonsdale 1992: 377).

A dead body was no longer synonymous with uncleanness, burial was no longer reserved only for those who had respected the ideals of the Kikuyu ethos, and all the spirits, without exception, joined the post-mortem life painted by missionaries. The question was no longer whether an individual survived as a person after death or not, but "simply" knowing where the person ended up: hell or heaven.

Burial location

Even though everyone needs to be buried today, not just any kind of burial will do. The reproach the first visitors to the Kikuyu made against throwing away dead bodies has today been taken up by the young people in the rural area of Laikipia—but against the Kikuyu who bury their dead in cemeteries! Our informants from the Nairobi suburbs of Kabete held much more "ecumenical" concepts about funeral practices and considered burial in a cemetery as the unavoidable consequence of the lack of land.

Several informants mentioned deathbed curses as the most imperative reason to bury a parent on family land:

> So if somebody says he should be buried at home he must be buried at home. If you turn down his request of being buried at home, then after one year, you will start hearing and seeing problems within your household, either a member can die as people think as a joke, so it's good to bury somebody where he wishes because it is like a curse.[26]

In rural areas, municipal cemeteries are considered to be the last recourse for poor families—so poor that they cannot even buy a few square feet of land to dig a grave:

> But when one is buried in the municipal cemetery, people will start saying that person had no land because all his money, he was taking beer and using them with women. So, one should buy land to avoid such accusations when one dies, to avoid being buried in the municipal cemetery.[27]

All the same, the first Kikuyu in Kabete to be buried in Langata cemetery was forced to do so out of poverty:

> He was called Kĩhuha and he had a very big land. What happened is that he sold it out [in 1958, after the apportioning of land]. So he was just left with a plot he could not even be buried in. So, he had to be taken to Langata. ... People said nobody would help him, because he had large tract of land and he sold it out in measure to have the money. And nobody was willing to offer a grave site.[28]

This is the very picture of failure for a Kikuyu man: selling so much of his property that he is unable to keep even a patch of land for his burial. If burial is proper only if it is done on family land for the Kikuyu in rural areas, it still involves the kind of classification that characterized precolonial funeral practices. Today, it is no longer a question of an ethical regulation related to personal socioeconomic achievement (*thaka, mũramati, mũhomori*), but rather a question of a purely economic status that is linked to personal success. Thus if someone ends up being buried in a municipal cemetery, it is clearly through a lack of foresight or through an inordinate desire for money.

The young people I met in the Laikipia Plateau were unanimous about wanting to be buried in their own land. The reason they gave is the disgrace—for the dead person and the family—that burial in a municipal cemetery implies and that is clearly associated with the former stain attached to the death of the *thaka*:

It's my wish that I would be buried at my own plot. ... Because if I will be buried in a municipal cemetery, this to me is a show that I am a failure in live and I have betrayed my stand to try to save as much as I could as to earn the respect of a successful man in the society. ... Also if I will be buried outside my family's plot, this is a show that they have termed me as an outcast in the family. [Man, ~18, Laikipia, 1994]

The disgrace hits the young man's self-image, but it means also a rejection of the dead person by family members that corresponds to the disappearance of the name of a person who died before having a child. Another young man put it this way:

I would like to be buried on my land because to be buried in municipal cemetery is like being thrown away. But customary, one is supposed to [be] buried on ones plot or their relatives plot. If you bury some-body in municipal cemetery is not good if at all he had said that he should be buried on that plot and he can have a curse ... What will my children say about it? Because they will ask where their relative were buried even it's their grandfather or grandcucu [grandmother], or mother, father, brother, or any relatives. [Man, ~20, Laikipia, 1994]

Remembrance and curse are paired together here. Remembrance is an es-sential point in the desire to be buried at home, for the migrants of the Laikipia Plateau live in fear of being forgotten by their descendants. They imagine—based on their own experiences as pioneers—that their children will have no roots because of the absence of grave sites for their relatives on family land. What will they say if they don't see the burial place of their grandparents? Moreover, certain events have reinforced a lack of respect for municipal cem-eteries: the mix-up of bodies that sometimes occurs when a dead person is buried in another's place (*Nation* 1995: 4), or the burial of anonymous bodies in groups of three in the same grave—the rumor claims they were given over to hyenas (*Target* 1995)[29]. In light of the lack of security associated with mu-nicipal cemeteries, burial on family land leads to the assurance of a successful death, since no one could imagine burying an unknown person in the spot reserved for one's father.

The importance of remembrance concerns not only the descendants, but also the wife of the deceased who could risk forgetting her husband. The hus-band's burial on land where the widow is living is also considered an effective way of preventing her remarriage. We need to clarify this fear of having the wife contract a new conjugal union, because it sheds light on the primordial bond that links the Kikuyu to the land. If the wife actually remarries, the chil-dren from the first marriage and members of the patrimonial family will live in fear of seeing the deceased's land inherited by another family. The new husband or his family could try to dispossess the children of the first marriage and take a portion of lineage land from the patrimonial family. One woman told us about this:

> I am planning to be buried in my own plot ... because in your plot, your children will be remembering you as they will see the grave. Also to be buried in your own plot is important as for a husband because the wife you left cannot go to be remarried in another household because when she sees the grave she will remember she had another husband. But if buried in a municipal cemetery, your wife will forget the husband, hence will be married again by another husband. [Man, ~18, Laikipia, 1994]

Remembrance and loyalty go together for this young woman who thinks that the frivolity of wives should be countered by the daily vision of their former husbands' graves. Another issue that emerges about the importance of the grave is the control that the spirit of the deceased could have over the living, according to precolonial spiritual concepts. This potential threat against bad behavior or the disrespect by the survivors is also associated with the positive influences that the spirit of the dead person can have on his close relatives. This aspect is brought up to justify the desire for being buried on one's own land rather than on holy ground in a cemetery consecrated by the church:

> I would like to be buried in my plot in Nyakinyua. When I am buried here, I will be seeing all what my children are doing. If they go on wrong way, I will be guiding them showing them the right way to follow. If I am buried in a government cemetery I will be very far away from my children and I will not be able to guide them. [Woman, ~40, Laikipia, 1994]

Nevertheless, burial on family land does not happen automatically. Despite the specific role that spirits continue to play, material circumstances are sometimes the determining factors. A teacher told us in a conversation:

> I was buying so that I can be buried there. But I was buying so the children have a place to settle. For buy ... for burial, even if I die now I can ask them to bury me where I die. If I die in a hospital like in Nyeri, they buy a cemetery there. [Woman, ~40, Laikipia, 1994]

This openness to being buried in a cemetery corroborates a concept that the older people in Kabete presented to me: the evolution of funeral practices, especially the burial location, does not adhere to an urban-rural distinction. In fact, a large number of Kikuyu participate simultaneously in urban and rural worlds because of the numerous migrations they make during their life.[30]

Nevertheless, these ideas also reflect the ambivalence of the Kikuyu concepts of death. On one hand, the spirit of the deceased goes to a Christian heaven; on the other hand, that spirit remains among the living and inter-venes in their daily lives. The deceased must be buried in family land, but if economic circumstances or the risks connected to the dead body's location require it, he can just as easily be buried in a cemetery and receive a Christian blessing—risking, of course, being derided. So the burial of a close relative in a cemetery can be considered acceptable if the journey to bring the body back home seems insurmountable. Civil servants transferred to distant and isolated regions of Kenya run the risk of being buried in those regions in case of a sudden death. Nevertheless, if the deceased worked in a place that is not be-yond the range of communication, the family will spend large sums of money to have the body brought back to the patrimonial land. The body of a civil servant who died in Mombassa was brought back to Nanyuki by his sister, a housemaid. She mobilized her entire social network to handle the cost of this. She was helped by her brother's former colleagues who pooled money for the transportation costs, and the body was interred on her parcel of land.

The idea of only acquiescing to burial in a cemetery as an exception begins to appear in urban areas just at the end of the twentieth century. Previously, the return of the body to one's home was mandatory for all the Kikuyu. So, in the 1960s funeral practices reaffirmed the religious affiliation of the deceased and distinguished Muslims from Christians:

> Death and burial suggest a crucial symbolic differentiation between Muslim and non-Muslim, although it is not common for non-Muslims to die in Pumwani [a poor section of Nairobi] since few of them are old. Occasionally a child dies, however, or someone meets with an accident. Invariably the body [of a non-Muslim] is sent back to the rural area, from which the deceased came, to be buried (Bujra 1970: 7).

Let us note incidentally that the costs associated with funerals, especially the return of the body to one's village of origin, also played a role in the uncom-mon decision to convert to Islam: "[In the mid-1930s, prostitutes] in Pumwani claimed that one of the main attractions of urban Islam was that the religion would arrange their burials" (White 1990: 115). This service provided by Islam was not negligible for the prostitutes in Nairobi who had often cut all ties with their families. They found themselves with two alternatives: conversion to Is-lam, or the complex organization of their funerals by their living relatives.

Authority and burial

Some aspects of funeral practices can be seen as an expression of power by older people over the young or of social control over each individual person by the neighborhood. Thus, an individual who refuses to participate in ceremonies for the death of a close relative or neighbor is at risk of being disowned—if not by the family, then at least by the neighbors. These individuals run the strong risk of having their bodies buried in a municipal cemetery:

> Also, if a person does not collaborate with relatives and neighbors during a burial of somebody else, even in turn people will not help in burying him, so the municipal council will do the burying.[31]

The individual who is not responsive to the demands of mutual aid in the case of emergencies is in danger of finishing out his own life in a pitiful way and of being considered a person who is "less than nothing." This is the ultimate vengeance by the family or the neighborhood for the disrespectful pariah. In the case of serious infractions of the rules of mutual aid, the deceased's family members may even refuse to take care of the dead body. This would leave no one to take charge of the funeral, and municipal employees will therefore take the body to the municipal cemetery.

The social control that precolonial funeral practices allowed has not disappeared. Precolonial funeral practices indirectly limited violence by listing those who die violent deaths on an index and refusing them burial.[32] The path to achieve the status of a *mũhomori* discouraged individuals from using violence after they had started families, since only those who died "in their own time" were buried. Death still offered one of the essential ways to monitor everyone's social practices. Today, only the people who show a minimum of reciprocity, whether in their patrimonial family or their neighborhood, have the right to proper burial.

The destiny of the dead body thus still involves a question of status, as much for the deceased who achieve their individual destinies as for the family's reputation and prestige. The conflicts that can arise over the possession of the dead body—whether to ensure ownership of a property or to show respect (or disrespect) to the deceased and his family—highlights the crucial importance of burial today.[33]

This evolution of funeral practices is corroborated by individual ideas about burial location. In rural areas, it is still necessary to bury the body on family land, a requirement that can stir up passionate emotions:

> About 400 members of two clans gathered at the local hospital mortuary in a legal dispute about where to bury the body of John Wanjohi Kiragu and his second wife, Rosemary Nyakio, who were murdered on March 16. His first wife and her only son want to bury the body. But the late Kiragu's senior clansmen and those from his wife want to be allowed to bury him (*Nation* 1994: 5).

Thus the ownership of land still constitutes a condition for a successful life because without it there is no proper burial. In rural areas, only people who die unexpectedly because of an illness or who die poor or rejected by their families are buried in a cemetery.

The concept of burial seems to have evolved rapidly in Kabete. Indeed, the majority of my informants hope to be buried "at home," whether it is in Kabete (for those who own land there), in their place of origin in the Central province, or in the Rift Valley. But they do not cast aspersions on those who are buried in a cemetery. Some assert: "If you will to be buried in Langata cemetery, it is upon you, if you wish to be buried in your shamba, in your land, it's upon you." However, it is still the case that "most of the people bury in the house [plot]." Beyond these options, interment in a cemetery can happen for other reasons: "For instance if the plot, the shamba here are very small, and the people cannot find enough land to be burying people. It is in those circumstances that they would prefer to go in cemetery." The hope of most of the Kikuyu is clearly to be able to be buried at home, but external constraints force some people to consider the cemetery as their last resting place, without this necessity arousing anymore ridicule. And the inhabitants of Kabete sometimes excuse themselves for this shift in the Kikuyu ethos by explaining this change as modernization:

> Some years back people would feel very bad if they had [to be buried] about Langata cemetery. Then people would be feeling very bad, being associated with a burying in Langata cemetery. So it is a matter of time, even those people [in the rural areas] when there would be pressure on land, then they would start … [to change their minds].[34]

It should be noted that a cemetery is called *kĩbĩrĩra* in Kikuyu today. Although the word used to designate the place where the dying and the dead bodies of the "incomplete" people were deposited, today the same word means the place where the bodies of people with "bad deaths" are "abandoned." Burial in a municipal cemetery is fitting only for incomplete people or for daring modern people. Despite this, our Kikuyu informants mentioned the cases of important men who had wished to be buried in cemeteries either to show how modern they were or because of their desire to conserve land for their descendants by not encumbering it with multiple graves. Such a "chosen" goal had to be written in a duly formulated will so that the group in charge of the burial would not quarrel internally over the body's destination.

The desire to be buried on one's own plot of land—a principle connected to a desire for immortality—constitutes an aspect of the Kikuyu ethos. In the ethical dimension, monetary wealth means nothing, at the end of the day, if it is not invested in basic property (i.e., for one's final resting place.) In rural areas, even a man with a lot of money would be completely discredited if he was eventually buried in a municipal cemetery. In addition, if the purchase of a piece of land coincides with the death of a family member, the deceased will inevitably be shamed, because the abrupt acquisition of property is truly a sign of poor investment strategies both by the family and by the deceased. To justify their reluctance about burial in a cemetery, our informants offered motives such as the children's desire to see the graves of their grandparents or their parents every day, the absence of "beauty" in a burial in a municipal cemetery, and even the inevitable confusion about how descendants will find an ancestor's tomb if it is located among dozens of other "anonymous" tombs.

Conclusion

The work of Christian missions—especially their vision of the destiny of the dead—and of the British colonial administration—especially its hygienist policies—deeply transformed Kikuyu concepts about funeral practices and the soul.[35] These Christianizing and sanitary efforts have been crowned with success. Precolonial burial practices have almost entirely disappeared, although the goal of keeping a dead body on family land recalls the classifying function that these practices performed, while at the same time securing the family's property. Modern burial locations and funeral rituals have replaced the former method of depositing bodies in the bush. The esteem enjoyed by the mūhomori was, in the past, expressed by their burial. Now, the simple fact of burial no longer provides a distinction between successful people and unimportant or poor people. Nevertheless, this practice has preserved some of its meaning today despite its Christian attire: men and women are still classified by the manner in which they are buried.

The body of the deceased only rarely belongs to its prior owner.[36] It is the family—and even more broadly, the community—that reclaims the deceased. A funeral still remains the indicator for assessing the deceased's life and deeds: in choosing the form and the location of burial, the group reclaims the individual and renders its judgment upon him.

Notes

1. For evidence of the disposal of the dead, see Gatheru 1964 or Routledge & Routledge 1910: 168–173.
2. Today, the size of a funeral still divides the dead according to economic status (Kariuki 2003).
3. For a description of the social organization of the Kikuyu society, see Droz 1999 and 2000b; also see Peatrik 1994. On the issue of rank and age-set, see Droz 2000a and Prins 1953.
4. Old man, about eighty years old, Kabete, 2001. During my field work (fifteen months between 1993–1995 in Laikipia, three months between 2000–2001 in Nairobi), I committed myself to preserving my informants' anonymity. Concerning the topic of this article, I questioned my informants about the meaning and practices of death and

burial for them today. In Kabete, I focused my questions on the differences between today's practices and meanings and the ones they witnessed in their childhood and youth.

5. See Leakey (1977: 937–991) for a detailed description of precolonial funeral practices. Louis Leakey's monumental ethnography of "precolonial Kikuyu society" is based on intensive conversations about precolonial time with Kikuyu conservative elders at the end of the 1930s in the south of Kikuyu country, north of Nairobi.
6. See also Lamont, this volume.
7. Nonetheless, her husband could still be buried.
8. See Leakey 1977 for the method the author used to "collect" information. Berman & Lonsdale 1991 presents a critical analysis of the invention of Kikuyu "tradition" and the bitter conflict between Louis Leakey and Jomo Kenyatta about who was allowed to speak in the name of "tradition." See also Lonsdale 1992 concerning the internal debates about the moral economy of Kikuyu colonial society.
9. Kabete today is a small town of around 301,000 inhabitants, about nine and a half miles northwest of Nairobi. The first Anglican mission station in Central Kenya was founded there at the turn of the century by Canon Leakey, Louis Leakey's father. At the beginning of the nineteenth century, it was rural, but today it has become part of the greater Nairobi area.
10. "Deaths due to violence, suicide, or accident, or even death that took place away from home, did not rank as normal" (Leakey 1977: 938).
11. The body was cleansed and stripped of its ornaments and clothes. It was considered necessary for the corpse to be as naked as it had been when entering life.
12. They lost any individual identity as beings, as opposed to those who were remembered individually.
13. For a detailed discussion on precolonial concepts of souls and funerals, see Droz 2003.
14. Old man, around seventy-five years old, Kabete, 2001.
15. See Lamont in this volume, KNA/LEG.14/21/Vol. 1 Native Authority Ordinance, 1920.
16. We find some succinct descriptions of the first burials in Weithaga in Karanja 1999: 26, 61. Derek Peterson describes the burials in Tumutumu this way: "John Muriuki, for example, was called home from school in the mid 1920s at the death of his grandmother. Working without the assistance of relatives, he dug the grave, wrapped the body in cloth, and placed it in the grave. He remembered that a few relatives assisted by throwing dirt into the grave. They were later cleansed by the elders, but Muriuki refused. He explained himself: 'When Christianity came from Tumutumu, cleanliness (*utheri*) was started as we came to know about it. It was the mission people who started the idea of burying the dead. They brought the light and we learned from them. When I was burying my grandmother, people would not come to help me, they feared being caught by *thahu*. Even after I buried her, my mother want a ceremony to be performed, but I didn't want that'" (Peterson 2000: 113).
17. The land issue lies at the core of Kenyan history. Land disputes appear from the beginning of the colonization and were "settled" by the Carter commission (Lonsdale 1992). During the Mau Mau, the Swynnerton Plan "consolidated" property rights in the central province, favoring Kikuyu loyalists (Sorrenson 1967). Today's land market is highly tense and most of the "tribal clashes" which have erupted in Kenya since 1992 have involved land.

18. The KCA was mainly formed of young Christianized and literate Kikuyu. They opposed the Kikuyu elders during the colonial period and fought a moral war with those Kikuyu who conducted the Mau Mau Uprising.
19. For the case of the Mbeere, neighboring the Kikuyu, see Glazier 1984.
20. Old man, about seventy-five years old, Kabete, 2001.
21. Old man, about eight years old, Kabete, 2001.
22. Very few Muslims lived in the Nairobi area. They were mainly families of the "Sudanese" battalion hired by the British administration.
23. Another informant gave me a more accurate date, 1914, for the last disposal of the body in Kabete.
24. Old man, about seventy-five years old, Kabete, 2001.
25. The notion of ritual impurity seems to have disappeared among the Kikuyu following the counterinsurgency measures adopted by the British army throughout the Mau Mau Uprising. During their villagization operation, they constrained Kikuyu people to break the rules that preserved them from impurity. See Elkins 2005 for a description of these measures. See Lamont in this volume for the concept of impurity among the Meru, who are closely related to the Kikuyu.
26. Young man, about twenty years old, Laikipia, 1994.
27. Young man, about eighteen years old, Laikipia, 1994.
28. Man, about sixty years old, Kabete 2001.
29. See also Lamont, this volume.
30. See Droz 1999; Droz & Sottas 1997.
31. Young man, about twenty-five years old, Laikipia, 1993.
32. See Heald 1989 on this issue concerning another ethnic group of the Bantu language group.
33. See for example the famous S. M. Otieno case (Cohen and Atieno Odhiambo 1992).
34. Man, about sixty years old, Kabete, 2001.
35. For an extensive study of the British welfare policies in Kenya, see Lewis 2000.
36. Having a will drawn up is not a guarantee that the individual's desire will be respected.

Bibliography

Berman, Bruce and John Lonsdale. 1991. "Louis Leakey's Mau Mau: a study in the politics of knowledge." *History and Anthropology* 5, no. 2: 143–204.

Bujra, Janet. 1970. *Ethnicity and Religion: A Case-study from Pumwani, Nairobi.* Discussion Paper N 13. Nairobi: Institute of African Studies.

Cohen, David William and E. S. Atieno Odhiambo. 1992. *Burying SM: The Politics of Knowledge and the Sociology of Power in Africa.* Portsmouth, NH: Heinemann.

Droz, Yvan. 1999. *Migrations kikuyus: des pratiques sociales à l'imaginaire. Ethos, réalisation de soi et millénarisme.* Recherches et Travaux no. 14. Neuchâtel & Paris: Institut d'ethnologie & Maison des sciences de l'homme.

———. 2000a. "Circoncision féminine et masculine en pays kikuyus: rite d'institution, division sociale et Droits de l'Homme." *Cahiers d'études Africaines* 158 (XL-2): 215–240.

———. 2000b. "L'ethos du *mûramati* kikuyu; Schème migratoire, différenciation sociale et individualisation au Kenya." *Anthropos* 95, no. 1: 87–98.

——. 2003. "Des hyènes aux tombes; Moderniser la mort au Kenya central." In *Les figures de la mort à Nairobi; une capitale sans cimetière,* ed. Y. Droz and H. Maupeu, 17–54. Paris: L'Harmattan.

Droz, Yvan and Beat Sottas. 1997. "Partir ou rester? Partir et rester. Migrations des Kikuyus au Kenya." *L'Homme* 142: 69–88.

Elkins, Caroline. 2005. *Imperial reckoning: the untold story of Britain's gulag in Kenya.* New York: Henry Holt and Company.

Gatheru, Mugo M R. 1964. *Child of Two World; A Kikuyu's Story.* New York & Washington: Praeger Publishers.

Glazier, Jack. 1984. "Mbeere Ancestors and the Domestication of Death." *Man* 19, no. 1: 133–147.

Heald, Suzette. 1989. *Controlling Anger: the Sociology of Gisu Violence.* New York: St Martin's Press.

Karanja, John. 1999. *Founding an African Faith: Kikuyu Anglican Christianity 1900–1945.* Nairobi: Uzima Press.

Kariuki, Joseph. 2003. "Funérailles kikuyu dans les quartiers de Nairobi." In *Les figures de la mort à Nairobi; une capitale sans cimetière,* ed. Y. Droz and H. Maupeu, 55–74. Paris : L'Harmattan.

Kershaw, Greta. 1973. "The Kikuyu of Central Kenya." In *Cultural Source, Material for Population Planning in East Africa,* ed. A. Molinos. Nairobi: East African Publishing House, 3: 47–59.

Leakey, Louis S. B. 1977. *The Southern Kikuyu before 1903.* 3 vols. London, New York and San Francisco: Academic Press.

Lewis, Joanna. 2000. *Empire State-Building: War & Welfare in Kenya 1925–1952.* Athens (USA): Ohio University Press.

Lonsdale, John. 1992. "The Moral Economy of Mau Mau: Wealth, Poverty, and Civic Virtue in Kikuyu Political Thought." In *Unhappy Valley, Conflict in Kenya and Africa; Violence and Ethnicity.* eds. B. Berman and J. Lonsdale. Athens (USA): Ohio University.

Nation. 1994. March 30.

Nation. 1995. April 7.

Peatrik, Anne-Marie. 1994. "Un système composite: l'organisation d'âge et de génération des Kikuyu pré-coloniaux." *Journal des Africanistes* 64, no. 1: 3–36.

Peterson, Derek. 2000. "Writing Gikuyu; Christian Literacy and Ethnic Debate in Northern Central Kenya, 1908–1952." PhD diss., University of Minnesota.

Prins, Adriaan Hendrik Johan. 1953. *East African Age-class Systems; Galla—Kipsigis—Kikuyu.* Groningen & Djakarta: J.B. Wolters.

Routledge, W. S. and K. Routledge. 1910. *With a Prehistoric People: the Akikuyu of British East Africa.* London: Edward Arnold.

Sorrenson, M. P. K. 1967. *Land reform in the Kikuyu country.* Oxford: Oxford University Press.

Target. 1995. April 1–15.

White, Luise. 1990. *The Comforts of Home: Prostitution in Colonial Nairobi.* Chicago: University of Chicago Press.

CHAPTER 4

Decomposing Pollution?
Corpses, Burials, and Affliction among the Meru of Central Kenya

Mark Lamont

Introduction

Due to their enigmatic status among the living, corpses are the source of great ambivalence and therefore also powerful goads to the human imagination. While I will return later to changing dispositions toward corpses in the specific ethnohistorical context I address in this essay—that of the Meru in central Kenya from the 1930s to the present—my opening concern lies with what Bilinda Straight (2006: 100) has called the "entangled agencies" between the living and the dead.

Many mortuary practices, from organ donors in the United States to double burials in Indonesia, are by definition only specific developments within broader historical processes. This chapter seeks to qualify the historical study of mortuary rites in central Kenya by demonstrating how a powerful complex of ideas and practices can be transformed, not only through changing historical conditions, but through the ways in which the "ontological status of persons—the living as well as the recently dead—is typically, even necessarily, in flux" (Straight 2006: 102). Prior to the 1930s, the Meru disposed of the dead and dying through surface exposure in uninhabited forests and through ejecting corpses and the terminally ill from domestic and agricultural spaces, a practice found throughout the central Kenyan highlands. This practice was linked to ritual action aimed at cleansing the bereaved from the pollution of death, the corpse being particularly dangerous in its decomposition until it was obliterated through carrion eating animals such as hyenas or vultures. The colonial government banned corpse exposure and through coercive legislation forced the Meru to bury their dead from 1934 onward. Taking this shift from corpse exposure to burial as my point of departure, this chapter discusses how complex negotiations with colonial government policies on hygiene, social space, and property produced new forms of corpse disposal and transformed the relationships that surviving Meru could have with the deceased. While the Meru have buried their dead for seventy years, apprehension over the status of the deceased—what anthropologists have conceptualized as "pollution"—is still a factor in Meru death practices, albeit one radically transformed from its pre-1934 forms.

What concerns me here is death pollution, or rather its seeming decomposition within Meru expressions of affliction and bereavement since the middle colonial period. In discussions about pollution with my Meru interlocutors, most of whom are Christian, I was told that such things were no longer of concern. Yet in my dealings with funerals and those involved in the bereavement process, I found that this stance was more apparent than real, and that while death pollution was not explicitly expressed, some people's corpses and the circumstances surrounding their deaths provoked anxiety about sickness and misfortune. The title of this chapter, "Decomposing Pollution?", is a heuristic question that captures something of the displacement of the Meru pollution complex through the combined and overlapping histories of forced burial, Christianization, and land reforms among the Meru.

Given the shortfall of convincing historical explanations of why central Kenyans rapidly adopted inhumation in the 1930s, this chapter seeks to refocus attention on moral panics about hygiene during this same period to argue that the Meru did not so much abandon pollution as find ways to incorporate colonial government and Christian concerns for hygiene into their own changing theories about the relationship between affliction and moral order. Decomposition, in this sense, is being used both as a heuristic device and as an analytic scheme.

By tracing a largely oral history of death practices before colonial sanitation policies forced people to bury their dead and conversion to Christianity sanctified interment, this chapter claims that Meru anxiety over the polluting effects of contact with corpses mirrored the panic about African hygiene among colonial officials and technocrats. In its broadest sense, and following upon Mary Douglas's (1966) work on pollution, hygiene is thought of here as a way of maintaining moral order, in this case definitions of "good" and "bad" deaths. By focusing on the polyvalence of both pollution and hygiene, I hazard the claim that the entanglements of Meru pollution complexes and European hygiene structures are not wholly dissimilar in their management of death and the dying.

Informed by ethnographic fieldwork undertaken in 1998, 2001–2003, and a brief revisit in 2007,[1] my argument is that the Meru turn to burials in the 1930s was contingent upon changing circumstances in the emergent colonial polity. Yet changes in the treatment of corpses and the management of their disposal were also the outcome of analytic work about the meanings of hygiene among those young Meru of the mid-1930s who converted to Methodist Christianity. Enforced by the Meru Local Native Council (LNC), mandatory burial initially sparked off debates between male elders, women, youths, and colonial authorities about where and how to bury the dead. These debates, however, were relatively short-lived. According to archived colonial documents and to conversations with older Meru who witnessed the change from corpse exposure to burial, interment was to become generalized throughout most of the Meru subgroups within a few years.

Colonial policies that enforced burial met with various local interpretations and anxieties about the effects closer contact with corpses would have among the Meru. While keeping sight of the coercion of the colonial system, one possible outcome of the shift from corpse exposure to burial was that the ontological relation between the dead and the living, based on a deep aversion to the pollutions of death and sex—affecting people, animals, and crops—came to be imaginatively challenged through new ideas about hygiene. The problem remains to account for how increased colonial intervention in Meru funerary practices provided a new context for rethinking how corpses could possibly threaten the well being of the living.

To wade into this problem, I've chosen to organize this chapter into five main concerns: the comparative ethnography of the central Kenyan region, a reconstruction of corpse exposure and forced burials, a discussion of the protests against burial and their implication for the concepts of pollution and hygiene, a reconsideration of the role of shifting land tenure and memory work, and finally an ethnography of contemporary ambivalences towards certain kinds of corpses and graves.

The regional context

For the central Kenya region, the shift from corpse exposure to burial has received a variety of recent scholarly interpretations (Droz 2003; Morovich 2003; Peatrik 1991, 2000; Glazier 1984). A re-examination of this history shows how changing mortuary practices connect with broader issues of colonial domination, shifting property, and social relations, as well as the making of new cosmologies through conversion to Christianity, and above all, the changing relationships between the living and the dead. Keeping the regional context in perspective, comparisons between the Kikuyu, Mbeere, and Meru illuminate how similar structural processes might produce different social effects in the management of death practices across the region. In a broader comparative perspective, however, the combination of corpse exposure with pollution complexes without elaborate postdisposal mortuary rituals appears to be something of an anthropological oddity.

I am drawing attention, here, to Robert Hertz's well known essay on the variety of mortuary rituals where mourning periods are organized to manage the pollution of death through double burials and the eventual preservation of the bones of the ancestors (Hertz 1960 [1907]). Hertz first linked the wetness of decomposing corpses to death pollution and intense mourning for the deceased, a process eventually brought to a close through the exhumation of dry bones and their reinterment in permanent tombs as ancestors. Focusing mainly on Indonesia, Hertz drew attention to societies that stress the eventual preservation of physical remains while remaining wary of the dangers of decomposition. The central Kenyan examples from the early twentieth century differ in many respects, but most strikingly in the deposition of the corpse in uninhabited forest areas for disposal by scavenging animals, often hyenas, with little or no further mortuary rituals taking place other than an intensive purification conducted after disposal and a limited period of postmortuary seclusion for the bereaved. And yet all central Kenyan peoples were highly expressive in their precautions against both sexual and death pollution, despite not recognizing the deceased as ancestors beyond one or two generations. Here were societies that would have confounded Malinowski's dictum "love of the dead and loathing of the corpse" (Malinowski 1954: 47–8). How have ethnographers of the central Kenyan region accounted for this striking ethnographic material?

Anne-Marie Peatrik's treatment of Meru conceptions of life and death is unequivocal on this matter (Peatrik 1991, 2000). Writing about Meru corpse exposure prior to their adoption of burial in the 1930s, Peatrik provides only exceptional cases of interment, where an elder in later life, a *mwariki*, was buried in a household's dung midden (*ikiara*), but all other deceased were taken to the forest and exposed to the hyenas or other scavengers. In discussing the place of death in the Meru life cycle, Peatrik (2005) asserts:

> In Meru conception, there is no belief in life after death; there are no ancestors, no ancestor worship, no genealogical mentality, a state of things that fits well with the absence of descent groups. This is the reason why the corpses of people who have died before the completion of the life-cycle are so feared. And the different death rituals were, and still are, performed according to the age of the dead person (Peatrik 2005: 295).

The bottom line of this interpretation is that there can be no development of a "cult of the dead"— that is to say, an extensive social and ontological relationship between the living and the dead—when there is no genealogical depth to social groups. Yet this raises some interesting theoretical problems, firstly about what happened to the Meru pollution complex, and secondly about the rather rapid adoption of burial starting in the 1930s among the central Kenya peoples.

As a complement to Yvan Droz's chapter on the Kikuyu in this volume, my chapter on the Meru points out some continuing ambivalences in the treatment of corpses and questions about the polluting effects of the dead upon the living. In particular, my centrally organizing concerns with pollution, corpses, burials, and affliction lead me to examine hygiene as a conceptual framework in changing mortuary practices among the Meru. In building upon the work of other anthropologists (notably Glazier 1984), who have stressed land and changing property relations along with conversion to Christianity, this chapter argues that attention paid to changing concepts of hygiene may avoid assumptions that death and sexual pollution have been wholly abandoned among the Meru. To qualify this claim, it is worthwhile to first present other interpretations of the shift from corpse exposure to burial in the central Kenyan region that stress shifting social relations to property, especially land.

As a brief starting point, it is useful to highlight Jack Glazier's (1984) examination of the shift from corpse exposure to burial among the Mbeere. The Mbeere are a small population culturally similar to other ethnic formations in the central highlands of Kenya such as the Meru, Embu, Kikuyu, and Kamba (see Droz 2003, and this volume). Glazier's hypothesis about the relations between graves, property, land, and memory work adds an important tension to the argument put forth in this chapter. Glazier's view of the shift from surface exposure to interment among the Mbeere pivots on how changes in land tenure transformed the relationships between the living and their ancestors. Since all land is owned by clans or individuals, including woodlands and bushy areas, Glazier argues that burial has "domesticated" death, insofar as the bush was increasingly dissociated from the ancestors in the form of spirits. In his own words, "burial has domesticated death and created more tangible connexions between a social group and a land parcel" (Glazier 1984: 133). The scope of this interpretation of changing death practices is wide and accounts for why graves could be used as evidence for long-term residence on land subject to legal dispute. Among the Mbeere, the ancestors would have, in time, less and less connection with the causes of affliction among the living.

Glazier's (1984) account of the social consequences of burial among the Mbeere touches upon many of the themes addressed in this chapter, such as the social effects of mandatory burial and changing conceptions of death and affliction. Yet the Mbeere analysis also presents some revealing sociological and historical differences with Meru experiences of the same political processes. Characterizing the Mbeere of the 1930s as "highly mobile, weak corporate descent groups," Glazier asserts that there had been a weak link between lineages and territory, land having been abundant and readily accessible among the agro-pastoralist Mbeere of the early colonial period. Glazier presents the case that the "unceremonious disposal of corpses," characterized by having "little attendant ritual," was an epiphenomenal feature of Mbeere social organization. Even though burial was made compulsory by the Embu LNC as early as 1930, Glazier attests that Mbeere remained ambivalent about inhumation until it proved to be beneficial in settling land cases some decades later. With the introduction of far-reaching land tenure reforms across Kenya Colony, beginning in the 1950s, the Mbeere entered into an "avalanche" of clan disputes over land in which "genealogical recall" increasingly played a vital role (1984: 136–7). Here, Glazier claims, the Mbeere found new social uses for grave sites. Such spaces previously did not have such value in litigation at colonial courts. According to this interpretation of the acceptance of burial among the Mbeere, the main social effect of burial was that graves established a "visible connexion between a particular territory and forebears buried within it" (Glazier 1984: 144). In this analysis, a very critical link between graves and shifting property relations is socially established, particularly with reference to land and lineage.

Glazier's analysis of burials and graves in furthering Mbeere land claims in colonial court settings rests on the argument that lineages are the structurally significant feature of their social organization. For the Meru, the structurally enduring feature of their social organization is their age-set formation. Despite the abandonment of the formation of successive age-sets among many of the Meru subgroups in recent decades, its idiom persists as a symbol of social continuity and culturally defines social death. Among the Nyambene Meru, to the north of the populous central Meru, the cyclic opening and closing of age-sets can be traced back at least four generations, spanning a period of roughly a century. As a cycle of eight age-sets, divided by alternate generation sets, the name of each age-set is recycled approximately every hundred years. And within this cycle of age-set formation, social death is achieved when the last surviving member of a specific age-set passes on. In terms of memory work, the persistence of age-sets is socially more durable than the grave of an individual. An individual's grave is often neglected or even forgotten within a few years. Trees and other permanent boundary markers have more relevance in settling land cases in Meru than graves. Once the last members of an age-set have died, they are rarely mentioned again. This feature of Meru social organization has importance when comparing their ideas about death with other central Kenyan peoples.

At this point however, in order to contextualize death practices prior to the 1934 colonial imposition of burial in Meru, it is necessary to historically reconstruct the Meru practice of corpse exposure and its attendant pollution complex.

Corpse exposure

To the Meru, the corpse (*kîimba*) was a rank source of dangerous pollution called *rûkûo*.[2] Any physical contact with a corpse required immediate purification and was likely to cause significant anxiety about one's own health or the contamination of others, particularly spouses and children. According to Meru notions of personhood—and they were changing in the interwar period—those at the very beginning and end of the Meru life cycle were seen as less polluted. Likewise, very elderly persons, *ntindiri*, especially those waiting out their days in the dark of their houses, are said to be as small children in this regard. Yet, to the Meru of a half century ago, all corpses exuded an unseen miasma that endangered people and animals, a pollution that could be infused into any physical object the deceased came into contact with while dying (*gwatithia rûkûo*).

The Meru theory of health and sickness rested upon a notion of pollution called *mûgiro*. This *mûgiro* pollution can be applied to many explanations of misfortune. It explained afflictions, but it was also instrumental in keeping people conscious of how their behavior correlated with their well-being and health. The polyvalence of this concept is evident in that it could be invoked both to refer to individual misfortune and large-scale disasters that impacted large numbers of people (Peatrik 1999: 366). In this lived relation to misfortune, everyday life was one fraught with the concern for minimizing one's exposure to pollution. Vigilant and frequent purification rites were observed on a daily basis.

Certain categories of persons were considered to be less affected by the taint of *mûgiro*, typically those who had little contact with others, who were not exposed to sexual or death pollution, or who did not have to kill. Infants and the very old were considered to be pure: the very young because they had not come into contact with *mûgiro*, the agent of sickness, misfortune, and death before one's time, the very aged because they had lived a fulfilled life and had long since ceased sexual activities. In noting that the very elderly could handle corpses without harm, Hugh Lambert (1956) claimed that the very aged men in *kîama kîa mbiti* ("the hyena council") "have no further intercourse with women and are consequently considered fit and proper persons to touch dead bodies, the general principle being that a person who is incapable of passing on the taint to the other sex is incapable of getting it" (Lambert 1956: 94). Today, this pollution concept is only occasionally invoked, although at a funeral I attended in 2002, I heard an older woman console the fussing of a small child with the proverb "*gûtî mwana ûrî mûgiro*" (no small child has impurity).

In most cases of death, those living within the neighboring homesteads would be required to abstain from sexual activity until all the adult members of the deceased family were publicly declared clear of their *mûgiro*. Neighborhood sexual abstinence was viewed as preventing the infusion of *mûgiro* into people's houses. If the death was a child's, parents would perform a ritual sex act (*gûteera mpanga*) and then shave one another, *gîkîî*, to cleanse themselves of pollution. Other sexual "cleansing" rituals were performed. Among those returning from the forest where the dead and the dying were placed, the pollution carried back to their houses could only be assuaged through specific sexual acts followed by shaving, said to "cut away" the pollution. Men and women who were not spouses, and often older persons, carried out both rituals (*kûtheria*) and were known as *batheria* (literally "cleaners," but *kûtheria* can also mean to commit adultery.) Special care was taken to sweep the passageways of house entrances and the openings of the fenced compound, an act also known as *kûtheria*. This was important because both death and sex pollution could be passed on through the living—including animals, plants, and foodstuffs—as well as the inanimate: house structures, tools, soil, waterways, clothing, beddings, vessels, and ornaments.

In the event of a death, especially of someone who had suffered a long illness, there was considerable concern for the polluting effects of the corpse. The body was considered hot, infused with a lifetime's effects of past transgressions (see also Peatrik 2000). Infused by death pollution and symbolically akin to the corpse, the houses themselves were permanently abandoned, left to ruin. If an individual died in his or her house, portions of the walls would be demolished to allow hyenas or other scavengers to enter and drag away the remains. I have known people to express serious anxiety for accidentally stumbling over ruined house sites (*maganjo*), as sometimes happens when clearing land or forest, although this may be no more than the remnants of a very old hearth.

There existed certain persons who were tasked with carrying out the dead and dying from settlements into the woodlands beyond. Called *eenji* (singular, *mwenji*), such persons were outcasts. One became a *mwenji* through punishment for deviant behavior or as an alternative to capital punishment. Their only social role was to dispose of the dead and dying. They lived on the fringes of settlements themselves, not unlike the dead. A kind of living dead themselves, these men and women had the tasks of disrobing, shaving, washing, and then carrying the corpse into the bush. Both men and women could become *eenji*, and they only undertook the disposal of corpses of their own sex.

If a person died at home, *eenji* came to the homestead of the deceased to remove the corpse from their house. Depending on the distance to the woodland area, *eenji* often tied the legs and arms of the corpse onto their own with rawhide thongs and carried the corpse's torso on their backs, bent over at the waist to accommodate dead limbs. In order to capture the macabre intimacy between the corpse and its carrier, a few of my informants demonstrated the slumbering, awkward shuffle of the *eenji* carrying their burden. These kinds of bodily memories invoke details about the avoidance relations between the bereaved, the deceased, and those who managed the disposal of the corpse.

The following two sections attempt to compare European and African sensitivities about the management of corpses in the 1930s and contrasting concerns with hygiene. Of interest here is the sense of mutual repugnance Africans and Europeans had concerning each other's funerary practices.

Of hygiene and hyenas

In August 1934, the dozen or so African men making up the Local Native Council (LNC) of Meru passed a resolution that banned the practice of corpse exposure and compelled the Meru, on pain of prosecution, to bury their dead. It was not, of course, their initiative. Beginning in 1920 in Kiambu, a Kikuyu district near Nairobi, orders fanned out throughout central Kenya banning the widespread practice of corpse exposure. Repugnant to European sensitivities towards the treatment of corpses and their threat to sanitation, the disposal of the majority of dead and dying in specially demarcated areas outside of residential space was widely condemned as unhygienic and, in cases where the terminally ill were quarantined in the bush, denounced as immoral (Blakeslee 1956; Hobley 1910). Although the 1934 legislation that forced internment was overshadowed by other localized controversies, such as the lowering of the age of initiation (see Thomas 1998; 2003), it raised important questions about the meanings "hygiene" would take among the Meru.

In the months that passed in the wake of this new legislation, enacted under the Native Authority Ordinance, senior European administrators wrote, with some satisfaction, that the order had been "generally obeyed" and made bureaucratic note of some eighty-three convictions for "non-compliance" (KNA/Meru DC/MRU/1/2). In anticipation of the November rains, however, an extraordinary event took place that arrested one district officer's imagination:

> When the November rains appeared to be failing some thousands of women of Upper Abothuguchi marched into the boma to protest against the order as in their opinion the failure of the rains was due to the act of burial. They had suggested to the Chief that corpses already buried should be dug up again. After a baraza they went quietly away. It rained heavily the following night.

This was an event that has been previously discussed in anthropological publications on the Meru (Peatrik 1991; 2000; Lambert 1956). As I saw these women's protest as key in preparing the material for this chapter, I was already aware of a major methodological problem: that those who participated in this protest, the women of the age-set *Tirindi*, were long since deceased. On a visit to Meru in November 2007, where I tried to follow up on this historical event, very few elderly women could recall in particular detail why their mothers had protested against the Native Ordinance Act. Harriet Ndegwa, a widow whose mother had taken part in the protest, told me:

Our mothers used to have *bîama* (elder's councils), very much like our *gîkundi* (credit societies), but they organized the timing of the plantings and harvests so that one family would wait until they were told to begin work on the land. That was women's work, no man would get in there ... but our mothers, those of *Tirindi,* they went to Mûtindwa (Meru Town) because there was no rain and the Chiefs were telling people to bury, like we do today. We can't know about those things today, but our mothers were very good at speaking with men ... especially the Whites.

Women's alarm and protest over the inhumation of corpses points to senior women's position in agricultural rituals and the place of managing pollution to curb the threat of looming social, bodily, and environmental crises. From the women's perspective, the act of burying corpses in the ground was unpropitious, unnecessarily calling forth the spiritual agency of the recently departed. Put into cultural context, Meru accepted that droughts, famines, pestilence, and epidemic were natural catastrophes, but thought that these were manifestations of deeper tensions in the relations between the living, on the one hand, and the living and the recently dead on the other. In historical context, these women would have experienced death first hand, especially following three major famines that made the postconquest period one remembered for its high mortality. As a woman of about ninety years old, Rael Kiringo recalled:

During famine, my mother used to play a trick on us to keep off the hunger. She boiled those hard, inedible roots and kept telling us, "wait now, wait now" and we didn't know there was no food. Eh, people died though. Old M'Ncebere can tell you how many people died in his father's sugar cane stands. They gorged themselves on sugar cane and died. Eh, *Kîaramûû, Kîaranduara,* and *Ngigi* ... all of these happened when I was small (Kirengo, Kaaga, June 12, 2001).

These were *Kîaramûû* (1918 famine and influenza epidemic), *Kîaranduara* (1921 "famine of eating leather skins"), and *Ngigi* (1926 "Locust famine"), the brunt of which fell upon women desperately trying to feed their families. The combined 1918 crisis was said by the district officer who wrote the annual political report in 1919 to have "decimated" the Meru. Even a conservative estimate based on the scanty demographic evidence available would suggest an excess of 10,000 deaths that particular year. *Kîaramûû* was of such cataclysmic proportions that it is small wonder with such a surplus of corpses that there might be a surfeit of explanations.

Climatic disasters were linked together with diseases in an etiology of affliction that accounted for the social dimensions of famine. Unlike the European concern for countering famine through occasional food relief raised through

LNC taxation, the Meru accepted the possibility that such misfortunes were being visited upon them because people were not behaving in appropriately moral ways. With explanations of illness and misfortune linked to an etiology of affliction in which recent ancestors' blessings and curses bore as much explanatory weight as exposure to death and sex pollution, the emergent sexualities and high mortality of the 1930s provoked something like a moral panic among the elders (see Thomas 2003). This protest against the burial of the dead came at a time of rapid, bewildering change and crisis.

This incident also, however, suggests how the Native Authority Ordinance was conceptualized and acted upon within the Meru ontology of the 1930s, particularly with reference to the bodily memories of some of the eldest living Meru men and women I have known. Older Meru did not convey to me their former fear and ambivalence to pollution with words alone. They enacted it with dramatic reference to their own bodies, touching themselves to indicate particular afflictions associated with sex and death. For instance, on one occasion when an old man coughed, he explained that in his youth, when a man was seized by persistent coughing fits, his age-mates would ask him to identify "the woman" linked to his affliction before he set into motion certain "cleansing" rituals. Likewise, children's croup was often explained as the outcome of their parents' mutual pollution, perhaps even an undisclosed incestuous liaison. In order to understand the ambivalence the Meru briefly showed to the burial of the dead, we should perhaps look at the relationships between Meru pollution ideas with European concerns over hygiene.

Europeans were clearly alarmed about corpse exposure, citing the threat these practices had to communal hygiene. In turn, Africans found the European treatment of corpses equally alarming, even dangerous, as they touched dead bodies and sometimes cut them open. This did not only apply to the central highlands but throughout other regions such as western Kenya and the coast, especially where post mortem autopsies and the handling of bones were seen as evidence of European cannibalism (see Mutongi 2007: 34–38).

Ambitious "village sanitation" programs were implemented by colonial officials and missionaries throughout Kenya Colony in the 1930s and 1940s. Hygiene was one of the marks of "civilization," drummed into missionary converts and promoted through a number of venues, including *baraza*, the open air meetings arranged by government chiefs and headmen. In Meru, "village sanitation" took two principal forms, the digging of pit latrines and the ban on corpse exposure. Not incidental to the work of translation in such *baraza*, the word used to describe pit latrines, *bîoro*, was semantically close to the word used to demarcate the disposal of the dead, *kîorone*. Indeed, in administrative reports the notion that the Meru "threw out their dead" was deeply ingrained, a conceit that would be quite alien to indigenous standards of moral and physical hygiene. The exposure of the dead and especially of the dying was, however, a special case of alarm for European observers. A year after the ban was introduced, a colonial officer would write:

> An order requiring burial of dead persons was issued last year, under the provisions of the Native Authority Ordinance … A somewhat ingenious attempt to circumvent the Order was recently brought to light. The native in question instead of burying his child, killed a goat and buried it and threw the body of the child into the bush (KNA DC/MRU/1/2, Annual Report, 1934).

In the years following the 1934 burial ordinance, no further mention is made about corpse exposure in the administrative records, the officials noting that "socially considerable advance has been made, particularly in regard to … village sanitation and burial" (KNA DC/MRU/1/2). At about the same time as the above missive was written, a self-identified group of young Meru women and men, the *Atemibanjîra,* the first converts to Methodist Christianity, were stirring up controversy within their communities by their new disposition towards matters of dirt and cleanliness.

The *Atemibanjîra,* or "Pathfinders" as the Methodist missionaries referred to them, are widely considered to be the people who first performed Christian burials. A number of these people are still alive, although they are now mostly elderly and quite frail older women. One of them, Gladys Tirindi, told me how her parent's generation called them "stinkies," because they washed their bodies with bar soap, the smell of which was repugnant to many others who still washed using dust and castor oil. It was burial, however, that defined them as a group separate from nonconverts.

Almost all of my interlocutors acknowledged that the "Pathfinders" shocked other Meru by washing the corpses of deceased Christians, a task performed by *eenji.* In addition to ablutions, they also clothed those to be buried. Initial burials witnessed clothed bodies being buried six feet down, wrapped in wool trade cloths and sheets of calico. The adoption of caskets came more recently, as did the consumption of food after the burial, but surviving *Atemibanjîra* stressed the significance of burials to further conversions to Christianity because "Pathfinders" did not get sick in the ways predicted by nonconverts. Moreover, women who participated in the missionary seminars of Mary Holding learned of the "three Bs"—baths, babies, and Bible—as part of the Methodist Missionary Society's welfare and hygiene campaigns. Holding was an educationalist and published a series of Kîmerû language pamphlets on household chores and women's hygiene that some elderly women remember having heard read out to them at such seminars. These were variously titled: *Utheru bwa Mucii* ("Cleanliness of the Home"), *Mucii Jumwega* ("The Good Village"), *Ngono cia Afya* ("Hygiene Games and Stories"). Washing with soapy water was emphasized, but indigenous Meru cleansing rituals had always involved ablutions. In addition, with very high child mortality during the 1930s, the issue of cleanliness was associated with child survival and maternity work, one of the missionaries' main targets of hygiene propaganda. Around the same time, the long serving District Commissioner Hugh Lambert wrote a tract, *The Meru Yet to Come* (later translated into Kîmerû), that directly attacked child-rearing practices with condemnations of Meru hygiene and reproductive strategies. Neonatalist in scope, Lambert's propaganda made out a hygienic future emerging from a fear-laden and polluted past.

Esther Naitore, another surviving *Atemibanjîra*, described for me how she became a Christian in a story that touches upon pollution, the pain of children's deaths, and notions of hygiene:

> Oh! Oh! The children died. I said, "I won't spoil again." My three children died and people were so surprised, saying it was my husband's pollution. I decided not to stay in Meru. We [another woman and me] went to Tigania and stayed, but then Tigania women said, "You are joking ... that place where your children died, go back there, so that you may also die!" They chased us away. At the church, we stayed, and then at the mass, we as a group, the *Atemibanjîra*, we all denounced sorcery. That is when Nguruwe was born [her son]. Praise the Lord! We saw the light and turned away from sorcery. We saw that the "Three Bs" were the way forward." (Naitore, Chûgû, August 17, 2002)

In the next section, we leave behind concerns about hygiene and turn to the places where the dead were disposed, antisocial spaces that were ceded to European and other foreigners and put to commercial and administrative ends.

Shady places

Time after time, my Meru hosts would insist that the landscape had changed dramatically since the 1930s, especially following colonial land reforms and demarcations. Following the commercialization of agriculture, the colonial administration's ambitious land consolidation programs lasted two decades, radically transforming Meru agriculture during the 1950s and 1960s. This was undertaken as a long overdue response to conflicts over land, agricultural development, and a growing anticolonial movement that would lead to Kenya's independence in 1963. Land consolidation programs more than any other historical process transformed the Meru environment, including the gradual deforestation of large sections of Meru District. The forested slopes remained uninhabited before this process, after which aggressive efforts to clear the forest for land, fuel, and timber opened up the higher zones for coffee and tea production.

A common (if not reflexive) response to my interest in corpse exposure and the introduction of burial was that Meru District had been "really bushy and forested, not like today." The forests were the domain of hyenas, they would repeat, where people feared to tread. Although fairly densely populated in comparison to other central Kenyan communities, the Meru continued to be able to access land readily until the commercialization of agriculture commodified land. In the 1930s, administrators frequently commented on the rising "land consciousness" among the Meru and other central Kenyan peoples most affected by the massive appropriation of land by European settlers.

Most inhabited areas (*ntûûra*) had clearly demarcated areas, called alternatively *kîorone* or *ibîrîra*, where the deceased were disposed of. Today's place names identify areas where corpses were exposed. These are rarely residential sites. Such locations were used for building markets, coffee factories, schools, government administration blocks, and in some cases churches. Today, with the price of land skyrocketing—exacerbated by real estate speculators and land grabbing—quite a number of highly sought after commercial plots sit on former *kîorone* or *ibîrîra*, glossed into English as "graveyards."

In the thriving town of Maua, origin point of much of the world's supply of the natural stimulant *khat*, the truck stops, motor pools, lodgings, bars, and mosques that cater to Meru and Somali traders sit on a site, Gacîongo, that was used to dispose of the dead. Near a school I taught at in Mikinduri, around the coffee factory, sits another such site. Recalled in the form of place names, mostly related to death or forest animals, these formerly polluted sites were often turned over to development.

Wide acceptance of burial is normally associated with the first large group of Christians, the *Atemibanjîra* ("Pathfinders," or "Pioneers.") Salome Nteere, a self-identifying "Pathfinder," commented on how her parents' generation had settled the Methodist Missionary Society on grounds where corpses were disposed. This was Kaaga, cleared of forest around 1912, and a number of stories about this event are still avidly told about the difficult, early years of the Methodist mission station. European missionaries and administrators were often given land on the sites of *kîorone*. While the intention of these now long deceased elders in giving these specific sites to Europeans cannot be known, today's elderly described to me how their parents' generation thought the missionaries to be itinerant, and looked with interest at the misfortunes the whites endured at Kaaga. In permitting Europeans to build and develop their mission station on the site of a *kîorone*, were these Meru attempting to manage the influx of outsiders brought through colonialism?

In Mikinduri market, where I lived for a year in 2002, I learned that the first administrative hut, which neighbored my own rented house, was built upon the site of a *kîorone*. Although it is impossible to determine whether the colonial administration was attempting to make a symbolic gesture by building there, or whether the elders sought to see what would happen if they did build there, the area in which I lived was spatially marked off from the houses and plots of local people. It dawned on me that this area included the mosque, the medical dispensary, the district officer's house, the police station, the telephone exchange, and the houses of the first Muslim traders to settle in Mikinduri: all foreigners in the eyes of the local population.

By the early 1930s, land alienation throughout Kenya had sparked off organized opposition to European settlement. While there were no settlers permitted to appropriate land in Meru District, designated as a "Native Reserve," news of agitation against colonial land policies quickly reached Meru. Growing tensions over the availability of land led the Kenya Land Commission of 1933 to note specific cases where Gikuyu used corpses to lay claim to land taken by white settlers. The case of the exhumation of Chief Koinange wa Mbiyu's grandfather's remains was an attempt by his descendants to demonstrate how much land they had lost (Lonsdale 1992: 110). Of all the explanations given for the generalized shift from exposure to burial in central Kenya, changes in property relations and the value of land has attracted the most attention.

Glazier's account of how Mbeere made the burial of the dead their own deserves recognition, but he perhaps attributes too much weight in his analysis on the permanency of grave sites. As noted by Kenda Mutongi for the Maragoli of western Kenya, graves rapidly erode in a few years due to heavy rains (Mutongi 2007: 170). Claims to land through "proof" that one's ancestors were interred on one's property is more likely to be based on the graves of the recently dead. In Mutongi's assessment of Maragoli dispositions towards the dead, once graves have been leveled off, their mounds recessed into the soil, the spirits are said to be at rest and no longer threaten the living. Land in this context is a critical factor, since "to leave land was to abandon ancestors," but the materiality of the eroding grave mounds, much like the process of decomposition of bodies to dry bones in other societies, posed a problem to those Maragoli who negotiated new forms of land tenure based on "evidence" of long-term occupation on particular tracts of land. Maragoli innovations in cementing graves, of course, made it more difficult for newcomers to purchase or exchange land that had belonged to others. In this fashion, graves that would otherwise wash away were turned into permanent tombs. To the Maragoli, this meant that the spirits were still materially tied to the land.

Based on the Meru evidence, I would suggest that the presence of burial sites as a sign of long occupancy or of claims to land is restricted to the recently dead, possibly only one or two generations back. Among the informants whose family histories I managed to document, their title deeds were acquired relatively recently, mostly in the late 1960s. In most cases, the oldest identified graves, when still remembered, are those who were first issued title deeds. When land adjudication and consolidation occurred in Meru, the Meru had been burying their dead for about three decades. The graves of the deceased prior to the 1960s are elsewhere and informants at pains to know their where-abouts. Based on both Glazier's (1984) account of the Mbeere and Mutongi's (2007) study of the Maragoli, the linkages between burial, the materiality of graves, memory work, and evidence of property rights are important in Ke-nya today. The Meru evidence would suggest, however, that the social uses of graves to mark out continued corporate rights to land are inconsistent and marked by ambivalence about graves themselves.

In order to explore Meru ambivalences about graves and burials, I turn to the ethnographic present of the early 2000s, some seventy years after the first burials in Meru District, in order to show some of the inchoate features of contemporary burials and attitudes towards the dead.

Grave ambivalences

In December 2002, Julia Nkatha was buried. I was close to Julia enough to know that she had silently, even stoically suffered the deep probing pangs of angina since I had met her in 1998. Julia was a celebrated individual within her location, a "Pathfinder" with the Methodist Church, and, typical of her genera-tion, the mother and grandmother of many educated and successful people.

Julia was held in high esteem. There was an obituary in a national daily newspaper and her funeral was announced over the radio. Her eulogy was dis-tributed widely throughout the community. The funeral committee had easily raised funds to purchase a quality coffin with a thick umber lacquer, bright brass handles, and a carved relief of a crucifix on its face. Vehicles to trans-port the body and the funerary party from the hospital morgue to the church were volunteered. People came together to cook food, set up PA equipment, tie wreaths and pick flowers, arrange transportation for relatives living at a distance, and diligently sweep her dirt courtyard.

Julia's funeral was well attended. I had observed this at the dozens of funer-als of elders I had gone to. In fact, these were the only funerals I attended at that time. Although quite a number of young people had died during my stays in Meru—from accidents, murder, disease, or suicide—few invitations to at-tend their funerals had gone out. These were in complete contrast to the buri-als of elders, whose funerals were well publicized, costly, and elaborate affairs. Such a contrast, of course, probed me to question the distinct differences in attitude between my European acceptance of the deaths of the elderly and the repugnance of a young life "cut short."

Asking about this, people would inevitably grow somewhat reticent and mull over how to answer what was, I am sure, a difficult question to address. "Well ... you see," started one, "the families usually keep those a quiet affair."

As it was explained by the brother of a young woman who died unexpectedly while on duty as a prison guard in Embu:

> When she passed away, it was a hard thing for everyone, of course ... and that's how Muriungi [the two year old son of the deceased] came to stay with us. I think there was about a week to organize her funeral. My father took care of the certificate in Meru Town ... then he went in a *matatu* to Embu Hospital, where she passed, and ... I was in Nairobi at the time ... they buried her soon after. You know, my parents were grieving a lot (Muriuki, Kaaga, June 6, 2001).

With respect to the death of parents or grandparents, people will make strident efforts to attend funerals from afar, even when living abroad in the UK, South Africa, or the United States (see Maupeu and Droz 2003). In the brief narrative above, Muriuki did not attend his sister's funeral, a women who was his senior by two years, even though he was living in Nairobi, a distance of about 125 miles from Meru.

In the case of a suicide of a young worker at one of Meru's commercial bakeries, it was rumored that his two brothers, acting alone, buried him expeditiously after securing the death certificate and retrieving the corpse from the hospital's morgue. Although rumor, such stories make clear that the death of a young person, especially someone who has taken his or her own life, is generally slated for an attenuated burial, without much in the way of obsequies.

How to understand this difference in burials between the aged and the young? One possible path of interpretation lies in how Meru conceive of their life's overall course, elders being accomplished through the triple rites of passage of marriage, parenthood, and the circumcision of their children. Young people who die "before their time" have, by Meru definitions, led a highly curtailed life.

Another way of understanding this, however, lies in the cause of death itself. With respect to elders, who may die of "old age" (a category that does not exclude the diseases that afflict the aging), their demise is inevitably shrouded in the notion of a "good" death. People killed by others, or who happen upon an accidental death, or who die as a result of their own behavior, are put into another category concerning their death. In common parlance and in the national newspapers, these are indexed as "taboo deaths."

Consider the case of a young hospitalized mother who died in childbirth with her infant. As recounted by a friend of the woman's husband, her death was the subject to an intense debate among her in-laws and her parents. After a placental abruption during childbirth, she bled out and died. The infant, delivered by emergency cesarean section, died shortly after. After this tragic event, the husband turned to friends and family faced with a dilemma. While he had already organized the death certificate and transportation of the corpses from the morgue to Nkinyang'a for burial, his kinsmen approached him and told him he could not bury her on his smallholding. The stated reason was that the baby had died and they had no other surviving child that could be present at the funeral. They argued that it would be impossible to bury her on land belonging to her in-laws, since such an act would be a portent for future calamity. "A woman who dies losing a firstborn child during childbirth and who is buried on the land will claim another's firstborn," went one refusal. Her own parents argued that she had died while in the care of her in-laws (*athoni*), crying that some foul play had been responsible for her death, and that they had not received the entire bride-price that they had expected before their daughter gave birth to a child. Amid such bouts of blame, both the husband and wife's families refused to have the woman and infant buried on family land. Reluctantly seeking an alternative to a "proper" burial, the husband had no choice but to apply to have her and the infant buried in the public cemetery outside the hospital morgue. At a cost of 2500 Ksh. (about $48), she was interred in what is widely regarded as a "pauper's graveyard," most Meru eschewing the very idea of being buried in a public cemetery, just as among the Kikuyu (see Maupeu and Droz 2003; Droz, this volume).

Such impasses as the case above demonstrate how personhood is intimately linked with burial. As in other ethnographic studies of burial in Kenya, being interred in a cemetery is a sign of some frustrated status, whether it be landlessness, alienation from kin, or poverty. In Meru, the public cemetery behind Meru Hospital morgue deserves special mention with respect to pollution, burial, corpses, and affliction.

As argued earlier, some sites associated with the dead are polluted. Behind Meru Hospital's morgue is a public cemetery on a slope that leads down into a verdant valley bottom. It lies within shouting distance from Majengo, Meru Town's oldest slum, a site that was first home to former Nubian soldiers who assisted in building the Catholic cathedral. As the public cemetery lies on one of the major shortcuts to town from the outlying rural areas, the footpaths make a conspicuous wide arc around the plot. This place evokes horror stories. These are tales of mass burials in which the identity of the deceased is obliterated. Bones wash up to the soil's surface. Skulls resurface during the heavy rains. Remains get mixed up with one another. Corpses are interred using a backhoe and burials are hasty and superficial. Walking this route frequently in the company of other Meru, I heard these macabre stories, real or not, that spelled out a marked ambivalence to being buried on no-man's land. On such occasions, we furtively kept our distance and the apprehension of my Meru companions was palpable.

In 2008, this cemetery featured in the *East African Standard,* one of Kenya's daily newspapers, with the headline "Cemetery where the dead won't rest." Since my first visit to Meru in 1991, the Meru Hospital morgue and the municipal council cemetery have been at the center of complaints and controversies, mainly over issues of hygiene. The morgue's refrigeration unit is capricious and defective and mourning parties, coming to collect their dead, come prepared for long waits with aerosol sprays. The cemetery is perhaps more controversial, as the idea of mass graves and exhumations is alarming to those who live near it. The article in the *East African Standard* cites an elder spokesperson for nearby residents:

> Mzee Nahashon M'Muketha, 80, finds exhumations of bodies disgusting. Not only is the practice a taboo but it would also attract a curse, he says. "Disturbing graves for whatever reasons is not good. When we were young, children were not allowed to view bodies," says M'Muketha, a Mau Mau veteran and a Njuri Njeke elder. He says graveyards were holy places. People feared a curse if they disturbed the dead. They dreaded walking in a graveyard, let alone exhuming remains of a dead person, says M'Muketha. He says expectant women avoided walking across graveyards. This could attract the wrath of evil spirits and lead to abortion (Mathangani and Muriungi 2008).

Local residents openly discuss the cemetery as a health hazard, and a public health officer, Julius Mutabari, gave the Municipal Council two months to fence off the site and maintain stricter adherence to sanitation codes. Yet this concern for hygiene is shot through with concerns about what kinds of persons are buried there. Muriungi, a one time research assistant, told me: "I fear this place, Mark. Do you know who's buried in there? Nobody really knows who is who, they're all mixed up. There's babies and criminals, lying next to people nobody wanted to bury." This comment in particular was an insight into the social displacement of death pollution (*rûkûo*) in the time since the advent of forced burials, Christianization, and land demarcations. Meru concerns about hygiene in this cemetery are also concerns about the pollution of different categories of people being buried together, but also grave ambivalences about the circumstances of their deaths. The unclaimed corpses of criminals gunned down by police, the young unemployed man who hung himself, and the women who died in childbirth are all unpropitious deaths. And together, they have their own *kîorone.*

Decomposing pollution?

By way of conclusion, the Meru case compares well with other ethnographic and historical studies of the shift from corpse exposure to burials in central Kenya. Undoubtedly, the changing property relations of the colonial period, particularly the connections between land and lineages, are critical pieces of the puzzle, but in this chapter I have tried to bring pollution and hygiene into focus as another dimension of this process. In Meru today, *mûgiro* and *rûkûo* are rarely evoked as explanations of afflictions in any explicit manner, yet I have argued that such a formerly powerful complex of ideas and practices as those surrounding death cannot simply vanish into the ether.

This chapter used the heuristic question "Decomposing pollution?" to query statements by contemporary Meru that while death pollution no longer inhibits the material contact with the dead and dying, many still express profound anxieties over certain kinds of deaths and spaces where people who have had "bad" deaths are buried. The bodies of the dead and dying are still unsafe to the living, not because they pose an etiological threat, as before the 1930s, but because corpses retain the painful memory of an individual's life until they are eventually forgotten. As one mourning wife put it to me following the funeral of her husband, "We must sweep away the pain," a metaphor that not only fixates on the incessant sweeping of the homes and living spaces of the bereaved before and after funerals, but that also points to the eventual memory work that does the opposite of commemoration: forgetting. Drawing on my field experiences, I've tried to argue that dead bodies are not inert to the Meru, but that they are—depending on who has died and under what circumstances—still threatening to the moral order and sociality itself. But it is a threat that is managed in part by notions of proper hygiene and in part by the interment of corpses in their proper social spaces. And, to return to Belinda Straight's (2006) comments that opened this chapter, this threat can only be managed by considering the "entangled agencies" of the living and the dead in a volatile and indeterminate social order.

Notes

1. Special thanks must go out to the province of Quebec's FCAR and Canada's SSHRC for funding the research this chapter was based upon. I wish to acknowledge the Wenner-Gren Foundation Inc. for awarding a dissertation fieldwork grant for fieldwork undertaken in 2002 and 2003. Finally, a brief period of fieldwork was possible in November 2007 while in the employ of the AHRC-funded project "Death in Africa: c. 1800 to the Present," based at Goldsmiths College, University of London, and at Cambridge University. Thoughtful suggestions have been made by Rebekah Lee, Megan Vaughan, Walima Kalusa, and David Graeber.
2. The Kîmerû word for death is *gîkûo*, also the term for a crack. Meru avoid drinking from cracked vessels, as an augury of death.

Bibliography

Blakeslee, Victoria. 1956. *Beyond the Kikuyu Curtain*. Chicago: Moody Press.
Douglas, Mary. 1966. *Purity and Danger: An Analysis of Concepts of Pollution and Taboo*. London: Routledge & Kegan Paul.

Glazier, Jack. 1984. "Mbeere Ancestors and the Domestication of Death." *Man* (N.S.), 19: 133–48.

Hobley, Charles. 1910. "British East Africa: Kikuyu Customs and Beliefs. Thahu and its Connection with Circumcision." *The Journal of the Royal Anthropological Institute of Great Britain and Ireland* 40: 428–52.

Lambert, Hugh. 1956. *Kikuyu Social and Political Institutions*. IAI: Oxford University Press.

Lonsdale, John. 1992. "Afterpiece." In *Burying SM: The Politics of Knowledge and the Sociology of Power in Africa*, eds. David William Cohen and E. S. Atieno Odhiambo. Portsmouth (NH) and London: Heinemann and James Currey.

Mathangani, Patrick and Patrick Muriungi. 2008. "Cemetery Where the Dead Won't Rest." *East African Standard,* February 24.

Maupeu, Hervé and Yvan Droz, eds. 2003. *Les figures de la mort à Nairobi. Une capitale sans cimetières*. Paris: L'Harmattan.

Morovich, B. 2003. "Pollution ou libération? Le dilemme de la mort dans les Eglises *akûrino*." In *Les figures de la mort à Nairobi. Une capitale sans cimetières*, eds. Yvan Droz and Hervé Maupeu, 127–142. Paris: L'Harmattan.

Mutongi, Kenda. 2007. *Worries of the Heart: Widows, Family, and Community in Kenya*. Chicago and London: The University of Chicago Press.

Peatrik, Anne-Marie. 1991. "Le chant des hyènes tristes; Essaie sur les rites funéraires des Meru du Kenya et des peoples apparentés." *Systèmes de pensée en Afrique noire* 11: 103–130.

———. 1999. *La vie à pas contés. Génération, Âge et Société Dans Les Hauttes Terres du Kénya (Meru Tigania-Igembe)*. Nanterre: Société d'Ethnologie.

———. 2000. "Life and Death: Traditional Religious Conceptions among the Meru of Kenya." *Les Cahiers de l'IFRA,* no. 19. Nairobi: IFRA.

———. 2005. "Old System, New Conflicts: Age, Generation and Discord among the Meru, Kenya." In *The Qualities of Time: Anthropological Approaches*, eds. Wendy James, and David Mills. New York: Berg.

Straight, Belinda. 2006. "Becoming Dead: The Entangled Agencies of the Dearly Departed." *Anthropology & Humanism* 31, no. 2: 101–110.

Thomas, Lynn. 1998. "Imperial Concerns and 'Women's Affairs': State Efforts to Regulate Clitoridectomy and Eradicate Abortion in Meru, Kenya, c. 1910–1950." *Journal of African History* 39, no. 1: 121–45.

———. 2003. *Politics of the Womb: Women, reproduction, and the state in Kenya*. Berkeley: University of California Press.

CHAPTER 5

The Rise of "Death Celebrations" in the Cameroon Grassfields

Michael Jindra

In the Anglophone Northwest Province of Cameroon, the practice that links the living and the dead to the greatest extent is called the "death celebration" ("cry die" in Pidgin), normally held months or years after a death, but varying from place to place (Page 2007; Jindra 1997). While some ritual mourning may occur, it is normally a festive event that can last for days, with the family of the deceased calling upon all of their financial and social resources to put on a successful event that involves feasting, performances by dance societies (Argenti 2007), gun firing, and other performances and rituals. Such events dominate social life in the Grassfields, drawing family and friends from far away. Whole villages turn out. As in other parts of Cameroon (Geschiere 2005; Jua 2005), they can be crucial for identity and politics, and a showplace for elites. While this event may seem "traditional" to most observers, it actually evolved into a very common, large, and crucial cultural event only in the last decades of the twentieth century (Jindra 2005).

Over the last century, the mortuary cycle has been radically transformed. Different parts of the mortuary cycle are now emphasized at the expense of others. There is less concern with pollution and purification, and there is more attention paid to honoring and beseeching the ancestors. The corpse and death itself were feared more early in the century. Death celebrations are bigger now, and people "celebrate" more than before. Many include contemporary popular music, and Christian choirs and clergy now play a major role. (Muslims are a relatively small minority in the province). As in other parts of Africa, refrigerated mortuaries are now used in some areas (Page 2007). The attitude toward masks that dance at funerary rites and other events is more casual, especially in more urban areas. In general, these changes indicate a decline in the perceived "pollution" of death, and a possible increase in beliefs about the power of the ancestors to bless, beliefs expressed most visibly in the rise of the grand death celebration, an event that is believed to involve the ancestors. The death celebration has become the central event of Grassfields social life, one in which all sectors of society can participate, traditionalists and Christians, young and old, men and women, rich and poor. This chapter will highlight how this celebration has been adapted over the years, offer the larger historical context within which it has changed, and explain the crucial and ongoing sense of ancestral presence, even in an area that has become largely Christianized.

Death celebrations range in size and duration from small and short to large and long (over several days), and the nature of a celebration depends on a number of factors, including the importance, age, and family status of the deceased, as well as the wealth of the family and supporters. To give the reader a sense of the event, I will include a description of a moderately sized death celebration held in November 1993 in the Bafut area, about twelve miles north

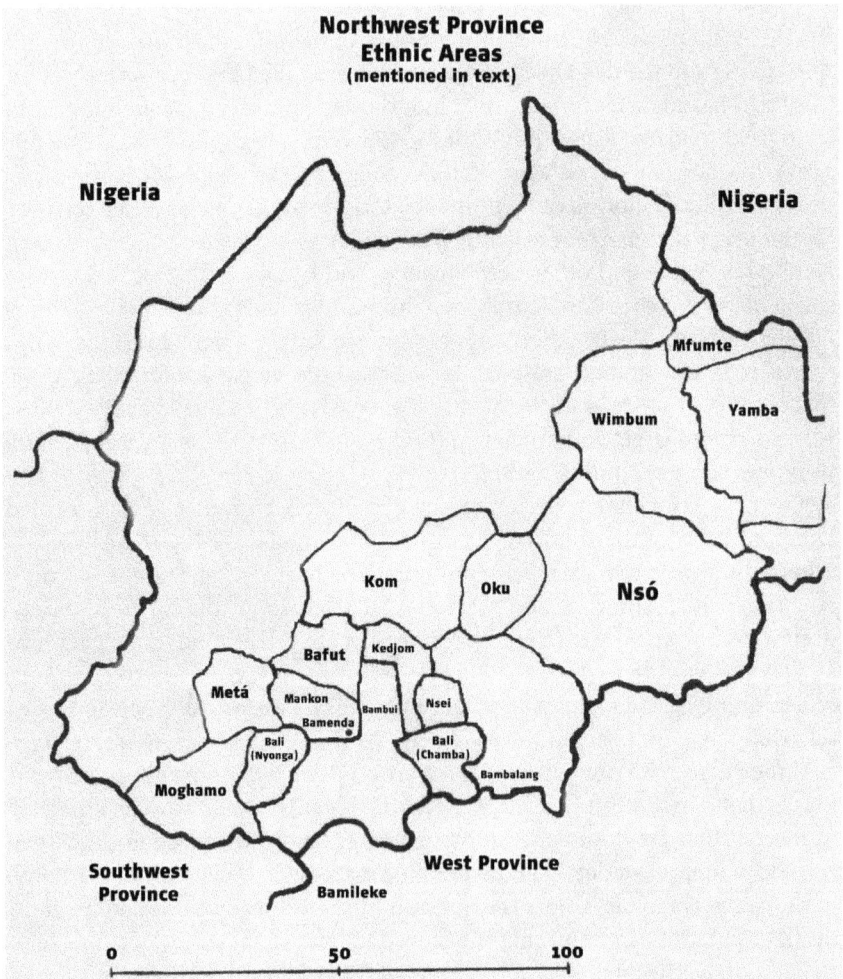

Map 5.1. Northwest Province ethnic groups.

of the provincial capital Bamenda. This celebration continued over two days and was hosted by two brothers, both lower to mid-level civil servants living in provincial capitals. One of them, Elias, lived nearby in Bamenda and made most of the arrangements for the event, which was held for their mother who had died three years earlier.

It began on a Saturday *Mumitaa* (a "country Sunday") in the early afternoon with a memorial church service at the local Presbyterian church. After the church service, which lasted about an hour and a half and included a biographical eulogy of the deceased, there was a procession, led by the pastor and by relatives carrying photos of the deceased, to the host's family compound about half a mile away. The pastor conducted a brief ceremony at the grave on the edge of the compound yard. The participants then proceeded directly to the yard and danced for another hour as photos of the deceased were held high in the air. The photos included images of the father whose death preceded the mother and whose death celebration had already been held. By midafternoon, all the adults had found a seat on the makeshift bamboo benches lining the yard. Palm wine, yellow pods (*akup*), corn, and groundnuts were distributed. Men and women for the most part sat separately. The main course was brought out, plantains and pounded cocoyams with goat meat. The "big people" at the death celebration ate inside, as is normal, while others feasted outside.

At around 5 p.m., the CWF (Christian Women's Fellowship, a local Presbyterian church group of about thirty women) performed, while the CYF (Chris-

Illustration 5.1. The procession to the grave. Bafut, November 1993. Photo by Michael Jindra.

Illustration 5.2. Feeding the guests. Bafut, November 1993. Photo by Michael Jindra.

tian Youth Fellowship) practiced near the grave. During the dancing, some dancers gave small change wrapped in cloth to other dancers. An hour later, the CYF formally entered the grounds, carrying *nkung,* a plant that indicates peace and fertility. They went to the grave, circled once, and then went to the yard to dance. The CWF watched them for a time and then went to visit the grave themselves. As dusk approached, many people left, some to their homes, but many to surrounding compounds where the festivities would continue all night long. Others, however, continued to arrive, for the main performance of the celebration was the next day. At 7 p.m., there was more eating and drinking, and a young man drove into the compound on his motorcycle with a cassette stereo strapped to it, which he promptly set up in the yard.

At 8 p.m., Elias went inside one of the huts, where certain family members were gathered around a fire normally used for cooking. Elias' mother's mother and mother's father's families, the key groups that must be satisfied at this occasion, were in this room. Throughout the night, they kept Elias busy with their demands for food, drink, and more space. If they had not been satisfied, they would have threatened to leave, and so Elias did what he could to please them by taking them crates of beer and chickens on a regular basis. The fowls were cooked over an open fire and eaten immediately. Other relatives sat in other compound buildings. Across the yard, Elias' father's family sat together, talked, ate, and helped Elias with arrangements for food and drink. Soon the stereo was blaring loudly, playing mostly African pop music to which children danced exuberantly.

Several other death celebrations were going on in this quarter and people came and went, making the rounds of these events. At 10 p.m. a *njang* music group began to perform, playing complex rhythms on the wooden xylophone that rested on a bed of plantain stalks. The group continued to play through the night, their performances alternating with blasts from the stereo. More food was served, and at 12:30 a.m., Elias and his brother took a tour of six surrounding compounds where people had gathered for the occasion. At each of the compounds there was music and dancing, and they joined in briefly at each place. They had returned to the main compound by 1:30 a.m., by which time young men dominated the *njang* dancing. The beat and steps were fast. Children selling cigarettes and peanuts hung around the edges of the compound.

This night is called the *ale niwo* ("vigil death") in this Ngemba-speaking area of the province. The reasons for this event are not always clear, but one Bafut man attending the event described it as a "reunion with the ancestors," when libations were poured to them. The spirits are said to be "stronger" at night, and this is why several masks, or "jujus" in local pidgin, may show up at night. Younger folk, however, do not generally pay a lot of attention to this, and during this night there was much entertainment while kin relations and responsibilities were recognized and played out through the seating arrangements and the giving of fowls. The *ale niwo* is even more important than the main, public part of the death celebration, since it is the time *par excellence* when kin obligations are met and actions taken to prevent conflict and misfortune.

Through the night, food continued to be distributed. Close family members who kept the vigil were entitled to a fowl, and more of these were given out at 3 am. Various people around the compound were slouched over in sleep, while in one of the rooms seven children slept on a bed. Some of the groups, especially the mother's family, demanded more food at this point, keeping Elias very busy. Elias later said he gave out between twenty and thirty fowls to these groups during the entire occasion, besides the large quantities of food and drinks (both bottled beer and palm wine) given to the general population. Most of it was provided by Elias, but additional food and alcohol came from his brother, and other relatives and friends also pitched in to support him.

During the rest of the night, and as the sky began to lighten, a number of groups from the surrounding compound began to appear at the compound to dance. Just after 4 a.m., a masked man called *mama'ko* showed up. The doors were shut so the women did not see him and his attendants. They circled the grave, blowing on a horn, pounding drums, and dancing. After about ten minutes, they left. At 4:30 a.m., Elias fired a gun. Elias's younger brother's age-set group arrived and danced first around the grave and then to the compound, holding leaves. They sang about remembering their father and mother, and they were also said to be "looking for the deceased" (whom they did not see, which augured well.) At 4:45 a.m., the mother's mother's family came out of their room and went to the grave, then returned to the yard carrying the *nkung* plant. At 5:30, groups from the other compounds began to show, deposited leaves at the grave, and then went to the compound. There was much gunfire until around 7 a.m. At this point there was another lull as people rested, washed, and ate. At 8:30 a.m., a group of older women from Elias's family went from compound to compound rhythmically banging sticks together and asking for contributions of food or money. There was another lull in the activities as people rested from the long night and the time for regular Sunday morning church services arrived. In the afternoon, more masquerade, dance, and church groups performed in the main compound. Many of these groups will have a whole series of appearances to make at different compounds during this popular dry season time for death celebrations.

Death celebrations in most other areas of the Grassfields are not all-night affairs, but most of the activities—from the church service to the ritual gifts, public feeding, and entertainment—are common across the region, with differences in exactly how these activities are conducted and what they mean (Jindra 1997). In many areas, the most public and well-attended part of the death celebration is held in the afternoon with group and general dancing, gunfire, and distributions of food and drink. Women dress up in their best patterned cloth wrapper or Western-style dress and proceed to the compound with big pots of food. Men may wear a colorful, embroidered "Grassfields gown" (Horner 1990). In some cases, families pick a colorful cloth pattern that is made into shirts and dresses and worn as a "uniform" in a visible demonstration of family unity. Men offer up a fusillade of their long, aged, flintlock Dane guns, pistols, or modern shotguns, or they may clash machetes amongst themselves. Big pots of plantains, pounded cocoyams, or rice can be found cooking in the backs of houses, tended by groups of women. Small markets spring up at the edge of the compound where vendors show up to sell snacks.

Drums, wooden xylophones, or other instruments provide the beat for the dancing, which can alternate between general public dancing and the organized performances of dance groups wearing uniforms or carved masks. Crowds gather around to watch groups perform and often join in the dancing. The audience expresses their approval of groups of individual performers by dancing out and laying money on the ground or by placing it directly on a performer's body, often on the forehead. Male groups demonstrate their agility on the dance ground in energetic or militaristic display, while women dance smoothly and gently, singing and swaying back and forth. Female choirs and dance groups sing verses with both serious and humorous themes. They will sympathize with the deceased, intone Christian hymns, incorporate local gossip into their songs, joke about wanting people to die so they can eat and drink at death celebrations, or complain if not given enough to eat. In the general dancing, dancers—young and old, male and female—join in a large circle and dance with shuffled steps.

As dusk falls, the death celebration may end in a joyous gathering of extemporaneous group dancing. As people leave, many are singing, dancing, and laughing their way home, exhilarated by the dancing and the buzz of the alcohol. Distant relatives, village residents, and those who just "came by" return home, leaving those close relatives "involved" in organizing the event to stay behind and finish the occasion. It is this exuberant atmosphere, this cornucopia of color, sound, smell, and taste, that give these events their name of "death celebration."

Illustration 5.3. Large death celebration in Bambui, December 1993. Photo by Michael Jindra.

Ritual and material changes

Though it might be regarded as the quintessential Grassfields event, significant changes in the mortuary cycle have occurred over the years. Perhaps the
greatest change in the last decades concerned the number of delayed death
celebrations. My first experience in the Meta' area from 1984–86 told me that
death celebrations were held at least a year after the death, often longer. My research found, however, that delayed death celebrations, while historically held
for some people, were by no means typical for most Grassfields deaths in the
past. Having a delayed death celebration is in fact a relatively recent phenomenon, one caused by the major cultural changes of the Grassfields. In most
areas large, delayed death celebrations were formerly restricted to "important"
and usually titled individuals or lineage heads, since these were the ones who
became future ancestors. These celebrations are now larger, delayed longer,
and held for almost any death. There are financial (money is needed to put on a
grand event) and seasonal (events are better in the dry season) reasons for this,
and more recently, the use of mortuaries in a few areas has allowed burials to
be delayed as well, so both burials and death celebrations are increasingly held
at some later date past the death (Page 2007).

Increased mobility has also played a major role in delaying death celebrations. The entire extended family is required to be present for the event. With
families spread out around the country and overseas, it is harder to get family
members together for mortuary events. Organizing one event when all family members can be present simplifies this. In the Meta' and Moghamo areas,
there used to be a separate day of celebration sponsored by each son or son-
in-law; each one had to prepare a dance (Dillon 1970). These events normally
took place within a year of the death. These events are now combined into one
big day, and more dances and activities are packed into a shorter period, making the celebration bigger but shorter. Presently, they often take place more
than a year after the death, when the successor and his family supporters organize a death celebration and the sons-in-law are "invited" to prepare a dance.
In fact, anthropologist Richard Dillon indicates that this change was occurring
around the time of his research in 1970, for his notes describe an argument between two relatives over whether to combine two mortuary events on the same
day. One argues that combining the two is against "native law," but in the end
it is agreed to combine the events (Dillon 1970). In Nso', the weekly memorial
celebrations have declined in favor of a large final celebration, as in the rest of
the Grassfields. Large death celebrations can last several days if the deceased
had many children and belonged to a number of organizations, each of which
would sponsor a dance.

As mentioned briefly above, earlier records indicate that death celebrations
were formerly much simpler and limited only to titled people or members of

societies or royal families. Some of the earliest accounts of what appear to have been delayed death celebrations were recorded in 1918 by L. W. G. Malcolm. He witnessed no large death celebrations, only the appearances of male societies in commemoration of certain deaths, such as that of a chief's son (Malcolm 1923: 400). Delays, when they occurred, were at most a year, according to most historical accounts (e.g. Ritzenthaler 1962; Schmidt 1943; Emonts 1927; and numerous British assessment reports such as Hawkesworth 1926).

As I will discuss below, Grassfields society is now more decentralized and less hierarchical, with much greater freedom for families to hold large events celebrating their own members. This freedom means that we now see death celebrations held for people at all levels of society, and we also see more and different resources utilized at these events. Death celebrations, for instance, now provide meat for all attendees. Domesticated cattle, brought by Fulani to the Grassfields early in the twentieth century, provide a ready supply of beef. Bottled drinks are a necessity for any family with any degree of wealth, and different kinds of food may be served, including more recently introduced foods such as rice. Gunfire has become primarily a means to honor the deceased at the later death celebration, and the rapid crack of shotguns now joins the loud blasting from the older, slower Dane guns.

Technology has also changed the death celebration, as it has mortuary events throughout the continent, as other contributions to this volume make clear. Photographs are now an essential element of the mortuary cycle. They are displayed at prominent places at funerals, on graves, and during processions, and they are used as central props by groups dancing at death celebrations. Photos may substitute for the displayed body when a death celebration is delayed until after burial. Pictures of elderly people are often taken with this purpose in mind, much as buildings are sometimes constructed primarily for death celebrations. The importance of family ties is symbolized by the numerous and ubiquitous pictures of relatives which form the main decorations in house parlors. Numerous photography studios in towns cater to this business, even though it is relatively expensive.

The videotaping of burials and death celebrations is a more recent phenomenon, but has taken its place alongside the photograph as an important part of death celebration planning for those who have the equipment or can afford to hire someone to film. Interviews with relatives are usually part of the filming, with reminiscences about the deceased or actions taken to help the deceased before death. In the videotapes I've seen, people describe their sadness and mention the accomplishments of the deceased, including the number of wives and children he had, or how the deceased supported people in the family. Not only is videotaping used to remember the deceased, but it also provides a way to record those present at the death celebration. The cameraman pans around the compound, filming everyone there. As mentioned above, it is important that all close relatives come, and anyone who does not may be suspected of witchcraft (though this is less likely to be the case for the larger, more secularized death celebrations that are more frequently filmed.)

Tensions between spending and regulating

Death celebrations consume a substantial amount of resources, with expenses routinely going into the hundreds of dollars (representing years of savings for many), and into the thousands for those with more resources. There have been cases where people have fled their villages because they could not afford to host death celebrations. Much of the money is spent on food and drink. It is not unusual for several cows to be killed to supply a death celebration, and crates of beer are a must for someone with any amount of money. A significant proportion of money also goes to the hiring and feeding of dance groups or church groups such as choirs or fellowships, as discussed below. Modern forms of transportation allow individuals to go long distances, so it is possible to bring greater numbers of dance groups to a death celebration.

Thanks to the modern economy, many individuals have someone in their extended family who either is an elite or is married to one. These elites are often called upon to provide the bulk of resources for the death celebration. Some of the expense is mitigated by the fact that people are more mobile now and have a wider circle of friends, including coworkers and classmates, whom elites can call on to "support" them. These friends will in turn call on their friends when they need to marshal support for a death celebration. In fact, in some cases these events can be used to actually make money. Several informants mentioned that a death celebration can be a ruse to make money when hosts call on a wide network of family and friends for support, and then fail to use all of the resources at the death celebration, keeping or reselling what is extra.

Death celebrations may also be stimulated by other factors, such as economic stress, which drives people seeking relief to the source of power, the ancestors, as discussed below (Diduk 1993). Economically, the net effect of the death celebration seems to be a redistribution of resources from elites to villagers through food and drink and through the payment of dance groups, choirs, and secret societies.

In recent decades, and in some cases even since the colonial period, the expense of funerary rites has become an issue not only in Cameroon but across Africa, as discussed in the introductory chapters of this volume. Already in the early 1960s local Cameroon governments were attempting to regulate expenditures on mortuary ceremonies (Chilver and Kaberry 1968: 80). This effort, however, must not have been effective, because the government and newspaper editorialists, among others, were still complaining about the tremendous expenditure and "fuss" of death celebrations in the mid-1980s when I first went to Cameroon (Ibrahim 1987; Bekong, n.d.). During fieldwork in the mid-1990s, several informants reported to me that local authorities (both traditional and state) had passed or were considering attempts to limit expenses and cut mourning times. For instance, in the early 1990s the *Fon* (chief) of Bambalang, through his *kwifon* (regulatory society), restricted the drinks at death celebrations to traditional types like palm wine, excluding the expensive bottled drinks. He also decreed that death celebrations should take place on a "country Sunday" (a rest day in the traditional eight day week) so as not to interfere with economic activities. In 1997, the traditional authorities of Mankon, near Bamenda, proposed a set of regulations meant to limit expenses at death celebrations (Acquaye 2000). And despite ongoing economic problems and stagnation, money is still poured into death celebrations, drawing repeated criticisms from various parties (e.g. Timah 2001).

Various elites have been part of this effort to limit expenses. Local cultural associations often propose that death celebrations be shortened and held within a certain period of time, such as one week. Some complain that the death celebration is a waste of resources needed elsewhere. Most likely, this kind of "public education" is ongoing, as any enforcement seems lax and temporary, with people quickly reverting to expensive practices. Unless backed up by strong authorities, these regulations and "suggestions" are not followed closely.

Death celebrations in the Grassfields are not just a "luxurious" form of consumption allocated after necessities, but actually compete with necessities such as school fees and medical expenses. It was repeated by different informants in different locations that if a person is sick and may die, relatives sometimes withhold money for medical expenses, preferring to save it for the death celebration in case the person dies. In some cases, the sick person himself may do this. One man told me he often saw children of families without money for school fees carrying beer to death celebrations. Churches regularly encourage people not to hold money back for death celebrations, but to use it to help people when sick.

This leaves us with the basic question of why people put their money in death celebrations and not elsewhere. Among other reasons, pressure from villagers is put on wealthy elites to hold death celebrations. Relatives obviously look forward to such occasions, since they provide food, drink, and sociality. Also, it is sometimes said that an elite's ancestors may be resentful of his wealth. Desiring to "share" in it, they cause misfortune until a death celebration is performed. However, poorer individuals are also told to hold these events, so the death celebration can't simply be reduced to a desire for the redistribution of wealth.

Diviners call for death celebrations, a call which the population accepts as plausible because of the long-standing and widespread belief in the power of the ancestors (which I discuss below). Ordinarily, important ancestors are "remembered" in the compound with libations poured or feathers thrown, especially if there are problems such as sickness. With the wealth now circulating in the economy, this is seen as insufficient, and people now are required to do full-fledged death celebrations, especially for close kin. One Wimbum elder reminisced that "in the old days, *ngambe* men (diviners) just said people should do a sacrifice with a fowl or goat, a small feast; only now they are supposed to do a big death celebration." One could speak of this, following economic logic, as an "inflation" of the ancestral economy.

Secularization of political authority

Another reason for the increase in resources put into funerary rites is the secularization and pluralization of political authority. In contemporary society, *fons* (chiefs) have lost much of their power to the modern state, a process—begun with German colonization—that led to a secularization of chiefly authority, Christianization of the region, and the establishment of a system of formal education. As described by one historian:

> A traditional economy based on control by the *Fon* and senior lineage heads of markets, external trade, and the allocation of prestige goods and communal wealth, encountered a monied economy, taxation … levies of food and workers for road building, the first contacts with a new world wide religion, hedge schools and catechists, [and] courts of law to which members of society could appeal above local leadership (O'Neil 1987: 360).

In this context, the political authority ceases to reinforce the reigning religious authorities (which now include the Christian churches), and vice versa, resulting in a divergence of these formerly more integrated spheres. Besides Christianity, the formal education system that was established in the twentieth century in the Grassfields, first by the missions and later by the government, played a major role in this process. The "present appears increasingly to rely on secular and Christian concerns," with fewer people joining secret societies or participating in other traditional rituals (Diduk 1987: 389). The increase in the number of businessmen and civil servants, along with the increased number of residents with relatives in Western countries, all mean that people are much less dependent on the traditional authorities and have more freedom to organize family events like death celebrations in the way they want.

In exceptional cases, funerals and mortuary events become locations for wider issues beyond the descent group. In the case of chiefs, succession issues for the chiefdom come about (Chilver and Kaberry 1968). Increasingly, the death of wealthy migrants brings into play the "politics of belonging" where the interests of family groups, traditional authorities, and villagers sometimes collide over the burial place of individuals (Page 2007; Geschiere 2005; Jua 2005). With "big men," funerary events can provoke political battles (Jua 2005), an issue found in other places on the continent (Maupeu 2003; Gilbert 1988). Where you are buried becomes the ultimate test of identity, and has implications for land claims, payments to local authorities for the right to bury, patronage, and other factors.

In general, Grassfields society has, through the relatively short period of a century, weathered massive social, religious, political, and economic changes. The traditional hierarchy at the beginning of the century monopolized trade and marriage negotiations and was legitimated by notions of historical primacy and contact with ancestors. But in many places the old hierarchy has been superseded by new elites that have either claimed the traditional titles or pushed them into irrelevancy. The mortuary cycle, the primary ritual cycle that summarizes a person's life, is the most visible reflection of this new hierarchy.

The presence of the ancestors

Despite the tremendous changes in the Grassfields over the last century, the power of the ancestors remains one of the strongest forces in the area. In fact, the presence and influence of ancestors may now be more pervasive because the decline in the authority of the traditional hierarchy and the increased access to wealth in the modern economy brought increased egalitarianism. This now permits more families to have regard for their own ancestors through events such as different types of death celebrations in order to obtain "good luck" in modern endeavors of school and trade (see MacGaffey 1986: 70–1 for similar changes among the Kongo).

Christianity has also had a significant impact, as it has become the dominant religion in the Grassfields (Catholic and Presbyterian being the two largest denominations). Changes include the softening of the threat of pollution surrounding death, the extension of death rites and burial to everyone, and—connected with this—an ironic "proliferation of ancestors" that is expressed most strongly in the increase in death celebrations. Some Catholics also connect concern for the ancestors with that of saints (see Jindra 2005 for the extended argument).[1]

The death celebration has become a way of remembering ancestors without having to do formal libations or sacrifices. There is a certain uneasiness among Christians over the pouring of libations, depending on how much they see certain traditional practices as "pagan." Christians prefer instead to have "memorials" and have thus made the "memorial service" a standard part of the death celebration. Indeed, the "remembering" of ancestors seems to have taken on Christian overtones (just as Christian overtones have been added to notions of gods, the land of the dead, and the ancestors or saints).

Tensions, however, between church and traditional authorities still occur, especially involving more theologically conservative churches such as the Baptist church (Yufenuy 2006). Pentecostal churches have become more popular, especially in the last ten years, and their rejection of tradition can cause some tension with family members who want to "remember" the deceased. Pentecostals are often adamant about not performing any traditional rites around burial or after, though years later other family members may perform a "cry-die" (often combining it with others), which Pentecostals may ignore since they do not believe it has any efficacy (Akoko 2007). These churches, and their attitudes toward tradition, are still a minority in the region, so the dominant outlook remains one where "traditional" elements are incorporated into mortuary events.

In this regard, the death celebration is, among other things, a festive gift to the ancestors. The feast is both literal and visual. The most important goal of the death celebration seems to be to "feed" and "entertain" both the living and the dead. The commensality of the death celebration is the most meaningful way of recognizing the kin links on which the Grassfields social structure is based. Eating and dancing are the most basic expressions of social bonding and entertainment, and in the context of the death celebration become the means by which the ancestors are kept involved in the society of the living.

Though the belief that the ancestors are present at the death celebration is common, there remains some disagreement over this, which is not surprising given the nature of the question and the ambiguity over the whole issue of the location of the ancestors, as well as the ambiguity of religious belief in the Grassfields in general (Pool 1994). Many deny that the dead actually come to the death celebration. In the Moghamo area, informants denied that ancestors participated in the death celebration, and located them instead at a ritual called *esu* (Jindra 1997: 254).

Others, however, mentioned that the dead are present at funeral ceremonies (Kebei 1983) or that a death celebration "calls the dead back." Some said that only the "good dead" are called back, especially family heads and *fons*, which is why there are no death celebrations for "bad deaths." There is a belief among many that the dead come to the death celebration to "take their share," after which they leave. Amongst the Wuli of Mfumte, witches are said to come to funerals and take on the form of the deceased (Baeke 1985: 182). The dead in general may also come back and "see" what is going on (Baeke 1995: 27), for "eating and dancing constitute the chief concerns of the spirit" among the Yamba (Gebauer 1964: 27).

Even if people are unsure about the nature of the participation of the dead, there is a consensus that the ancestors can see what is going on or are at least aware of "how they (the living) are doing it," in the words of one informant. One Kom man, at a death celebration for his father-in-law, told me that a seer came up to him and said that his father-in-law was present at the occasion. The seer even pointed to a bird singing on a branch, and told the man that it was his father-in-law enjoying the event. Ancestors witness the death celebration, and have the power to assist the living if they are happy that the death celebration was done right. The same applies to the pouring of libations, or for any sacrifice or putting of food or feathers on the grave or stone of an ancestor. In Kom, the ancestor's names are mentioned as goats are presented, and it is believed that the ancestors can see all the contributions that are made. In fact, if a person makes a contribution to someone who had failed to contribute to the giver's own death celebration in the past, the ancestors are said to "query" the person for making the contribution. In Oku, those who come to a death celebration present a fowl to the hosts, pull out a feather, and call out the ancestor's names. It is said that the ancestors can see what the people bring, and those who don't contribute risk misfortune (Argenti 1996: 204). In Oshie, I was told that the dead are at the final death celebration and receive food and drink placed on the ground. The death celebration sends the spirit away "in a blessed way." It no longer stays around in a "bad faith, but it can come in a good faith" and can be asked "why things are going wrong."

These conceptions, of course, vary from place to place and even among people in the same location. In some contexts ideas about the ancestors are more specific, and in others their general sense of power and influence is more implicit. This depends on many factors, including the socioeconomic and religious contexts of particular locations.

The significance of dance and masquerade

After eating, dancing is the most essential practice of the death celebration. Through the dances and songs of various groups, a number of themes are expressed, including mourning, death, and family (Doh 1990), and these performances may also contain commentaries on wider themes such as history, social structure, and politics (Argenti 2007). Dancing is a visible demonstration of the unity and solidarity of the kin groups and their relationships with others at the event. Dancing follows acceptance of the food provided, since dissatisfaction with food causes arguments and complaints and could prompt guests and groups to refuse to dance, causing an end to the death celebration. Both relatives and societies to which the deceased belonged must be pleased with their share of food, since both have the potential to cause future problems, and diviners are always ready to point this out if future troubles befall a family.

Occasionally, informants were specific about the relations between dancing and ancestors. In Kom, one informant said that the masked dancing "takes away" the ancestors and makes them see that the death celebration has been done properly. The dancing of the death celebration can be conceptualized as a call to the dead to participate and see what the living are doing for them, enabling them to go in peace and not to bother the living, but instead to favor them and bring them blessings. Dancing pleases the ancestors, promotes good feelings, and brightens the atmosphere, keeping away ill feelings associated with witchcraft and other misfortunes, including death itself. "Dancing makes people seem happy and as if the death were a thing near them such that they could cut it with a cutlass or shoot it. The people dancing is like the people preparing for war" (Dillon 1971). The drumming that is integral to these events is also crucial, for throughout Africa drumming plays a key role in ritual and social events and can be thought of as the "voice" of the ancestors (Chernoff 1979: 150).

In the Grassfields, as in some other parts of Africa, masking is one of the more dramatic elements of funerary rites. The appearance of certain feared masks like *Nko* at a death celebration is an honor for an elite deceased and his family, and is one of the highlights of the event. Jokesters may also appear at death celebrations, stealing food, mocking other dancers, and turning other cultural norms upside down by wearing rags or cross dressing. In places in the Grassfields such as Oku, a sole masked figure "cries" in an angry manner just after deaths, while at delayed funerary events, masquerade groups "dance" (Argenti 2007: 216). This latter is a more joyful, celebratory occasion, however, and is done with the entire group present.

At contemporary death celebrations, relatives and friends sponsor dance groups to honor the deceased and also to increase their own status and to fulfill responsibilities owed to others. For instance, a dance sponsored by a son in-law is the final expression of the debt he owes to the family for taking a daughter. A dance group will also perform at the death celebrations of one of its own members. These performances are part of the cycle of reciprocal exchanges that are the basis of the Grassfields social system.

The symbolic meanings of masked dancers, however, are also important. Throughout much of Africa, masked dancers are thought of as representatives of ancestral or other spirits (Gausset 2001; Vansina 1992: 25). This is also the portrayal in Chinua Achebe's popular novel *Things Fall Apart*. In the Grass-

Illustration 5.4. Dance group in Mankon, November 1993. Photo by Michael Jindra.

fields, there has been a certain amount of uncertainty on this matter. Chilver and Kaberry, in their seminal Grassfields monograph *Traditional Bamenda,* said that their informants denied that masks represented spirits (1968: 44). The masks, they argue, are more "aesthetic expressions" than "functional" in purpose.

From her sojourn in Nsei in 1937 and 1938, however, anthropologist Agathe Schmidt noted that a dead person in Nsei was buried with a woven net placed over the head like a masked dancer. She theorized that dancing is a "protective magic to avoid the evil power of the dead, since the masks themselves may represent a relation with the dead," making them more benevolent towards the living (1943: 138, 159–60). Also, the full dance group performing their synchronized dance steps at the final death celebration is a visual demonstration of unity for the ancestors. In this sense there is communication between the living and the dead, but not a direct representation of the dead in the masks.

Before the rise of the modern economy, dance groups were not as numerous at death celebrations. These groups are no longer "owned" only by chiefdom societies or by powerful lineages and titled men, among whom wealth used to be concentrated. The right to have a group can now be bought by many more people, and performances have become common. Thus, masking is still both an attractive feature of death celebrations and an important entertainment industry, and in areas that have a stronger chiefdom authority and associations like Oku, masks can still evoke fear, authority, and power (Argenti 2007).

In general, however, masks do not command the respect or symbolic authority they once did. People no longer bend down to them as often or fear them as much, and in some areas masks can be handled by anyone. The young simply do not join societies (which normally owned the masks and dances) to the extent their elders did (Diduk 1987: 389; Geary 1979: 58, Nkwi 1976: 199). This should not be too surprising, given the influence of modern education and Christianity, and the recent (1985) introduction of television, which provides more visual stimulation and attraction than masking. Before television, schools, and churches, the masks were among the most visual and important cultural creations, indicative of the strongest human institutions known, those of the *fons* and the societies. They now, however, compete with the other significant attractions of contemporary Grassfields life.

Conclusion

The death celebration is both ritual and festival, religious and secular, serious and playful. Anthropologists Robert Brain and Adam Pollock (1971: 65), writing about similar death celebrations among the Bangwa in the Southwest province, argue that in many ways it is a "theatrical performance rather than a rite." The event has always had purposes other than ritual or sacrifice. But there is certainly more diversity and pluralism in the worldview, education, and lifestyle of the Grasslands than there was one hundred years ago. These kinds of changes have significantly affected ritual events throughout Africa. Meyer Fortes returned to Ghana decades after his research to find that the religious meanings of ritual festivals had "faded out" (Fortes 1987: 64). In the DRC, André Droogers conducted a meticulous analysis of a 1970 Wagenia initiation ritual. He found that "no one could explain any longer why things were done that way" (Droogers 1980: 368). The ritual had largely become the expression of "tribal identity" and could last for years because it was simply "fun."

In the Grassfields, some of the symbolic meanings of death celebrations are lost, but people still have notions of what the event is about; they are clearly held in memory of an ancestor or ancestors, and they are necessary to avoid "bad luck." However, as among the Wagenia, much of the enthusiasm of the event is generated out of a sense of fun. The 1970 Wagenia initiation was the first one performed in fourteen years. Before the tremendous changes in the Congo of the 1960s, they were performed more often. These events, because they have lost their religious moorings, have lost their urgency. But the death celebration remains a necessary event, even more so now than in the past, largely because of the ongoing importance of the connection with ancestors. It has also remained popular because it lends itself to other, more secular concerns of cultural identity, prestige, family unity, and entertainment. Death celebrations help unify the family and please the ancestors (notions that are intimately tied), while also fulfilling community obligations and raising or maintaining social status. Mobility has separated families, but the complex activities of the death celebration, along with the requisite family meeting, keep family members close. The decline of traditional hierarchy and the rise of new wealth are expressed and even stimulated by death celebrations, where the performances of societies show family relationships and where the wealth of the family is put on display and consumed. The death celebration also allows the exhibition of the differing traditions of the Grassfields, both those based upon historical primacy in land and ancestors and the currently more overt expressions of belief in God that Christianity has stressed. The death celebration has proven itself to be adaptable to different worldviews. Death celebrations are also prime venues for displaying the aesthetic abilities of Grassfields peoples in all classes, whereas formerly such displays were limited to those of a certain title or those with a certain status as parents.

Through significant changes in social structure, religion, and politics, the death celebration has emerged as the quintessential Grassfields event, allowing residents to give due attention to the most important impulses of kinship, the expressive dimensions of life, the ancestors, and now Christianity. "This is our tradition," as one participant at a death celebration proudly told me. It may not be as traditional as outsiders think, but it certainly expresses some of the most basic elements and impulses of Grassfields life.

Notes

1. As in other parts of Africa, where the cult of the dead may have actually been introduced by certain forms of Christianity such as Catholicism (Spijker 1990: 95), or Christian practices may have unintentionally reinforced a cult of the dead (Bernault 2006: 234–5f.).

Bibliography

Acquaye, Florende Shu. 2000. "Death Celebration ("Cry Die"): A Conundrum for the Legislator in Cameroon?" *Tilburg Foreign Law Review* 8: 347–354.

Akoko, Robert. 2007. "'You Must Be Born Again': The Pentecostalisation of the Presbyterian Church in Cameroon." *Journal of Contemporary African Studies* 25, no. 2: 299–315.

Argenti, Nicolas. 1996. "The Material Culture of Power in Oku, Northwest Province, Cameroon." PhD diss., University College London.

———. 2007. *The Intestines of the State: Youth, Violence, and Belated Histories in the Cameroon Grassfields*. Chicago: The University of Chicago Press.

Baeke, Viviane. 1985. "Les Objets Rituels des Sociétés Initiatiques Chez les Wuli Du Cameroun Occidental." *Systèmes de Pensée en Afrique Noire* 8: 177–199.

———. 1995. "Wuli Witchcraft." *Journal of the Anthropological Society of Oxford* XXVI, no. 1: 21–41.

Bekong, Fondong. n.d. "Death Celebrations in Our Society." *Cameroon Tribune.*

Bernault, Florence. 2006. "Body, Power and Sacrifice in Equatorial Africa." *Journal of African History* 47, no. 2: 207–239.

Brain, Robert and Adam Pollock. 1971. *Bangwa Funerary Sculpture.* London: Gerald Duckworth.

Chernoff, John Miller. 1979. *African Rhythm and African Sensibility.* The University of Chicago Press.

Chilver, E. M. and P. M. Kaberry. 1968. *Traditional Bamenda: The Pre-colonial History and Ethnography of the Bamenda Grassfields.* Buea, Cameroon: Ministry of Education and Social Welfare and West Cameroon Antiquities Commission.

Diduk, Susan. 1987. "The Paradox of Secrets: Power and Ideology in Kedjom Society." PhD diss., Indiana University.

———. 1993. "Twins, Ancestors and Socio-economic Change in Kedjom Society." *Man* (N.S.) 28: 551–571.

Dillon, Richard. 1970–71. Notes from Cameroon fieldwork (with thanks from article author).

Doh, Emmanuel Fru. 1990. "Funeral Poetry in the Bamenda Grassfields (Cameroon)." PhD diss., University of Ibadan (Nigeria).

Droogers, André. 1980. *The Dangerous Journey: Symbolic Aspects of Boys' Initiation among the Wagenia of Kisangani, Zaire.* New York: Mouton.

Emonts, Johannes. 1927. *Ins Steppen und Bergland Innerkameruns; aus dem Leben und Wirken deutscher Afrikamissionare.* Aachen: Xaveriusverlag.

Fortes, Meyer. 1987. *Religion, Morality and the Person: Essays on Tallensi Religion.* Cambridge: Cambridge University Press.

Gausset, Quentin. 2001. "Masks and identity : The significance of masquerades in the symbolic cycle linking the living, the dead and the bush spirits among the Wawa (Cameroon)." *Anthropos* 96, no. 1: 193–200.

Geary, Christraud. 1979. "Traditional Societies and Associations in We." *Paideuma* 25: 53–72.

Gebauer, Paul. 1964. *Spider Divination in the Cameroons.* Milwaukee: Milwaukee Public Museum.

Geschiere, Peter. 2005. "Funerals and Belonging: Different Patterns in South Cameroon." *African Studies Review* 48, no. 2: 45–64.

Gilbert, Michelle. 1988. "The Sudden Death of a Millionaire. Conversion and Consensus in a Ghanaian Kingdom." *Africa* 58, no. 3: 291–309.

Hawkesworth, E. G. 1926. *Notes on the Bafut Area* (British colonial assessment report).

Horner, Alice. 1990. "The Assumption of Tradition: Creating, Collecting and Conserving Culture Artifacts in the Cameroon Grassfields." PhD diss., University of California-Berkeley.

Ibrahim, Ahmed. 1987. "Death Celebrations." *Cameroon Tribune.* May 26.

Jindra, Michael. 1997. "The Proliferation of Ancestors: death celebrations in the Cameroon Grassfields." PhD diss., University of Wisconsin-Madison.

———. 2005. "Christianity and the Proliferation of Ancestors: Changes in Hierarchy and mortuary ritual in the Cameroon Grassfields." *Africa* 75, no. 3: 356–377.

Jua, Nantang. 2005. "The Mortuary Sphere, Privilege and the Politics of Belonging in Contemporary Cameroon." *Africa* 75, no. 3: 325–355.

Kebei, Jervis Kewi. 1983. *The Weh Concept of the Soul.* Thesis, St. Thomas Aquinas Major Seminary, Bambui.

MacGaffey, Wyatt. 1986. *Religion and Society in Central Africa.* Chicago: The University of Chicago Press.

Malcolm, L. W. G. 1923. "Notes on the Birth, Marriage, and Death Ceremonies of the Eyap Tribe, Central Cameroons." *Journal of the Royal Anthropological Institute* 53: 388–401.

Maupeu, Hervé. 2003. "Enterrement des *big men* et nation kenyane." In *Les Figures de la Mort á Nairobi,* eds. Yvan Droz and Hervé Maupeu. Paris: L'Harmattan.

Nkwi, Paul Nchoji. 1976. *Traditional Government and Social Change.* Fribourg, Switzerland: University of Fribourg Press.

O'Neil, Robert. 1987. "A History of Moghamo." PhD diss., Columbia University.

Page, Ben. 2007. "Slow-Going: The mortuary, modernity, and the hometown association in Bali-Nyonga." *Africa* 77, no. 3: 419–441.

Pool, Robert. 1994. *Dialogue and the Interpretation of Illness: Conversations in a Cameroon Village.* Oxford: Berg Press.

Ritzenthaler, Robert and Pat. 1962. *Cameroons Village: An Ethnography of the Bafut.* Milwaukee Public Museum.

Schmidt, Agathe. 1943. "Totengebräuche in Nsei im Grasland von Kamerun." *Wiener Beiträge zur Kulturgeschichte und Linguistik* 5: 125–163.

Spijker, Gerard Van't. 1990. Les Usages Funéraires et la Mission de L'Eglise: Une étude anthropologique et théologique des rites funéraires au Rwanda. Kampen: Uitgevers-maatschappij J.H. Kok.

Timah, Njei Moses. 2001. "Speech To Moghamo Traditional Rulers." Accessed May 2, 2007. http://www.njeitimah-outlook.com/articles/article/2076046/34490.htm.

Vansina, Jan. 1992. "Kings in Tropical Africa." In *Kings of Africa,* eds. E. Beumers and H. J. Koloss. Maastricht: Foundation Kings of Africa.

Yufenuy, Jeff Ngawe. 2006. "CBC Pastor Warns Kwifon Against Interference In Church Business." *Cameroon Post,* November 20.

CHAPTER 6

Funerals and Religious Pluralism in Burkina Faso

Katrin Langewiesche

In a country characterized by religious pluralism like Burkina Faso, death as a social event provides an opportunity for confirming and updating the boundaries between the different religions. Not only are funerals occasions that reflect religious dynamics, but they are also ideal spaces for religious rapprochements. The following descriptions of burials and funerals in rural Burkina Faso, collected during my field research in the Ouahigouya region in Yatenga Province, help us to understand the everyday functioning of this religious pluralism and to describe the forms of interaction at play (Shaw and Stewart 1994; Peel 1990). Additionally, the analysis suggests that the "traditional" religion, despite its problematic label,[1] is just as dynamic and plural as Christianity and Islam.

Following the presentation of historical and sociological data on the Yatenga region and its *chef lieu* (county town) of Ouahigouya and the presentation of historical information on the development of religious pluralism in Burkina Faso, I will present two case studies:

- the funeral of His Grace Durrieu, First Bishop of Ouahigouya in 1965, as described by one of the priests in the logbooks (*Diaire*) of the parish of Ouahigouya, and
- the burials of the chief of Sonh in 1997, as related by some of the protagonists involved and observed by the author.

These descriptions will act as a basis for understanding how local interpretations of Christianity and Islam evolve and the way in which the population appropriates the world religions. These stories highlight the everyday approximations through which individuals attempt to give meaning to and organize the diversity of religions with which they are confronted. The main argument in this chapter is about the dynamics of religious contacts observed in funeral practices. These dynamics, which can be syncretic or ecumenical at any given point in time and which become proselytizing or exclusivist at another, show us how the intergenerational relationships are redefined, how the relationships between the autochtonous people and the newcomers are negotiated, and how the religious institutions position themselves in relation to each other in a pluralist religious field.

This research combines classic ethnographic (semidirective interviews and participant observation) and historical methods. The analysis is based on the "Diaires" of the parish of Ouahigouya (1955 to 1971), which are logs or diaries which were kept by the superior general of the mission station and regularly forwarded to the mother house. In the first diaries, up to 1936 approximately, the missionaries refer both to the customs and the local history of the country; in the subsequent diaries, they refer increasingly to events relating to the parish. The aim of the compilation of these diaries was to inform the superior generals about what was going on in the different stations, to establish a connection between the religious brothers, and to create a basis for the production of publications aimed at a wider audience, with a view to promoting the achievements of missions in France. It is in this last context that these diaries are critically utilized for this research.

The Yatenga Province

Yatenga Province is a densely populated (ten to fifteen inhabitants per square mile) and arid Sahelian area located in the northwest of Burkina Faso, near the Mali border. Its inhabitants, the Mossis, are the majority in Burkina Faso and speak the Moore language. Around the Yatenga capital, Ouahigouya, is a huge wooded and shrubby savanna, with some hills emerging here and there. Because of poor soil and difficulties with earning one's living in the overpopulated area, almost half the men aged between twenty and forty have migrated to Côte d'Ivoire or to other regions in the country. For several decades now, the Yatenga has been a region of emigration. This dynamic has not only transformed the Mossi economic system, but also its religious practices. Many migrants converted to Islam while they were abroad.

The Muslims increasingly impose their authority in the province. Although many political leaders in the period after independence were Catholics, the Church's influence in everyday life—an influence felt mostly in rural areas—remains limited. Although the Catholic influence is visible in the public space (as education and health care), in Yatenga rural areas, dynamic Catholic communities are rare. Nowadays, they have been replaced by Pentecostal groups that attract many young people.

The religious situation in the Yatenga Province is not significantly different from that of the rest of the country. Here, as everywhere else, religious diversity exists under Muslim domination, even if the importance of the Muslim majority varies depending on the region of Burkina Faso (see Barbier 1999):

some regions are still, for instance, "traditional bastions" (Barbier 1999: 166), and Islam is generally better represented in urban than in rural areas.

Historical development of religious pluralism

Religious pluralism exists less in the quantity of religious traditions available in a society than it does in the interactions and boundary lines between these traditions. In this sense, it may be said that although different African religions and Islam had coexisted in the area for centuries, religious pluralism (as distinct from a plurality of religions) was only established in Yatenga with the arrival of the Christian missionaries in the early twentieth century. The new concept of Christian proselytism changed the relationship between members of the different religions and between religious institutions. Missionaries and marabouts,[2] competing against each other, together questioned the traditional religion.

In contrast to the arrival of the first Muslims after the fifteenth century, the Christians' evangelization was supported by the theological mission and religious doctrine established by an ecclesiastical hierarchy. The growth of Islam over the past several centuries came largely through the everyday interactions of commerce, to which religious activity was often subordinated. Muslim tradesmen and chiefs have found a balance based complementarity, each group having its responsibilities. The Mossi states needed to open up to the outer world, notably toward the big cities of the inner delta of the Niger River. They offered therefore their protection and permission to practice their religion to the Muslim traders' caravans. In exchange, the Muslim traders developed a "praxis of coexistence" (Wilks 2000: 98) toward the unbelievers, one rooted in the conviction that conversion to Islam could not be enforced and that submission to nonMuslim rulers was acceptable as long as the Muslims could keep their faith. However, Islam has had a profound influence on West African cultures, even ones where conversion did not take place (Werthmann 2008; Launay 2006). Islamic elements seem to have been incorporated ever since Islam made its first inroads into the West African Sahel zone (Saul 2006). From the second half of the seventeenth century onwards, the royal elites started to convert (Levtzion 1968: 166; Skinner 1962: 663), and it is only in the course of the nineteenth century that conversions gradually touched the villages as well as the autochthonous population. As in many regions of French West Africa, the colonial system generated situations that contributed to the Islamic breakthrough (Cissé 1993: 192; Diallo 1985: 36). The rapid increase in conversions during the colonial period can be explained mainly by the anti-colonial attitude of some Muslim groups (Otayek 1984, 1988; Audouin and Deniel 1978). These proponents of Islam, who were considered to be a bastion against the colonizers, their religion, and the social and economic upheaval it brought, attracted many people. In contrast to neighboring West African regions, Sufi orders such as the Tijaniyya and the Qadiriyya were almost entirely lacking in Burkina Faso until the colonial period (Otayek 1988: 107). To the present day, few locations can be found in Burkina Faso that contain the tombs of Muslim saints, as well as few settlements that had been intentionally established or renamed for the purpose of highlighting a Muslim identity (Werthmann 2008: 133).[3]

The attempts of priests and pastors to convert the local population during the colonial era awakened the proselytizing ambitions of the Muslim leaders. Stewart suggests that when the colonial governments assumed the judicial and legal functions of Muslim clerics, they created a space for those Muslim leaders who focused their message on the mystical experience and for the Sufi brotherhoods these leaders promoted, both of which became the prime movers of the expansion of Islam in the twentieth century (Stewart 1997). After the arrival of the first missionaries, the marabouts committed themselves for the first time to conquering new adherents in order to thwart the increasing influence of the Christians upon the local population and political life (Kouanda 1997: 33). In contrast to the Catholics, who had already begun to found schools at the beginning of the twentieth century, the Muslims started to open their own only in the 1950s. In the 1960s, several *médersas* combining religious instruction and modern secular education in Arabic or French opened their doors in present-day Burkina Faso. The *médersa* of Ouahigouya was created in 1965 (Cissé 1990: 60). Significantly, the Catholic Church had to renounce the educational ambition it had during the colonial period when it was forced to put the private Catholic primary schools in the hands of the government at the end of the 1960s (Otayek 1997; Compaoré 1993; Audouin 1982). From 1969 to 1990, Catholic education in Burkina Faso only existed in the secondary schools, most of which were managed by religious congregations. However, the Catholic Church has since renewed its involvement in primary school education (Compaoré 2003).

After the independence of the country, the "old Islam" of the merchants (*Yarse*) and the nomads (*Fulbe*) was joined by a Muslim community composed of a traditional wing of marabouts and imams and a "progressive" wing of Arabized intellectuals, the reformist current of the Wahhabis and the movement of Ahmadiyya (Otayek 1984, 1993; Kouanda 1988). Today Muslims are divided by several trends. Most of the Muslim associations that exist in Burkina Faso have been united under the umbrella of the *Fédération des Associations Islamiques du Burkina Faso*, created in 2005. But since its founding until today (2011) this Federation struggles to be operational and thus reflects the internal divisions of Muslims.

Finally, the first Protestant missionaries were American Pentecostals (Some 2006; Laurent 2003). They began to settle in rural areas in the 1920s (Some

2006). Rural Pentecostalism is often limited to healing through prayer and promising youth freedom from traditions considered old and outdated. The support of a community that allowed people to free themselves from parental values was and is a decisive element of the Protestants' religious lives. In popular urban circles, there is an increasing fascination with deliverance prayers, healing ceremonies, and demon hunting (Fancello 2006; Laurent 2003). Although less visible in other countries of the subregion, the evangelists have begun to assume increased prominence in the Burkinabé political arena. This politicization of Pentecostalism is in line with a general trend that concerns all West African countries in a variety of ways (Strandsbjerg 2005; Mayrargue 2004; Corten and Marshall-Fratani 2001; Gifford 1998). The numerical increase of Evangelicals is fast. Between 1960 and 2006 the rise of the number of Evangelicals is five times larger than that of Muslims and two times more than that of Catholics.

Based on this brief historical overview, including various religious trends, we can now assess the following descriptions of burials and funerals in Burkina Faso. These stories reveal the process of syncretization as experienced in Burkina Faso. Syncretization is understood here as the collision or interaction of several symbolic and religious practices (Peel 1990: 338).

Tradition and folklore: the 1965 funeral of the first Bishop of Ouahigouya

Following unproductive attempts to safeguard its political influence (in particular after the schools were taken away in 1969), the Catholic hierarchy adopted new pastoral strategies for providing the masses with access to Catholicism in Haute-Volta in the late 1970s. The "inculturation" of the Catholics in their milieu became one of the aims of the representatives of the Catholic Church, who tried to transform the Mossi tradition into a kind of folklore liberated from its pagan meaning. A good example of this phenomenon may be found in the records of the parish of Ouahigouya, which report on the funerals of His Grace Durrieu, First Bishop of Ouahigouya in 1965. The priests of the parish wanted to stage an imposing ceremony to impress the Muslims and Protestants and to win over the followers of the traditional religion. This example shows that Catholics did not wait for the 1970s to "inculturate" burial rituals, but that the interaction of religious practices or meanings is a common and ordinary phenomenon in many pluralistic societies.

The funeral was carefully prepared so as to be "really dignified, prayerful and, at the same time, a means of attracting new converts, in particular among old men and women who attach such great significance to the kuré (funeral) ceremonies."[4] The Catholics wanted the funerary procession "to look like the kuré of a great chief, to whom one wishes to give the last honours" (Ibid.). The preparation committee tried to remain close to the traditional symbolism without generating any misunderstandings. Thus, the record reports:

> The idea of two young girls, dressed in mourning, walking by the coffin and carrying a basket, into which people would throw money for the church services is rejected, because of what the pagans and the Muslims may think (i.e., feeding the deceased, giving the ancestors water to drink). A basket will be placed in front of the coffin at the cathedral for this purpose.[5]

The basket (*peogo*) has a particular symbolic meaning in the traditional ceremonies. A married woman belonging to the family of the deceased (*wemba*) carries it on her head in such a way that the public can see its contents. It contains all of the deceased's belongings, which have to be distributed to specified people after the funeral. When a woman dies, all her belongings (crockery, *pagnes*, etc.) are returned to the *peogo* (i.e., her father's family), otherwise her *siiga* ("soul"[6]) will not be able to rest. The preparation committee aimed on the one hand to avoid any close contact with the pagan *peogo* while on the other hand trying to remain close to the traditional form of expression so as to attract the interest of the public. Despite the restrictions proposed by the preparation committee, it would appear that the objective of replacing the traditional symbolism with a Christian meaning was attained, at least in the opinion of the record writer, who wrote after the ceremonies that:

> The crowd increased in number right along the procession of His Grace's body. Religious hymns dominated, often drowned out, however, by the drums, the rifle shots, the women's yan-yan and—especially during the stops—the funeral laments taken from the exclusively African folklore.[7]

The records indicate that the missionaries considered at length the possible effects of the rituals on the local population. Each group of actors that participated in the ceremony was trained by the missionaries to conduct a perfect ritual. And, to the great joy of the missionaries, without any agreement about a potential intervention during the funeral, the Yatenga Naaba[8] spontaneously performed the symbolic task of throwing a blanket, traditionally reserved for the next Yatenga Naaba, on the coffin of the late bishop.[9]

The Christian and traditional messages were mixed, intentionally or not, as much by the Catholic clergy and traditional hierarchy as by the believers who participated actively in the event through their chants, gifts, and performances. Thus the believers do not appear to have awaited the theology of "Africanization" to reconcile traditional religion and Catholicism in accordance with their own interests and values.

Illustrations 6.1 and 6.2. 1965 funeral of the first Bishop of Ouahigouya His Grace Durrieu. (*General Archives of the Missionaries of Africa:* Rome.)

After Vatican II (1962–1965), Burkinabe theologians engaged actively in the theology of "Africanization."[10] They tried to find similarities between pagan and Christian institutions, similarities such as customary initiation and Christian baptism, or funerals and the feast of All Saints. Their works are based on the presupposition, implicitly acknowledged by an entire generation of theologians, that the local religions reach fulfillment in Christianity.[11] Consequently, their writings focus on the Christian background of the African religions and their possible adaptation to Christian requirements. This concern with combining the concepts of traditional religions and Christian ideas contributed to an acceptance of double practices on the part of the Catholics, an acceptance not found among Muslims and Protestants. This doesn't mean that Muslims or Protestants conduct fewer traditional rituals than Catholics: the point doesn't have to do with actual practices, but with discourse about these practices.

Having examined the example of the "Africanization" of the funeral of a Catholic bishop, which reflected the desire to bring local religious concepts and Catholic ideas closer to each other, we shall now observe how a group of protagonists managed to reconcile traditional religion and Catholicism during the funeral of a village chief some thirty years later. According to the census made between 1960 and 1961 in Haute-Volta, 3.7 percent of the population adhered to Catholicism, and by 1996 it rose to 16.6 percent.[12] In the 1960s, Catholics were a minority group seeking converts, and were confrontational with both Islam and traditional religion. In the 1990s, the Catholics were still a minority group—but one that was well established and growing less by means of adult conversions than by children's baptisms, indicating a "natural" increase of a hereditary Catholicism.[13]

Religious compromise: the two burials of the village chief of Sonh in 1997

The chief of Sonh died during the winter season, and his family buried him without making his death official. The death of an important man becomes official from the moment it is made public. In everyday language, the burial following the public announcement is the "official burial." The families seldom organize an official burial during the rainy season, because everyone is busy with work in the fields and because the millet required to make the millet beer (an essential component of the funerary rites) has not yet been collected. In such cases, the family buries the deceased immediately after the death, then announces it publicly and organizes an official burial a few months later. This burial is a symbolic one, because what is buried on this occasion is not a body but a board, a stone, or another object that symbolizes the corpse. In the *Mooré* language, this kind of burial is called *ku-maasga*, which literally translates as "cold burial."

According to various villagers, the *naaba* of Sonh was around one hundred years old and had "followed the Catholics" for twenty-three years without being baptized. He was married to two women. He had six children with his first wife, who had died a few years earlier, and did not have any with the second, his widow. Several people confirmed that it was the *naaba* himself who introduced the Catholics to Sonh and caused several people to convert. When he died, there were approximately forty Catholics in Sonh, which was visited by a priest from Ouahigouya around once a month.

When the *naaba* felt close to death, he told his children his last wish: he wanted a Catholic burial and not a "customary" burial, which would have necessitated displaying his body for two to three days before burying it. When in the throes of death, the *naaba* insisted on seeing Pascal, the catechist of Sonh, to be baptized before he died. He died the day after his baptism. His family immediately informed the *naaba*'s daughter and her husband who lived in the village of Lago. This daughter had to attend the burial because she would replace her father as a *Na-poka* until a new *naaba* took office.[14] The presence of her husband (*bikeepoka-sida*), Philippe Sawadogo, was also essential. Tradition required that he bring a goat, a straw mat, and cotton bands, without which the *naaba* could not be buried in the right way.

The Catholic burial

As soon as Philippe heard about the death of his father-in-law, he rushed to gather together the necessary items. The grave had already been dug when he arrived in Sonh. The family wanted to bury the *naaba* with honey, salt, a cat, and a cock. These offerings had been prepared and everyone was waiting for Philippe to proceed with the burial. In the meantime, however, the catechist Pascal had told his colleagues in Ziga, Rigue, and Leba about the *naaba*'s death, and they came to support him in his demand that the deceased's last wish be respected; he would have a Catholic burial, which would mean the interment of his body without the items required by tradition. Following some consultations between the catechists and the elders, the family decided to respect the *naaba*'s last wish and quickly complied with the view of the Catholics without expressing significant opposition. They withdrew the honey, salt, and animals and attended the Catholic ceremony.

The Catholic funeral took place in the afternoon and lasted approximately one hour. Certain aspects of the Catholic ritual clashed with the traditional rites. Pascal—the catechist—highlights them explicitly in the account of the ceremony that he made for me. The account explains that during the Catholic burial, the older nephews of the *naaba* washed his body, whereas during a customary burial this task is usually carried out by the *lagdba* (old men and women). Each village has its *lagdba* who take care of all of the dead people in the village; they do not necessarily have any family ties with the deceased.

Pascal continues his description by highlighting another major difference between a Catholic burial and a customary burial: other nephews carried the body and left the compound through the main door to display it on a catafalque outside. The four catechists recited psalms and prayers in front of the catafalque. In contrast, during a customary burial the body of the dead person must leave by a hole in the wall of the compound created expressly for this purpose (*ragnobega*, a bad luck door or evil door). As soon as the deceased leaves the compound in this manner, he is subject to interrogation. According to Pascal, this entire element of a customary burial is unacceptable to Catholics. Thus, during the Catholic burial of the *naaba*, the body left by the normal door. The funeral cortege was important. Led by the eldest daughter, who was followed by the eldest son, the procession escorted the body to the cemetery of the chiefs. The order of the procession followed that dictated by custom. The body, which was wrapped in an ox skin, was placed in the grave without any of the customary objects, and the grave was simply covered with soil. There was no mass. The catechist said a prayer to ask allowance for the deceased just before the grave was covered with soil.

The customary burial

Approximately five months after the Catholic burial of the *naaba*'s body, his family organized a symbolic ceremony in order to fulfill some of the customary rites that had not been carried out due to the opposition of the Catholics. Salif Bobodo Ouedraogo, one of the few Muslims of this lineage and the future chief of Sonh, was among those who insisted that the family organize a second traditional burial. He was personally interested in ensuring that the funerary rites proceeded according to custom, as he would be the late *naaba*'s replacement: it is said that if the funeral does not proceed as it should, the next *naaba* will not remain in office for long and will die quickly. Moreover, any other misfortune that might befall the family (i.e., the death of a child or young person, a bad harvest) would be related back to the failure to implement the customary funeral rites correctly. Despite being a Muslim, Salif had a particular interest in ensuring that the customary ceremonies were completed correctly. He actually took part in all of the events in the village and in Ouahigouya. When asked in an interview about the compatibility of a *naaba*'s duties with the practice of Islam, he answered:

> I can still pray and be a *naaba*. If I die, the Muslims will bury me and my children will conduct the funerals. Once you are the chief, even if you are not a Muslim, you will have traditional funeral when you die (*rog-miki*[15]). So what difference does being a Muslim make?[16]

When I meet Salif three years after he became *naaba* of Sonh, I asked him the same question about the compatibility of his duties as chief and the practice of Islam. This time he told me:

It is awkward (being *naaba* and a Muslim); I'm not Muslim any more now. I have become a Catholic. It is not forbidden for the Catholics to prepare and drink the *dolo* (millet beer). There are times when I have to prepare and pour some *dolo* ... Only me and my wives cannot be Muslims, the other people in the compound can.[17]

A customary burial comprises several steps which are supposed to be similar in all of the villages of Yatenga province, though details vary from one village to the next. A traditional burial starts with the cutting up of a live animal in the deceased's courtyard, a rite referred to as *tamuku* in the Mooré language. The protagonists then lay a mat surrounded by a blanket symbolizing the dead person in the ancestor's house (*kiim-roogo*). They dig a hole in the wall of the compound, through which the eldest daughter, eldest son, and the deceased (i.e., the catafalque on which the blanket symbolizing the deceased lies) will exit.

Goats, money and cotton strips are presented to the dead person. The throats of animals may be cut. The deceased is then interrogated (*sãenga*): a few men lift the deceased and someone starts to ask questions about the reasons for his death. The bearers walk back and forth, guided by the movements of the deceased. A man asks: "Have you hidden anything? Where did you hide it?" The "corpse" indicates several places by his movements. Some-

Illustration 6.3. Village of Sonh, 1996. The *na-poka* stripped to the waist in front of the compound of the deceased. Photo by Katrin Langewiesche.

Illustration 6.4. Village of Lago, 1997. Procession of a young *na-poka*. Photo by Franck Pourcel.

body digs in these places and pours water there. The interrogation continues: "Who killed you? Did you die because of your wives? If so, come here. Did you die because of your children? If so, come here. Was your life finished? If so, come here."

In the end, the bearers of the corpse leave for the cemetery, followed by the *na-poka* and its cortege. The men dig a hole into which they put salt, honey, money, a cock, and a black cat, both alive; the cat cannot be seen, as it is in a bag to prevent it from escaping. The men break the wooden stretcher on which they had carried the body and put the pieces into the grave. Most of the crowd does not follow the cortege to the cemetery and the remainder disperses at this point. They say goodbye: *Wend na kōd beoogo !* May God grant us a good night! *Amina!*

In summary, the main differences between the Catholic and traditional rituals lie in the presentation of sacrifices and in the rites relating to the status of the ancestors. The Catholic ceremony has the basic structure of a traditional ceremony but does not involve any sacrifices (the *tamuku*, the objects that accompany the "dead" in the grave, etc.), any of the rituals carried out in the house of the deceased (*kiim-roogo*), or the interrogation of the deceased on the causes of death (*sãenga*). The Catholic ceremony mobilizes as many people as the customary burial. Both rituals take place in the same locations. There is no church building and no special graveyards for Christians in Sonh.[18]

The boundaries of the religious arena

These individual accounts—be they of the funeral of Bishop Durrieu or the two burials of the *naaba* of Sonh—clearly demonstrate that the different religions constitute a "whole" within which individuals navigate. Some of the actors involved in the two burials cannot be characterized as Muslim, Christian, or "traditionalist," but—depending on the situation—as simply pluralist.

The analysis of the parish records showed that for the priests, the ceremonies held during the funeral of Bishop Durrieu not only offered a way of honoring the deceased but also provided the priests with a tool for converting the rural masses. The ceremony is part of this general movement within the Burkinabe Catholic Church, which is attempting to build a Catholic identity that is as close as possible to traditional symbolism.

The current archbishop of Bobo-Dioulasso, Mgr. Sanon, in his theology thesis of 1970, gives another example of this tendency. Mgr. Sanon recounts an experiment carried out by a priest in a village close to Pabré which reflects the Catholic Church's preoccupation with inculturation after Vatican II, here addressing the question of how the transformation of the customary initiation rite into Christian baptism could best be approached. The priest in question introduced the Christians into the village initiation rite, but requested that no immolations or chicken sacrifices be performed for the Christian participants. The elders accepted this request. Under these conditions, the elders and the bishop sanctioned the participation of the Christians in the ancestral rite of initiation and baptized the Christian participants immediately after the traditional rite when the initiates came back to the village, thereby retaining a spatial and temporal separation between the two rites (Sanon 1970: 210).

The first Catholic missionaries created a "moral" typology of pagan rites in order to evaluate the various levels of paganism. Thus, the traditional funeral (*kuuré*) was accepted by the White Fathers (*Pères Blancs*) as "a family and social duty." They accepted belief in God and in natural forces, but did not accept the pagan sacrifices, which were regarded as directly opposed to Christian beliefs (Audouin 1982: 197). This typology, accompanied by ecclesiastical punishments, enabled the faithful to identify the elements of tradition that conformed with Christian law and practice. The behavior of the missionaries in relation to customs varied from one area to another. In West Volta, the wearing of masks by Christians has been tolerated since the 1950s. People were simply asked to pray to God instead of the fetish when wearing masks (Audouin 1982: 360). As also illustrated by the story of Mgr. Durriez's funerals, since Vatican II the general tolerance of traditional rites and the search for an "African Christian way" have encouraged Catholics to practice their traditional rites so as to avoid a brutal rupture with their traditions.[19]

The attitude of the Catholics to polygamy is both an illustration and consequence of this acceptance of cultural traditions. The church hierarchy never allowed polygamists to be baptized. However, due to the large number of polygamists, this became a serious problem and necessitated an accommodation adapted to the conditions of real life. Therefore, the priests and catechists take initiatives and make exceptions in certain precisely defined cases (e.g., those involving the elderly or chiefs.) Thus, in spite of his polygamy, the old *naaba* of Sonh was baptized before he died. Because it is not regarded as a personal choice but as an obligation related to the chief's status, a chief's polygamy requires a different register. Fathers sometimes give their daughters in marriage to the chief in order to prove their respect to him, to thank him, or to honor him. The latter cannot refuse the women. Without tolerating it officially, the Catholics have always adapted to polygamy. Not only does the Catholic hierarchy tolerate the polygamy of the chiefs, but also that of men taking a second wife in the form of a levirate marriage. Among the Mossi, if she so wishes, the wife of a deceased man remains in her husband's family. She is married to a younger brother of her late husband, even if he is already married. The Catholics who "inherit" a woman in such manner remain Catholic, but are restricted from practices such as confession or communion.[20]

This flexibility with respect to the mixing of Christian and traditional values is obviously not adopted by all Catholics. Depending on circumstances, an individual may alter his or her behavior over the course of their life. For example, Pascal, the catechist of Sonh, adopted a different position on the death of the *naaba* as he became involved in the defense of Catholic orthodoxy. Pascal's position as catechist in Sonh, where he has been living since 1984 with his wife and children, is his first. He and his family come from another village of Yatenga Province. The Catholic community in Sonh is relatively large compared with those of the surrounding villages, and this gives Pascal a certain social importance in the village. Thanks to his authority as a *karemsamba* (master) of a rather large Catholic community, Pascal, who is just thirty years old and also an outsider in Sonh, has been able to assert himself vis-à-vis the old men who make the decisions regarding funerary rites. In this particular situation, his religious affiliation and status (as catechist) are more important to him than his status in traditional Mossi society, which does not allow outsiders to participate in decision-making on village matters. His religious affiliation allows him to play a social role which he could not otherwise have played.

Just as all Catholics do not accept the mixing of Christianity and traditional religion, all Muslims do not adopt a *tabula rasa* approach to Mossi customs, as our informants would often have us believe. They are not all uncompromising in relation to local influences. The master of the madrasa accepts, for example, that his own wife consults the soothsayers. As an educated Muslim he finds it easier to accept the local influences than the village imams. He insists on the fact that the rigor expressed by many village Muslims towards traditional customs is more a matter of community than of belief:

> Many people converted to Islam so that if they die, they get their burial, or if a woman gives birth, so that people come to the baptism, or to marry. Personally, I think that is the way it is for some people. It is to belong to the community. It has nothing to do with faith.[21]

What the madrasa master is observing here is the overlapping praxis—one which can be observed by an outsider—that many village Muslims carry out in relation to their rites and individual beliefs. However, these "hybridizations" or "adjustments" are not accepted by some village imams and some strong devotees. Their need for conformity with beliefs, rites, and behavioral norms takes precedence over the personal authenticity of the believer.[22]

The critical period following the death of a person clearly reveals the way in which the religious and social fields overlap. In order to control this event, the individuals or religious communities invoke both their cultural roots and religious affiliations (Catholic or Muslim in this case). These two facets are superimposed on each other and the boundaries between them are fluid. The situation faced by Salif, the future chief and one of the family's few Muslims, during the burials of the chief of Sonh, enables us to explore the way in which the Muslims we encounter see the boundary between Mossi and Muslim identity and how they "update" this boundary. Having been a Muslim, Salif acts as a Catholic because in his current situation, the rules of that religion are more compatible with his role as chief. The quotations above suggest that Salif cannot imagine going back to traditional religion. In the current context, he needs a universalist religion to assert himself in this world and to fulfill his functions as *naaba*. He sees the traditional religion more as a foundation than a "proper" religion. Salif adheres to the norms that prohibit Muslims from participating in both traditional rites and Islamic practice, and when this prohibition goes contrary to his interests, he converts to Catholicism.

These quotations also indicate that we are in presence of "a publicly oriented animism" (*animisme de charges publiques*) (Olivier de Sardan 2003: 14). The notables are in charge of rituals carried out publicly in the name of the village or lineage, even if one or the other is ninety-nine percent Christian or Muslim. It is sufficient for the chief or *bugo* (priest/soothsayer) to celebrate the traditional ceremonies to ensure the wellbeing of the village or lineage.

Historical explanations and strategic analyses

The few ethnographic examples presented in this chapter show that in the context of the current religious landscape—in which the multitude of religious groups makes it possible for each individual to follow several religious orientations at the same time or to alternate between them in the course of their lives—attitudes to religious syncretism differ significantly among Muslims and Catholics. Of course, it is also possible to observe nuances in behavior and attitudes within these two religious communities, as evidenced, for example, by the attitudes of Pascal, the catechist. during the burial of the *naaba* of Sonh and of the madrasa master. In general, Catholic priests and educated Muslims find it easier to accommodate the local influences than the village catechists and imams. However, it is possible to observe divergent tendencies among the Catholics and Muslims vis-à-vis syncretism. The question that arises here, however, is why—within the same current context of religious diversity— many Muslims refuse to engage in religious *bricolage*, while the majority of the Catholics accept it or tolerate it. In other words: Why are the boundaries between one religion and another different from the people involved within one and the same environment (i.e., Yatenga Province)?

Historical explanations can help interpret these differences. While the first Catholic missionaries in the Haute-Volta refused categorically and sometimes violently to accept any compromise with the traditional religion (Audouin 1982: 195), today there is far greater tolerance for this *rapprochement*. This change in the approach to the traditional religion around the 1970s was not limited to the missionaries of Haute-Volta. The more or less simultaneous Africanization of Catholicism after Vatican II may be observed in other African regions (Bureau 1996; Baum 1990). The "inculturation" of the Catholics within their environment became one of the goals of the representatives of the Catholic Church. They hoped to attain this goal by creating "Basic Christian Communities" (Boillot 1990; Laurent 1984), by encouraging a large-scale Africanization of the clergy, and by reinforcing pastoral work in urban areas and generally increasing their social involvement. During the 1970s, the spreading of the gospel in African societies demanded by the theology of inculturation became a major concern within the Burkinabese church. The thoughts of the priests in relation to the burial of Bishop Durrieu, which can be read in the parish record, provide a striking example of this phenomenon.

In contrast to this, the first Burkinabese Muslims accepted the country's customs, whereas contemporary Muslims mainly display an attitude of intransigence towards the traditional rites. The first Muslims in Yatenga Province were primarily foreign tradesmen who did not have a shared strategy for proselytizing. Over the course of the following decades, this professional specialization became a constraint, not only for the foreign Muslims but also for the Mossi Muslims: due to being educated in a Qur'anic school, they were unable to access the public service. If one agrees with Goody's (1971) view that none of the West African populations can be studied without considering their former links to Islam, it would appear nonetheless important to stress that a true project of Islamization developed in the Haute-Volta from the missionary period at the beginning of the twentieth century.

It was not until the 1970s that the Muslims organized and developed a real Islamization project in Haute-Volta. There was a noticeable change in the situation from the 1980s; Muslim elites educated in the West and an Arabized Muslim elite both gradually emerged, which developed real conversion strategies (e.g., the allocation of grants, the coaching of the young, the building of madrasas, the planning of radio campaigns).

The power struggles between the great religious institutions evolved over the past century with the arrival of the first Catholics and the massive wave of Islamization. This explains why the consequences of the conversion process are different today. What we have here are two inverse historical movements. The dynamics of the religious field unfold in two opposed directions for the two universalist religions. The origin of this opposition lies in their relationship to traditional society and to the dominant theology. The return to the letter of the Qur'an for Islam and the desire of Christianity to achieve immersion in Africanicity became the starting points for the opposition of Muslims and Catholics.

Apart from these historical elements, an explanation based on the strategic analysis of the interests at work here can help us interpret the attitudes of the various groups about these practices of religious *bricolage*. The interest that a group or a class develops in a type of belief or religious practice depends on its position within the social organization. In the case in question, the group that develops an interest in resuming traditional rites does not constitute a social group, such as "women," "elders," or "tradesmen." Instead, it is a group of individuals that transcends religious or sociological characteristics. It is not established once and for all, but rather forms and disbands depending on the prevailing situation. Evers and Schiel (1988) use the term "strategic group" to describe such configurations. The empirical analysis confirms that in a given community, for example, all of the "Muslims of a village" do not have the same interests or the same representations and that depending on the context, these interests and representations form differently, yet not in any random way. Individually speaking, none of the attitudes of the various people faced with the death of the *naaba* is of lesser importance. Considered together and integrated into the historical and contemporary context, they enable us to identify the outline of a bigger social game. In the case under examination, it is the dignitaries of Mossi society (the future *naaba*, the *na-poka*, and her husband), be they Muslims, Catholics, men, women, tradesmen, or farmers, who show an interest in returning to the traditional religion. This interest in the traditional religion is of course grounded in personal dispositions and in their socialization, as well as in their situational interests of the moment. For instance, the first daughter of the chief has assumed since her youth that some day she would be *na-poka*. The individuals who do not have a precise function within the Mossi traditional organization mostly display their religious orthodoxy, if they are Muslims, and mostly accept religious syncretism, if they are Catholics.

Reference was made in passing to the variety of attitudes among the Muslims with respect to traditional religion and its rites. Whereas the master of the madrasa displayed an attitude of tolerance under pressure from the village Muslim community, Salif gave up Islam so as not to have to mix the religion of the Prophet with traditional rituals. This diversity shows that behind the almost unanimous disapproval of syncretism on the part of Muslims lies the religious "mix" experienced in everyday Muslim life.

As opposed to this, the fact that Catholics accept this mixing of religions appears to reflect their will to display an image of tolerance. The weight of religious history of the region, briefly evoked in the beginning of this chapter, still influences the relations and interactions between the contemporary faith communities and their members.

Both religions need each other to display their specific features. They are defined at least as much by their relationship with the traditional religion as by their respective characteristics. However, even within the framework of their antitraditionalism, many non-practicing Catholics and Muslims either still feel Christian or claim to be Muslims.

The burial: a motive for conversion

In the Yatenga villages, the most frequent reasons for conversion mentioned by my informants are marriage, healing, burial, and above all the fear of not being buried in the right way.[23] Religious experience is undoubtedly an intimate and personal event that cannot be entirely apprehended sociologically. However, it is socially structured and generates social effects. When considered as a social phenomenon, religious conversions throw light on the nature of the transformation of values, such as the processes of individualization and modernization already underway. Conversion occurs between freedom and constraint, individual destiny and collective future, intimate conviction and public expression. The religious motivation for conversion is seldom as pure as that conveyed by the word "conversion" itself: it combines with social, economic, and political considerations. For this reason—and in order to go beyond the theological meaning of conversion—the Comaroffs introduce the concept of "conversation." They analyze the two concepts, conversion and conversation, both as historical practices and as analytical categories. The conversation metaphor refers to the dialogue and dialectics inherent to all individual conversion and to general religious transformations (Comaroff and Comaroff 1991). The encounter of individuals with different religious practices and beliefs creates new possibilities and significations. In this vein, other authors tackle religious change and conversion as a "creative process of intercultural communication" (Blakely and van Beek 1994: 5), a "translation" requiring compromise of the two partners or a "passionate communication process" (Peel 1990: 339). Although stimulating, the analysis of religious change in terms of "co-writing" (Van Der Veer 1996) may sometimes omit the situation of domination within which the first conversions—conversions to Christianity in particular—took place (Hock 2006; Hefner 1993).

The comparison of the different waves of conversion to Christianity and Islam shows that conversion is a process of influence, the outcome of which depends on the distribution of power between the various groups of the society in question (Peel 2002). Men and women, young and old of one and the same society do not share the same concerns and are not incited to convert for the same reasons. Thus conversion is a significant component which influences the transformations of relationships between generations and the genders (Masquelier 2001; Leblanc 2000; Launay 1992). Conversion enables the individual to manage his or her fate or to forge a path through several identities, and conversion reveals tensions that characterize historical and contemporary societies (Hervieu-Léger 1999).

In the parish records of Ouahigouya of the 1960s, the White Fathers appear to be completely clear about the motivations for conversion and the strategies adopted by the population. In several villages, the fathers note both "a solid group of old men who really want us to be here" and a feeling of hostility from the young adults.[24] They are perfectly aware that the elders join them because they are seeking a counterpower to oppose the increasing economic and social influence of the Muslims, as represented by the young adults. The power of the elders is particularly oppressive for the younger members of society, especially given that the latter reach the most productive age of thirty-five to forty without gaining any access to decision-making powers. Migration—and the frequent subsequent conversion to Islam—offers the young people a way of escaping from the control of their elders (Miran 2006; Ouedraogo 1997; Schildkrout 1978). The money young adults earn in Côte d'Ivoire or Ghana gives them far more rapid access to a form of economic independence than they would gain if they had remained in the Mossi village. The elders are well aware of the fact that this migration (and the conversion to Islam that accompanies it) accelerates young people's access to independence and reduces the elders' own power over the youth. Thus they use the Catholic priests as a barrier against Islam, which increasingly threatens their rights as the representatives of tradition and the holders of resources and decision-making powers.

In the 1960s, the elders wanted the Catholics to become established in their villages firstly because they sought a counterpower to the social and economic hegemony of the Muslims and secondly because they feared that their sons who had become Muslims would not bury them in accordance with the traditional rites (*kuuré*). The Catholics, who understood this fear well, tried to comfort the population by claiming that traditional funerals were accepted by the White Fathers as "a familial and social duty." In the Yatenga region, they confirmed this attitude during Bishop Durrieu's funeral in 1965 by bringing the symbolism of Christian funerals and the Mossi *kuuré* as closely into sync as possible. This determination to find a religious compromise is updated regularly and in different ways, for example in the toleration of polygamous Christians and double burials (e.g., both Catholic and traditional), as in the case of the chief of Sonh.

The tensions, conflicts, and individual sufferings that a conversion can cause are exemplified by a sixty-year-old Catholic woman who lost her husband and who lives with her only son. This son, a Muslim, has told his mother that he will not organize a Catholic burial after her death, but rather a Muslim one. The desperation of the woman is so great that she called on the priest of Ouahigouya to ask about the possibility of living far away from her son. Otherwise, she feels compelled to convert to Islam. She would prefer to convert to Islam and receive a burial in accordance with the religion of the Prophet than to stay Catholic and have a burial which is not appropriate to this religion. The effectiveness of the burial depends on the extent to which the traditional, Christian, or Muslim norms are respected, as any failure in this regard means that the deceased will neither be able to join his or her ancestors nor rest in peace. In the opinion of those involved, a Muslim burial without the recital of the funeral *surahs* is as useless as a Christian burial without prayers or a traditional burial without sacrifices. In this "ritualist" approach of religion, the way a ritual is performed has a very important impact on its effectiveness. For some people the passage to the afterlife is dependent on sacrifice, while for others access to paradise is only possible if the prohibition on sacrifice is observed.

Funerals are times at which Catholics and Muslims must locate their position vis-à-vis the other world religions and traditional religion. They are spaces in which individuals and groups display their ideas with respect to religious frontiers and pluralism through concrete and observable actions. Thus when it comes to explaining a religious landscape composed of several religious traditions, a landscape characterized by individual religious mobility and complex processes involving the reorganization and rebuilding of community identities, the analysis of funerals proves a particularly fertile source of information.

Notes

1. While "traditional" suggests a static and closed character, alternative labels—"indigenous," "local," "African"—are also problematic, given that Christianity and Islam can be all of these things too.

2. The term *marabout* includes Qur'anic masters and imams, diviner and healer marabouts, and well-read theologians. On the ambiguity of this notion, see Robinson and Triaud 1997.
3. Ramatoulaye near Ouahigouya in the Yatenga province is one of these settlements. It was founded in the early twentieth century.
4. *Diaire,* June 5, 1965.
5. *Diaire,* June 6, 1965.
6. *Siiga:* vital principle, one of the various components of the person, often translated as "soul."
7. *Diaire,* June 12, 1965.
8. *Naaba, naanamse* (plural): chief. The term *naaba* refers to a chief, irrespective of the territorial unit which he rules. The chief of the former Yatenga kingdom and of the present-day Yatenga province is called Yatenga Naaba.
9. *Diaire,* June 12, 1965.
10. See *inter alia* Sanon 1991; Sanon and Luneau 1982; Leroy-Ladurie 1965.
11. This theology of inculturation, which is criticized by Messi Metogo (1985) and many others, starts from exalted traditional cultural values and neglects the economic and political issues of current African reality.
12. *L'enquête démographique par sondage en République de Haute Volta de 1960-61.* Vol 1, INSEE, Département coopération: 104; *Analyse des Résultats du Recensement Général de la Population et de l'habitation de 1996,* Vol 1, INSD, Ouagadougou 2000: 54.
13. The statistics of the diocese of Ouahigouya show 1,204 child baptisms and only 758 adult baptisms in 1996.
14. *na-poka, na-pokse* (plural): Eldest daughter of the chief, who succeeds her father for a short time and takes over his functions. The term *na-poka* is also used as a title when addressing the person.
15. Literally translated, *Rog-miki* means "born found" or "what we've found as we came into this world." *Rog-miki* combines notions of identity, religion, and all things that have been transmitted by the ancestors, be they religious rituals or celebrations, ways of preparing the millet, building a house, or dancing, as well as ways of dealing with in-laws or with the distribution of political power. In this context, *rog-miki* means traditional funerals.
16. Salif Ouedraogo, interview, 1996 and 1997.
17. Salif Ouedraogo, interview, 2000.
18. There are generally several graveyards in the Mossi villages: one for the chiefs, another for the *bugba* (healer-priests), one for the adults, one for the children, and one for the *sāpogba.* The *sāpogba* are the "bad dead," those who died as a result of an accident or drowning, women who died when pregnant, or people who committed suicide (*sāpogba* literally means "wound").
19. With one exception: the immolation of animals. Catholics, Protestants and Muslims all are disturbed by the pagan aspect of the sacrifices.
20. Interview with Abbé G., 2000.
21. Interview with, Abdoulaye, the master of the madrasa, 1995 and 1996.
22. Shaw and Stewart (1994) draw attention to antisyncretism, the erection of rigid boundaries against other religions.
23. For more details on the other motives for conversion, see Langewiesche 2003.
24. *Diaire,* January 11, 1966.

Bibliography

Audouin, Jean and Raymond Deniel. 1978. *L'islam en Haute-Volta à l'époque coloniale.* Paris and Abidjan: L'Harmattan-INADES.

Audouin, Jean. 1982. *Evangélisation du Mossi par les Pères Blancs, approche socio-historique.* PhD thesis, Paris: EHESS.

Barbier, Jean Claude. 1999. "Citadins et religions au Burkina Faso." In *Dieu dans la Cité. Dynamiques religieuses en millieu urbain ouagalais,* ed. René Otayek. Bordeaux: CEAN.

Baum, Robert, M. 1990. "The emergence of Diola Christianity." *Africa* 60, no. 3: 370–398.

Blakely, T. D., Dennis L. Thomson and W. Van Beek (eds). 1994. *Religion in Africa. Experience and Expression.* London: James Currey.

Boillot, F. 1990. "Les communautés chrétiennes de base au Burkina Faso." *Politique africaine* 39: 176–182.

Bureau, René. 1996. *Le prophète de la lagune: Les harristes de Côte d'Ivoire.* Paris: Karthala.

Cissé, Issa. 1990. "Les médersas au Burkina. L'aide arabe et la croissance d'un système d'enseignement arabo-islamique." *Islam et Sociétés au Sud du Sahara* 4: 58–72.

———. 1993. "L'islam et le christianisme durant la période coloniale." In *Burkina ... 2000. Une église en marche vers son centenaire,* ed. Jean Ilboudo. Ouagadougou: Presses Africaines.

Comaroff, Jean, and John Comaroff. 1991. *Of Revolution and Revelation: Christianity, Colonization and Consciousness in South Africa.* Chicago: University of Chicago Press.

Compaoré, Maxime. 1993. "L'enseignement privé catholique en Haute-Volta (1901–1960)." In *Burkina ... 2000. Une église en marche vers son centenaire,* ed. Jean Ilboudo. Ouagadougou: Presses Africaines.

———. 2003. "La refondation de l'enseignement catholique au Burkina Faso." *Cahiers d'études africaines* 169–170: 87–97.

Corten, André, and Ruth Marshall-Fratani, eds. 2001. *Between Babel and Pentecost: Transnational Pentecostalism in Africa and Latin America.* London: Hurst.

Diallo, Hamidou. 1985. "Islam et colonisation au Yatenga (1897–1950)." *Le mois en Afrique* 237–238: 33–42.

Evers, Hans-Dieter, and Tielman Schiel. 1988. *Strategische Gruppen.* Berlin: Reimer Verlag.

Fancello, Sandra. 2006. *Les aventuriers du pentecôtisme ghanéen. Nation, conversion et délivrance en Afrique de l'Ouest.* Paris: IRD-Karthala.

Gifford, Paul. 1998. *African Christianity: Its public role.* London: Hurst.

Goody, Jack. 1971. "The Impact of Islamic Writing on the Oral Cultures of West Africa." *Cahiers d'études africaines* 11, no. 43: 455–466.

Hefner, Robert W., ed. 1993. *Conversion to Christianity.* Berkeley: University of California Press.

Hervieu-Léger, Danièle. 1999. *Le pèlerin et le converti. La religion en mouvement.* Paris: Flammarion.

Hock, Klaus. 2006. "Translated Messages? The Construction of Religious Identities as Translatory Process." *Mission Studies* 23, no. 2: 261–278.

Kouanda, Assimi. 1988. "L'état de la recherche sur l'Islam au Burkina." *Islam et Sociétés au Sud du Sahara* 2: 94–105.

———. 1997. "Marabouts et missionnaires catholiques au Burkina à l'époque coloniale (1900–1947)." In *Le temps des marabouts,* eds. David Robinson and Jean-Louis Triaud. Paris: Karthala.

Langewiesche, Katrin. 2003. *Mobilité religieuse. Changements religieux au Burkina Faso.* Münster: LIT-Verlag.

Launay, Robert. 1992. *Beyond the Stream: Islam and Society in a West African Town.* Berkeley: University of California Press.

——. 2006. "An invisible religion? Anthropology's Avoidance of Islam in Africa." In *African Anthropologies: History, Critique and Practice,* eds. Mwenda Ntarangwi, David Mills, Mustafa Babiker. Dakar, London, New York: Codesria.

Laurent, O. 1984. "Les communautés de base en Afrique. Points de repère pour une évaluation sociologique." *Spiritus* 25, no. 95: 115–128.

Laurent, Pierre-Joseph. 2003. *Les pentecôtistes du Burkina Faso: Mariage, pouvoir, et guérison.* Paris: IRD-Karthala.

Leroy-Ladurie, Marie. 1965. *Pâques Africaines: De la communauté clanique à la communauté chrétienne.* Paris: Mouton.

Levtzion, Nehemia. 1968. *Muslims and Chiefs in West Africa: A Study of Islam in the Middle Volta Basin in the Pre-Colonial Period.* London: Oxford University Press.

Masquelier, Adeline. 2001. *Prayer has spoiled Everything.* Durham: Duke University Press.

Mayrargue, Cédric. 2004. "Trajectoires et enjeux contemporains du pentecôtisme en Afrique de l'Ouest." *Critique Internationale* 22: 95–109.

Metogo, Eloi Messi. 1985. *Théologie africaine et Ethnophilosophie.* Paris: L'Harmattan.

Miran, Marie. 2006. *Islam, histoire et modernité en Côte d'Ivoire.* Paris: Karthala.

Olivier de Sardan, Jean-Pierre. 2003. "Préface." In *Mobilité religieuse—Changements religieux au Burkina Faso,* Katrin Langewiesche. Münster: LIT-Verlag.

Otayek, René. 1984. "La crise de la communauté musulmane de Haute Volta. L'islam voltaïque entre réformisme et tradition, autonomie et subordination." *Cahiers d'Etudes africaines* 34, no. 3: 299–320.

——. 1988. "Muslim Charisma in Burkina Faso." In *Charisma and Brotherhood in African Islam,* ed. Donal B. Cruise O'Brien. Oxford: Calderon.

——. 1993. "L'affirmation élitaire des arabisants au Burkina Faso." In *Le radicalisme islamique au sud du Sahara,* ed. René Otayek. Paris: Karthala.

——. 1997. "L'Église catholique au Burkina Faso. Un contre-pouvoir à contretemps de l'histoire." In *Religion et transition démocratique en Afrique,* eds. F. Constantin and C. Coulon. Paris: Karthala.

Ouedraogo, Jean-Bernard. 1997. *Violences et communautés en Afrique Noire.* Paris: L'Harmattan.

Peel, John D. Y. 1990. "The Pastor and the Babalawo: The interaction of religions in nineteenth-century Yorubaland." *Africa* 60, no. 3: 338–369.

——. 2002. "Gender in Yoruba Religious Change." *Journal of Religion in Africa* 32, no. 2: 136–166.

Robinson, David and Jean Louis Triaud, eds. 1997. *Le temps des marabouts.* Paris: Karthala.

Sanon, Anselme Titianma. 1970. *Tierce Église, ma mère, ou la conversion d'une communauté païenne au Christ.* PhD diss., Institut catholique de Paris.

——. 1991. "Jesus, Master of Initiation." In *Faces of Jesus in Africa,* ed. Robert J. Schreiter. Maryknoll, NY: Orbis.

Sanon, Anselme Titianma and René Luneau. 1982. *Enraciner l'Évangile. Initiations africaines et pédagogie de la foi.* Paris: Editions du Cerf.

Saul, Mahir. 2006. "Islam and West African Anthropology." *Africa Today* 53, no. 1: 3–33.

Strandsbjerg, Camilla. 2005. "Les nouveaux réseaux évangéliques transnationaux et l'Etat: le cas du Bénin." In *Entreprises religieuses transnationales en Afrique de l'Ouest,* eds. L. Fourchard, A. Mary and R. Otayek. Ibadan and Paris: IFRA-Karthala.

Schildkrout, Enid. 1978. *People of Zongo: The transformation of ethnic identities in Ghana.* Cambridge: Cambridge University Press.

Shaw, Rosalind and Charles Stewart, eds. 1994. *Syncretism/Antisyncretism: The politics of religious synthesis.* London: Routledge.

Skinner, Elliot P. 1962. "The Diffusion of Islam in an African society." *Annals of the New York Academy of Sciences* 96, no 2: 659–669.

——. 1967. "Christianity and Islam among the Mossi." in *Gods and Rituals,* ed. John Middleton. New York: Natural History Press.

Some, Magloire. 2006. "Les missionnaires protestants anglo-saxons face au nationalisme français en Haute-Volta de 1920 à 1939." *Le fait missionnaire* 18: 73–108.

Stewart, Charles. 1997. Colonial Justice and the Spread of Islam in early 20th century. In *Le temps des marabouts: itinéraires et stratégies islamiques en Afrique Occidentale Française,* eds. Robinson, David and Triaud, Jean-Louis. Paris: Karthala: 53–67.

Van Der Veer, Peter, ed. 1996. *Conversion to Modernities: The Globalisation of Christianity.* London: Routledge.

Werthmann, Katja. 2008. "Islam on both Sides: Religion and Locality in Western Burkina Faso." In *Dimensions of Locality: Muslim Saints, their Place and Space,* eds. Georg Stauth and Samuli Schielke. *Yearbook of the Sociology of Islam* 8: 125–127.

Wilks, Ivor. 2000. "The Juula and the Expansion of Islam into the Forest." In *The History of Islam in Africa,* eds. Nehemia Levtzion, Randall L. Pouwels. Athens: Ohio University Press.

CHAPTER 7

Funerals and the Religious Imagination

*Burying and Honoring the Dead in the
Celestial Church of Christ in southern Benin*

Joël Noret

> "If I have joined the Celestial Church of Christ, it is because,
> as a philosopher, I have seen that what they did was
> a bit like what our ancestors used to do."
>
> G.-B. A.

Introduction

In contemporary southern Benin as in other parts of Africa, funerals are major social events. However, even though some significant evolutions have been experienced in the last decades, research on the topic has until recently often seemed disconnected from research on social change in this region of Africa, as well as in many others. Funerals and social change were in fact two domains of research, the first more or less focused on the permanence of "traditional rites," the other on the forms adopted by "modernity" in the African field. In what follows, I will try to focus both on social dynamics and on social continuities through the study of funerals in the Celestial Church of Christ, a Beninese prophetic Church which has today become the second largest church of the country in terms of membership, right after the Catholic Church.

This chapter is organized around two main issues. In the first part, after introducing the Celestial Church, I will show the implications of the fact that Celestial funerals always take place in the broader social context of a differentiated society. In the second part, after the presentation of the cycle of funeral rites introduced by the church approximately fifty years ago, I will show how Celestials are involved in a *bricolage* of the status of the dead between "traditional" ways of thinking and schemes of thought inherited from missionary Catholicism. Also, drawing on my southern Benin materials, I will show how the focus on displaying one's social and economic capital as the real driving force behind the importance and extravagance of contemporary African funerals (see in particular van der Geest 2000) should be supplemented by other perspectives.

The Celestial Church of Christ in southern Benin

The Celestial Church of Christ was established in the city of Porto-Novo in southeastern Benin in 1947, approximately twenty years after the beginning of the *aladura* movement. In the 1920s, the *aladura* movement had seen the birth of a series of prophetic churches, especially in the regions of Lagos and Ibadan in neighboring southwestern Nigeria. Samuel Bilewu Joseph Oshoffa (1909–1985), the founder of the Celestial Church of Christ, was first a member of the Sacred and Eternal Order of Cherubim and Seraphim, one of the main *aladura* Churches, implanted in Porto-Novo in the 1930s. According to him, in 1947, Oshoffa—a carpenter at that time—had a vision after getting lost in the swamps of the low valley of the river Ouémé, near Porto-Novo. This vision ordered him to establish a church that would become "the last vessel" for salvation. He met his first success in the villages of the lagoon surrounding Porto-Novo, and the Celestial Church experienced a fast growth in the following decades.

Nevertheless, the importance of this somehow millenarian starting point should not be overestimated. Both the Celestial Church and the other *aladura* churches require the faithful to wear white robes during the services, and both involve themselves heavily with the religious concerns of the "traditional" religious system, especially with the problem of finding an effective protection against the dangers of occult aggression such as witchcraft. Christian influences, however, cannot be reduced to a simple "mask" over traditional religious logics (see Mary 2000; Bastide 1970), and going back to the literal meaning of the Bible has been another obsessive concern since the origin of the church. Samuel Oshoffa was raised in a Methodist environment and attended a Catholic school for a few years during his childhood. Moreover, the Celestial Church bears the imprint of Islamic influences from the Yoruba environment of Porto-Novo in which the young Oshoffa was educated, which included for numerous decades a significant number of Muslim lineages. I will return to the question of the interplay between these different influences while analyzing the Celestial rites for the dead.

Finally, the source of religious legitimacy is double in the Celestial Church of Christ: it derives both from the Bible and from dreams and visions. "Visionaries" actually represent an important category of church member (see Henry 1998; Mary 1999). In every church compound, these people offer day and night religious consultations to all those who need it; their visions, normally free, perform a divinatory function similar to that of traditional diviners. The Celestial Church thus ensures in southern Benin a religious service open to everybody and aimed at providing a solution to concrete problems of everyday life: visions are often followed by a "prescription" of "spiritual works" that imply a series of more or less long prayers and appeal to more or less important ritual materials (candles, incense, palm branches, holy water, holy sheets, etc.). The strong materiality of the majority of the Celestial rites is indeed widely acknowledged in contemporary southern Benin, and this, together with the divinatory activities of the visionaries, largely nurtures the accusations of "fetishism" regularly formulated against the church, especially among the circles of Pentecostals and fervent Catholics.

Today, despite the fact that it now represents the second largest church in Benin (after the Catholic Church) in terms of membership with more than 1,200 parishes (of which the vast majority are located in the southern part of the country), the Celestial Church of Christ has neither obtained a legitimacy comparable to that of the historical missionary churches (Catholic and Methodist) nor to that of churches like the Assemblies of God, the main Pentecostal church in Benin (Noret 2004c). Finally, after the sudden death in 1985 of the "prophet pastor founder" S. B. J. Oshoffa soon after a car accident, the church, at that time already established in many African countries (especially in Nigeria and the Ivory Coast with a few thousand and several hundred parishes, respectively, but also in Europe and the United States), experienced increased division. After the death of the prophet, a brief division occurred between two of Oshoffa's main collaborators, one from Benin (B. Agbaossi) and the other from Nigeria (A. Bada). The death of the latter in 2000 then led to new divisions and new conflicts and alliances between the ethnonational leaders of a church that its founder had declared "one and indivisible."[1]

Funerals in a differentiated society

The society of southern Benin is now incontestably differentiated. By this I don't mean, of course, that there are no more continuities between the social and religious worlds that constitute this society. Funerals in particular are a place of important social investment in the whole society (see also Noret 2005). However, this investment can be ambiguous and controversial. Indeed, the sumptuous dimension of these "ruinous ceremonies," as they were termed in particular during the Marxist-Leninist period of the country (1972–1990), is frequently criticized as socially irresponsible by those same people—the great majority of the population—who organize them when they are in a position to do so, a contradiction resulting from the importance of internalized social norms and pressures. Additionally, the wide sharing of this social investment in funerals within the population does not mean that the norms that shape how burials should be organized are shared in the same way across the different social worlds of southern Benin society (see Noret 2010).

In fact, the differentiated character of the society goes back to the period of the development of kingdoms and "precolonial" urban centers with the diverse social hierarchies to be found in each. But, just to briefly mention here one very complex evolution, the differentiation of the society of southern Benin developed in particular from the nineteenth century with the gradual establishment of the Afro-Brazilians (see among others Guran 2000; Giordano 2001) and the expansion of Muslim and Catholic minorities, with these two phenomena only partially overlapping. This differentiation then obviously increased in the twentieth century during the colonial era and all the consequences and dynamics that it brought about in every sphere of social life.

Today, if lineages often remain at the heart of the management of death and organization of funerals, the exertion of authority by customary chiefs on these occasions is no longer recognized as easily as before. Social actors are today more and more committed to different social worlds and networks, especially in urban environments, and this happens in a context characterized by the growing priority of religious affiliations and identities. Therefore, when funerals are organized, several groups are often able to claim an active role (even slight ones) in the decision making process. These groups include the different components of the paternal and sometimes maternal lineages of the dead, the lineage of a female deceased person's husband, and also eventually the members of the religious group of the deceased and in some cases even members of his or her profession, although this last is found to a much lower degree.

However, it is especially within the different components of the paternal and maternal families of the dead (children, brothers and sisters, uncles and aunts, and lineage authorities) that conflicts are likely to originate, especially when these groups or parts of them (i.e., children, siblings, etc.) don't agree on the same funeral "scenario." In most cases, these struggles are resolved either by the surrender of certain parties or by the formation of a compromise, even a minimal one. Alternatively, people will typically say that "the family imposed itself" (where "the family" often refers to the deceased's brothers and sisters or the lineage authorities), "the children imposed themselves," or—in order to stress the fact that an agreement has been found—that "we came to an understanding."

Conflict plays a changing role in funerals depending on the situation, as the different groups that try to find their place in the funeral "scenario" are likely to encourage the formation of both relations of concurrence and those of affinity. Nothing prevents, for example, a form of political liturgy of the elites from cohabiting with any religious register. This is how in November 2000, during the funerals of an important Celestial "Senior Evangelist," different religious, political, and even lineage-related demonstrations coexisted without major tensions in the context of a Celestial-dominated ritual. Different elements, however, were added between the display of the corpse in the house of the deceased in Cotonou, the economic capital of the country, and the burial ceremony and the moment of inhumation in the deceased's region of origin two days later. As it is not uncommon in the case of prominent people's burial rites, these funerals involved different groups claiming the departed as a honorary member.

The deceased had recently passed away in Paris, and on the night of his arrival in the mortuary house there were Celestial drums and trumpets in order to ensure the night vigil. The day after was dedicated to different forms of homage. Since the deceased was a retired *"instituteur de classe exceptionnelle"* in a family involved in the highest levels of state power, an official speech that reiterated his state service as a teacher—and thus also his contribution to the moral edification of the nation—was pronounced in the morning. Later, a delegation of the departed's maternal lineage, a royal family originating from Togo but equally settled in Benin, performed traditional funeral songs, while the carrier of the *récade* (the emblem of royal power) that accompanied the delegation was left highly visible. Since there were no sacrifices to be offered in this sort of lineage homage, their coexistence with the Celestial Christian identity of the dead was clearly easier. Some of the deceased's children, Celestials as well, even danced during the performance of the songs, while other members of the deceased's parish, embarrassed because of the confusion that could be generated by this performance of lineage rituals, and desirous of avoiding accusations of "syncretism," explained that what I was witnessing was in no way a part of the burial ceremonies organized by the Celestial Church. A certain tension was then perceptible, as lineage rites are easily condemned in a church like the Celestial Church of Christ. Finally, later in the afternoon, the former president N. Soglo officially came to pay honor to the corpse, since one of the departed's brothers was at that time an important government minister in Benin.

During the wake that took place that night, the same kind of cohabitation of rituals occurred. The trumpets of the *gendarmerie* were the first to be heard, as another brother of the deceased was a colonel in the Beninese army. Afterward there was a Catholic wake because another brother of the dead was a priest (all the brothers, with the exception of the deceased himself, were Catholic). It is only after these first two wakes that a Celestial vigil took place. In fact, at the beginning of the church, Celestials generally would not organize wakes on the day before the burial. However, since the habit of organizing wakes is now so widespread in contemporary southern Benin (with the exception of Muslim people, who bury their dead on the same day of the death or on the day after), Celestials themselves also started organizing music performances on the day before the burial. These performances—both those that take place within the framework of Celestial funerals and those that take place in a different context—now enable the Celestials involved in burial ceremonies to be involved in the ritualization of the night before the burial. Additionally, such performances also enable the church choirs to show their musical *savoir-faire* to non-exclusively Celestial audiences, assisting in the promotion of the Church.

The next day, accompanied by Celestial prayers, a long motorized procession headed towards the deceased's region of origin, where he would be buried. Nearly forty-five miles later, after a stop at a local school where the deceased had taught when he was young and another one at his father's house, the corpse was brought to the land where the deceased man had intended to build a parish before suddenly dying, the land that he would be buried in. The few hundred people gathered for the event gradually took their places on the plastic chairs aligned under the huge canvas that covered a vast part of the land on which the parish would be built. The burial ceremony was hardly started when another moment of political liturgy occurred: Mathieu Kérékou, then-president of the Republic, had travelled in support of the brother of the departed who was then a government minister. The entrance of Kérékou, who took a seat in the first row in one of the armchairs reserved for the deceased's immediate family and for the political authorities expected for the occasion, was obviously solemn, that is, according to Pierre Bourdieu (2001: 176), "legitimate and extra-ordinary": a hedge of policemen and bodyguards, the audience partially standing either for curiosity or for respect, etc. The Celestial liturgy proceeded normally until the very moment of the burial, when a Catholic prayer pronounced by the priest brother of the deceased joined the prayers performed by the Celestials.

However, when the rituals involved are not solely Christian, their cohabitation can also turn out to be more difficult, even if the incompatibilities are often practically limited by the concern of keeping a form of entente between the different groups involved in the organization of the funerary "scenario." Entente and a sense of compromise, particularly in the familial sphere, remain important social values, even if in practice these values do not exclude, in the "backstage," tricks and cheating performed against other groups also involved in the organization of the funerals.[2] Nevertheless, a real attitude of exclusion towards lineage rites, one anchored in open demonization and moral disqualification, exists today among the Christian elites (and among Muslim ones) of each denomination, including a large number of Catholic priests. Indeed, despite their not truly having power over the widespread double practice of church services and of traditional lineage rites, Catholic priests have come to play more and more on the growing social value of Christian funerals, using these moments to deliver speeches that openly discredit lineage rites. Such speeches can even take place during the funeral itself, as I have regularly had the opportunity to notice in recent years.

In the Celestial Church, the desire for a radical break with the lineage rites has been obvious since the origins of the church. Most recently, a document called "Testament" has even been created for this purpose by the ecclesiastical authorities of the Beninese branch of the church. This allows the members of the church to write down their wish to be buried according to the rites of the Celestial Church instead of their lineage traditional rites. This document can then serve as legal evidence during the meetings for the organization of funerals. However, I have not yet encountered a case where such a "Testament" had actually been drafted. In fact, the recourse to written documents to serve a testamentary purpose seems to be quite rare within the society of southern Benin. And this phenomenon of course multiplies the struggles regarding the more or less legal appropriation of inheritances, and frequently leads to—or feeds—serious family conflicts.

The radical refusal that Celestials oppose to "traditional" lineage ceremonies clashes sometimes with an equally radical refusal on the part of the lineage authorities to abandon these practices. In such cases the conflict can become open, with more or less explicit threats of magical aggression or with recourse to the local *gendarmerie*. However, conflict does not normally lead to this extreme, and the reaching of a compromise is more frequent. The main issue is that each involved group must reach a compromise without compromising itself, according to the expression of Luc Boltanski and Laurent Thévenot (1991: 338–343).

In March 2004, in Abomey (the historical capital of the precolonial Dahomean kingdom), the discussions that surrounded the funerals of a founding figure of the Celestial Church in the town were relatively tumultuous. The dead was a member of an important Yoruba family of the town that didn't want to be marginalized in the organization of the funerals. Indeed, the lineage authorities rather wanted to use the occasion to recall and celebrate the deceased's lineage and to glorify the lineage identity of a person known throughout the town. But such a position (along with the concern for reaffirming the lineage right to the corpses of its dead "children" regardless of their religious affiliation) was not unanimous among those members of the family who could express their own opinion. A regular informant and a friend who described the scene right after it happened affirmed that he took the floor at a family meeting in order to remind everyone that the deceased had been sick for months before dying and that the influential lineage members had been at that time much less worried about him than they were acting today; they were claiming the right to bury him according to lineage rites and yet they had not done anything for him during his long illness. However, this intervention only served to confirm the independent spirit of my friend, and the lineage authorities maintained their claims.

On their part, both the children of the departed who were members of the Celestial Church and those who were members of other Christian Churches, as well as the church congregation headed by the deceased intended to bury the dead according to the Celestial rites. But this scenario also implied that the burial lineage rites would not be celebrated around the corpse and that the lineage authorities would not be given the fingernails and tuft of hair of the dead that have become in southern Benin, at least since the nineteenth century, a conventional metonymic substitute for the body. Such opposition could have degenerated into open conflict and the involvement of the police, but a form of compromise accepted by both parties ended up emerging. This compromise illustrated quite well the pragmatism of both the people fighting for tradition and of the Celestial negotiators.

Indeed, after the parties had privately agreed on this compromise, the parishioners of the deceased's church solemnly came to ask the lineage authorities to let them bury the dead. This saved the "face" of the latter, who were thus recognized as the final decision makers in the funeral scenario. However, in order to avoid any open conflict, they knew that they had to allow the parishioners (and the children) to organise a Celestial burial without even asking for the fingernails and the hair of the dead. This kind of removal from the corpse is exactly the kind of activity that Celestials want a radical break with. Claiming these substitutes for the dead would have been unacceptable to the group of the children and the parishioners.

But the lineage authorities could not surrender all rights to the organization of the funeral, and therefore the children handed in a large amount of money (400,000 CFA francs, according to my informant, or nearly 900 dollars) so that the lineage funeral for their father could be organized. Since they could not obtain the fingernails and the hair, the lineage ritual experts had resorted to a convocation of the dead man's spirit similar to the rituals used when there is no available substitute for the corpse (in precolonial times, this was particularly the case for the warriors who had died during the raids of the Dahomean army.) Also, the complete cycle of funeral and ancestralization rites was organized with money the children had given. Of course, the amount given to the lineage authorities was actually higher than necessary for the organization of the lineage rites, allowing the remaining amount of money to be shared as compensation for allowing the children and the parishioners to have the use of the corpse, which was finally buried on the parish land that the dead man had acquired during the last decades of his life in Abomey.

In this case, both parties actually managed to keep a part of what seemed essential to them, but at the same time they had to surrender on other essentials. The children and the members of the dead's church obtained the right to organize the Celestial funerals without having to give the fingernails and hair of the dead to the lineage authorities, and the latter obtained the reaffirmation of their right to have the use of the bodies of lineage members and to organize lineage funerals. But simultaneously, the Celestials surrendered on the fact that only Celestial funerals would be organized, and the lineage authorities dropped the idea of organizing lineage funerals for the corpse or its conventional substitute.

The pragmatism of the different groups, however, isn't the only reason for the cohabitation that arises at such funerals. In fact, the compromises that come out of concern for lineage and social entente also lead to forms of agreement that can remain tense and that unquestionably contain a share of violence. In urban environments at least, lineage authorities often know that the contemporary law in Benin does not really support their claims on bodies, and that the recourse to police forces by the deceased's children would probably not work to their own advantage. But on the other side, the magical capital of the traditional elites often remains decisive in dissuading direct opposition to lineage authorities: the fear of magical aggression that often bears upon those who try to break too radically with lineage ceremonies certainly plays a role as important as the concern for lineage "entente" in leaving open the possibility that the different groups involved will be able to negotiate. Therefore, the pragmatism of the latter is perhaps less linked to tolerance of other ways of conceiving funerals than to the prudence and concern of both sides for not being involved in a spiral of physical and magical violence.

The Celestial way of death

Burying the dead in a Celestial manner

In 1974, a brochure entitled *Lumière sur le christianisme céleste,* written by a well-educated person from the circle of the prophet Oshoffa, was released. It was particularly meant to answer the criticism directed in those days at the church, as well as to clarify the organization of the ecclesiastical hierarchy. But a small chapter was also devoted to funerals, entitled "*Le Christianisme Céleste assure les obsèques de ses membres.*" The brochure answered the criticism about the way the church was supposed to bury its dead. Because the Celestial Church refused the performance of the "traditional" lineage rites on behalf of its members, it was at the time accused of abandoning bodies without proper burial rites. The chapter on funerals justified the establishment of Celestial funeral rites, as well as the break with lineage funeral rites, which were considered evil practices. Specific funeral rites have been practiced since the first decades of the church's existence, and I will now briefly describe their present form.

As I already stated, a music performance often takes place on the night before the inhumation, even though it is not really part of the Celestial liturgy established by the prophet Oshoffa. On the morning of the burial, the corpse is showed for one or two hours in the mortuary home (which is very often the house where the dead used to live when he was alive), and after a series of prayers and songs around the corpse, the deceased, dressed with his or her Celestial robe and the rank insignia of the ecclesiastical hierarchy, is brought directly to the cemetery or to the lineage grave for the burial service proper. Celestials do not bring corpses inside church compounds because the latter are considered impure, and unless otherwise indicated the floor of the parish should not be soiled by their presence. However, some exceptions are likely to occur, as in the above-mentioned events in which the two important "Evangelists" of the church were buried, one within the walls of a parish under construction and the other inside the parish he had established.

Upon taking the corpse towards the grave, a procession starts behind the faithful carrying the cross, the blessed water, and the incense, and a holy song begins. It retrieves a conventional metaphor from the Fon (the main ethnic group in southern Benin) and Yoruba worlds: "We come to the market, we come to the market in this world." The fact that a deceased person, especially an old one, "goes back home" when (s)he dies is indeed a conventional way of regarding death and the relations between the world of the living and the world of the dead, even though it of course does not constitute a religious be-

Illustration 7.1. Celestial prayers around the corpse of a *Senior Evangéliste* in Cotonou, 2002. Photo by Joël Noret.

lief as such. Next to the grave, the coffin is positioned on wooden logs placed through the grave or right beside it, and many different ritual actors and attendants gather around it.

Individual or collective prayers, canticles, collective recitations of psalms, and readings of the Bible commence one after the other until the "announcements" that enumerate the places and dates of the wakes and the services for the dead that will follow the inhumation. Afterwards comes the preaching, very often dealing with conventional themes that refer to ideas shared in the different Christian worlds and even (for some of these themes) in the traditionalist world of southern Benin: the ignorance of people regarding the moment of death, the fact that man is dust and that the soul is property of God, the concern that the dead will find a "good place" in the afterlife and will continue to be benevolent towards the people left behind, etc.

After the preaching, the conductor of the ceremony performs the purification and the sanctification of the grave with incense and blessed water. These rites can be regarded as a rather direct continuity with "traditional" practices of purification, even though the fact that Catholic cemeteries are also considered to be blessed ground must also be underlined. At that moment, a eulogy of the deceased may take place (especially in educated circles) before the conductor incenses the coffin. At that moment the choir, positioned just beside the grave, begins a canticle sung in a language which was unintelligible at the beginnings of the church and considered to be the "language of the angels." Catalyzed by this specific canticle (which, unintelligible, perfectly illustrates a paradox very frequent in ritual languages) and the simultaneous incensing of the corpse—a gesture which is used *in loco verbi*, quoting Levi-Strauss (1971: 600)—the soul of the dead is said to rise towards heaven, carried (according to many Celestials) by angels.

After the incensing of the corpse, which is a fundamental moment that will be recalled again during the services for the dead on the eighth and the forty-first day after the burial, the conductor improvises a short prayer before picking up a handful of soil or sand and spreading it on the coffin while remembering with a conventional formula that man is dust. As the coffin is lowered, those who wish can throw another handful of sand on it, or take turns using the sprinkler to pour blessed water. The ceremony is then finished.

In the vast majority of cases, and unless the dead died young and in tragic circumstances, a reception is organized after the burial ceremony. This event represents one of the most significant expenses, if not the most significant, as the reception is also the moment of the funeral attended by the largest audience: some people indeed arrive just after the ceremony of inhumation, either to save time or because they have to attend two burials on the same day, these events being concentrated more and more on Thursdays and Saturdays (on the organization of time in funerals, see Noret 2006: 113-119; 2004b). Also, the re-

Illustration 7.2. Celestial burial liturgy in the largest cemetery of Cotonou, November 2000. Photo by Joël Noret.

ception is increasingly organized separately by the different children (though some of these can still join together to "receive their guests" in common) and by the other categories of relatives. Each child indeed fears to be obliged to pay for the others in some way by contributing to receive the "guests" of the other people, and this at the expense of resources that could be used for his or her own "guests."

This quite general evolution shows of course only one aspect of the contemporary restructuring of familial solidarities, but from this point of view at least the conception of "African solidarity" as unproblematic and noncalculated is in contemporary southern Benin most obviously "a myth to be revisited" (Vidal 1994). However, a part of the reception always remains almost by necessity organized with the help of contributions from the different children of the dead, since there are people in attendance who are neither the "foreigners" nor the "guests" of someone in particular. It is to this common reception that, for example, the members of the choir and of the parish of the dead will be invited in the case of a Celestial funeral, even if the highest religious personalities that attend the event might also be received and given food afterward by some children of the deceased.

However, despite the fact that the postburial receptions often mobilize substantial resources when compared with the income of those who organize them, arguing that the lavishness of funeral expenses means that these organizers take death as an "excuse" to perform a ceremony for the living's symbolic benefit (see van der Geest 2000) probably underplays the tensions in which people are caught while engaging in such expenses, and the true burden that funerals represent. Having different social roles (as child, but also as spouse, as parent, etc.), a man burying his father, for instance, often knows the difficulties the expenses he is incurring will cause in his household for months (or even years) after the event, and people may be in such occasions really divided between parts of themselves (on the plural nature of the self, see Lahire 1998 and 2002). Funerals are rarely desired or welcomed, and while they are certainly a "passionate sociodrama" where making use of one's social and economic capital can take an existential turn (Vidal 1986), I have often seen my informants involve themselves in such events with apprehension, anxiety, or even anguish (see also Bähre 2007; Englund 2001).

Also, to ensure important funerals for one's parents is a key moment in the construction of the feeling of the accomplished filial duty, and funerals may in this respect prove to be a key moment of the grieving process (see Noret 2010). I remember, for instance, a regular Celestial informant, unquestionably a religious virtuoso in the sense of Max Weber, who used to live permanently within the walls of a parish and devoted himself to praying and to helping people accomplish the "spiritual works" prescribed to them by the visionaries of that parish. Hence, he used to own very few things, and had almost no money. When his mother, Celestial as well, died a few years ago, he could not contribute to any expense incurred by the funerals, and suffered at least for a few months from a genuine and persistent regret. Not being able to contribute to the funerals, as he should have done as a son of the deceased, definitely did not facilitate his grief.

The postburial rites

On the night of the third day after the day of the burial, the first of the three wakes organized by the church takes place. The second and the third wakes will be organized on the fifth and the seventh day, before the eighth-day service. Actually, the whole week following the inhumation is marked by liturgical ceremonies, and the Celestial way of death proves to be ritually dense, a fact that constitutes an evident continuity with the "traditional" handling of death and its numerous successive rites that lead to ancestralization (see, among others, Herskovits 1938: 352–402; Jamous 1994; Noret 2006: 286–413). The precise codification of the wakes, however, is absent from the first written documents issued by the Church, and the systematization of the current way of doing is then probably quite late in the elaboration of the ecclesiastical liturgy.

The wakes, organized most of the time in front of the house of the deceased, start with the sanctification (with incense and blessed water) of both the ritual space and the person in charge of the service, an event common to Celestial ceremonies in general. Previously, a cross, two candles, and a Bible containing a paper that mentions the name of the dead have all been placed on the little altar provided for the occasion, which is usually a chair in front of which the person who leads the service celebrates with his back turned towards the audience. The wake starts with a series of prayers, readings of psalms, and songs. The canticles which are likely to be sung are of course numerous, but some of them are very common. The first canticle, in the Gun language, states for instance that "we work in order to clean our spirits." Another very popular one is meant to communicate to the dead that he is not forsaken: "Oh dead, I come with you (bis), there where you eat, there where you drink water, there where you drink a beverage, there where you sleep; oh dead, I come with you!"

Afterward comes the reading of the Bible and more songs. If the deceased was wealthy, held a high rank in the ecclesial hierarchy, or held significant social capital, there is usually more than one choir, and more songs. Indeed, if the scripts of the wake and the inhumation ceremonies are strongly codified, this does not imply that the gap is trivial between, for instance, (a) the well-attended funerals of an old male or female member of the Church who was wealthy and advanced in the ecclesiastical hierarchy and whose adult children succeeded in life and (b) the scarce obsequies of a young faithful who comes from a poor family and who was scarcely involved in the Church. Economic, social, and proper religious capital all interlace here and together define the importance of the funeral in the eyes of the church congregation.

But let us return to the wakes. After the reading—drawn from the Old or the New Testament and read most of the time in a local language and sometimes in French—comes the moment of the announcements, followed by the preaching. It is only afterward that the choir is again asked to "animate" the wake. Its rhythmic hold on the audience can obviously vary depending on the case, but at least a part of the female audience often starts to dance when the "battle" rhythm of the church, symbolising its continually renewed fight against malevolent spirits, is launched by the drummers.

Prayers close the wake, and afterwards the audience is often offered a bowl of "coffee" (condensed milk which is diluted and then flavored with instant coffee) with a piece of bread or a cereal mush before slowly leaving the place. The day after the third wake (the one with the highest attendance, because those who can not attend the first two wakes make the effort to participate in this one), the eighth-day service closes the ceremonies of the week following the inhumation.

As stated above, a religious service for the dead, called the eighth-day service when it takes place one week after the burial, is organized after the three wakes. As a noticeable part of those in attendance will not be Celestial on this day, the ban on wearing shoes inside the parish walls is softened, but the parish will have to be "purified" after the service. Before the service, a *catafalque* (an empty wooden structure that represents the coffin) is placed between the nave and the chancel. In the Celestial temples altars are normally oriented towards the east, and according to this ideal geography the "head" of the *catafalque* is oriented towards the south with its "feet" toward the north. This *catafalque* is also initially covered with a black cloth with a white cross in the middle and then with a white cloth with one or three blue crosses. A candle is placed at the head and another at the feet.

As a sign of its solemnity, the service starts with the entrance procession of the different categories of members: the choir, the upper ranks of the Church hierarchy, the male and female faithful, and finally the members of other religions that attend the ceremony. Next, prayers, songs, readings of the Bible, and psalms come one after the other. The preaching follows and is often as lengthy as in the majority of the Celestial services, which can last three or four hours. After the preaching comes the moment of the offering accompanied by the choir, and after this finally comes the crucial moment of the ceremony: the incensing of the *catafalque*.

At that moment, the wooden structure welcomes the soul of the deceased for whom the service is celebrated: the dead receives there the blessings contained in the incense and in the songs and the prayers that are being performed. At the beginning of the incensing, the two candles placed at the head of the *catafalque* and at its feet are lit. The white cloth is removed to disclose the black cloth with the white cross. The faithful in charge of the incensing then incenses the *catafalque* while the choir solemnly sings the canticle revealed in the "language of angels" that had already been sung around the grave during the burial. But this time, the translation of the canticle into Gun (the main language used in Porto-Novo's region, where the church was established), revealed to the prophet after the apparition of the canticle itself, is sung promptly after the original one, and then the entire canticle is restarted again: "Let's come to the Lord (bis)! Up there in Heaven, besides the Archangel Michael! Oh, brothers, let's come to the Lord!"

The "elite" faithful who know the biblical justifications of the church activities concerning the incensing of the *catafalque* make reference here to the beginning of the third chapter of the book of Zachariah. There, after his death, Joshua appeared in front of God wearing filthy clothes, at which point these clothes were turned into clean ones by the "Angel of the Eternal" as a sign of the remission of his faults, Satan having failed to highlight Joshua's iniquity. The fact that the white cloth is again placed on the black one after the incensing could here be a metaphor of the remission of sins expected from the ritual action. The mastery of this biblical justification is however unequally distributed among the faithful, and the meanings the services for the dead often take on are more complex, as we will see later.

Illustration 7.3. Incensing of the *catafalque* at a Celestial eighth-day service in Cotonou, November 2000. Photo by Joël Noret.

The moment of the incensing, however, is extremely solemn. It is forbidden to move (adults take children's hands if necessary), especially in the central part of the temple, because that is the path that the soul and the angels carrying it follow at that moment. Being hit by the soul or by one of the escorting angels would necessarily lead to sickness, accident, or death, depending on the informant asked. Given that the faithful in charge of the incensing might find himself on the path of the soul or of the angels, he must be (at least according to some informants) both full of spiritual power and praying in order to avoid this plight. These contact precautions, the attention paid to keeping the world of the dead and world of the living separate, clearly recall the precautions traditionally taken in order to avoid the contact with the spirits of the dead. And during the ceremony, the *catafalque* also becomes a way of making the dead present, evoking in some respects the ancestors' altars but also certain artifacts which materialize in a provisional way the presence of the spirits of the dead during the rites of ancestralization that can be found in the different ethnic traditions of the region (on those rites, see, among others, Jamous 1994; Noret 2006: 286–402). A form of dialectic thus appears here that makes the *catafalque* a complex synthetic object. Actually, the form of the artifact clearly shows, like the majority of the objects employed by the Celestials, the Christian filiation and identity claimed and experienced by the participants in the ceremony. But by bringing back the spirits of the dead in the *catafalque*, the

Celestials also introduce some habits of thought that can hardly be considered to be inherited from missionary Christianity and that rather recall the convocations of the dead found in "traditional" lineage funerary and ancestralization rituals.

Finally, after the white cloth has been put again on the *catafalque,* the members of the family of the deceased are invited to kneel in the central part of the temple as seven ranking faithful start to pray for them. A last song and some prayers finally close the service. Most of the time, the mourners organize another small reception for the attendees within the church compound itself or, for those who care to organize a new "separate" reception, in the place arranged for receiving "foreigners." Such a service for the deceased is still organized on the forty-first day after the burial.

The *bricolage* of the status of the dead

Conversion to Celestial Christianity, often motivated by the quest for a solution to concrete problems, is never really followed by explicit education as to the systematized doctrine of the Celestial Church. Discussions on the interpretation of the rites may take place among the faithful or be raised during preaching, but in the majority of the parishes "biblical classes" are either embryonic or nonexistent. It is therefore not surprising that the religious imaginations of Celestials differ according to their previous religious socializations, and that the kinds of relations with the dead they conceive of depend on those influences.[3]

Moreover, my discussions with Celestials about the status of the dead always happened within the framework of questions about their religious life. My research may thus fail to give a full account of "the lack of consistency and systematic rigor in people's beliefs" (Astuti 2007: 234) since, just as among the Vezo evoked by Rita Astuti, one can also hear in southern Benin—among Celestials as among the population in general—judgments according to which "when one is dead, one is dead." Such assertions often seemed to be quite rare, and very probably, according to my ethnographic experience, they are less frequent in southern Benin than among the Vezo in Astuti's account. But those opinions clearly exist, even if the question of their precise extent and contexts of enunciation and validity are beyond the scope of this chapter. In brief, what follows is an account that relies specifically on the religious discourses of Celestials and not on all of their discursive and tacit practices.

In general, many faithful think that when the *catafalque* is incensed, the soul of the dead receives the prayer for the remission of sins, which is one of the results expected from the canticle and the ritual action in general. In such interpretations, the ritual aims at obtaining the peace of the deceased's soul (and consequently, the peace of his or her family). However, one must also underline the fact that Celestials, like the vast majority of Christians in southern Benin (Evangelicals, Pentecostals, and Catholic and Celestial militants excepted), don't talk much about heaven and hell (see Noret 2004a). The souls for which things go wrong are those who can't rise towards God, those that remain "down" and roam among the living, or simply those that have not found "a good place on the other side." In this particularly, the religious questioning of the Celestials most obviously bears the mark of the traditional religious system: it is at the same time a concern for redemption or salvation and a concern for the departure of the soul.

By this, I don't mean of course that the image of such a departure was absent from missionary Christianity, or that departure isn't present as a simple conventional metaphor for death in the Christian worlds of southern Benin. I would rather underline the gap existing between the orthodox issue of missionary Catholicism, which is a religious concern for redemption and salvation of the soul, and the concern of the lineage funerary rites, which is a concern for the aggregation of the deceased to the group of his forebears. And the conceptions of the afterlife held by the majority of the Celestials are marked by these two religious issues at the same time. You can typically hear that the peace of the soul is linked to its departure towards God, to the fact that it does not remain "down." This kind of popular interpretation does not spontaneously recall the question of damnation: even if this interpretation exists, it hardly appeared spontaneously in conversations with my informants. Rather, it is much more frequent to hear oscillations and entanglements between concerns for the aggregation of the soul to the group of its forebears (which evoke a scheme of ancestralization) on one side and for the soul's peace and salvation (which evoke a scheme of redemption) on the other.

However, focusing on the interpretations of the incensing of the catafalque does not provide a full picture of the ambiguity of the status of the dead in the Celestial Church. Actually, this ambiguity most clearly appears when you discuss with the Celestial faithful the reasons motivating the regular organization of religious services for the dead (such services, whether responding to the demand of a member of the faithful or of a family, have exactly the same liturgy of the eighth-day services). Many Celestials then recognize that the dead can sometimes act to benefit the living. As one *Vénérable Senior Evangéliste*, a high-ranking man in the Church hierarchy, put it in a discussion that we had near the town of Abomey in August 2007 while evoking how souls guard some people: "You know, it is said that the dead are not dead. Perhaps something [bad] would happen to you, and that soul fights for you"—and finally the bad thing does not happen to you any more. It is common for informants to evoke in the same interview both the problems that the souls may have and the need to thank souls for what they do in order to explain why religious services are organized for them. As a Celestial choir member of approximately twenty years old, a member of the Church since his early childhood, told me in Cotonou in August 2007: "When one asks a mass [a religious service] for a dead relative, it is because perhaps this dead relative has many difficulties there [in the afterlife], and [we do that] so that this dead relative may have peace. Perhaps he deserved to go to heaven and because of some sins he cannot be accepted in heaven, and thus it is necessary to organize masses in order for him to be accepted." But five minutes later, he added, in a slightly different perspective: "I think that dead relatives help. I really believe that ... I take my own case for instance. It was said to me that my [dead] older sister helped me a lot, and that it is not finished, and that I really must ask a mass [a religious service] for her. And that she will always help me."

Such narratives often show quite different ways of thinking about the dead, evoking one after the other the precariousness of their situation and their usual power to help the living. Moreover, when considering this second scenario, it seems that the religious relations Celestials weave with their dead oscillate between two different configurations. Some faithful indeed recall the benevolent or malevolent actions of the dead in the world, as if they were some kind of independent entities, while others more systematically place the dead in the position of intercessors who may pray to God in favor of the living. This ambiguity over the autonomy of the dead appears clearly in the prayers pronounced during the funeral rites. It is common to hear on these occasions in reference to the dead: "May he not forget his wife, may he not forget his children," and so on—statements very often followed, however, by "May he pray for them": the figure of the interceding dead is reintroduced after the invocation of his or her protective action. When the prayer is said in the Fon language (the main vernacular language of southern Benin), it is addressed to the dead in an even more direct way, the conventional expression being "*ma won asi towe kpo vi towe lɛ kpo*" which means "do not forget your wife and your children." This is a popular way of praying to the dead that can be found far beyond the Celestial Church. In this case, the prayer is more directly addressed to the deceased, before it may be specified that he or she is asked to pray for spouses and children. Thus we see how a position of intercessor or even of autonomous entity is regularly attributed to the dead, these formulas being pronounced at almost every funeral (with the variants that, for instance, the deceased's gender and age impose.)

Additionally, the same people can in some contexts evoke their relations with the dead as if the latter were independent entities and in other situations evoke them as if they were intercessors. This potential instability or relative ambiguity of schemes of thought has long been highlighted by anthropologists. The hesitations or oscillations that can be found in the original syncretic or synthetic religious productions among the Celestials should of course not be considered without reference to the *"logique de l'à-peu-près et du flou"* (Bourdieu, 1980: 146) of the practical reason. But those hesitations and approximations must also be considered in relation with the heterogeneity of many people's (and thus many Celestials) religious socialization, which often confront social actors with different religious universes, notably those of "traditional" divinities (the *vodun*) and those of Islam and Christianity in their various forms.

Actually, the kind of *bricolage*—in the sense here that the "preconstraints" of the symbolic materials involved in the process fully act (see Lévi-Strauss 1990: 30–36; Mary 2000)—of the status of the dead in which Celestials are engaged is certainly not unique to them. Many Christians (Catholics and Methodists) in southern Benin are indeed involved in a similar symbolic work regarding how they consider the status of their dead: sometimes as recourse figures that recall the ancestral type, sometimes as deceased who implore their prayers in order to improve their condition "on the other side." Furthermore, the Celestial Church is the only church (probably with other small churches derived from it) in southern Benin where the dead periodically return to an artifact like the *catafalque*. In that way, the Celestial services for the dead perhaps illustrate better than other liturgies the work of synthesis accomplished on the figures of the dead in contemporary southern Benin, where the Christian religious materials unquestionably constitute an evermore important source of inspiration in the reshaping of categories and the transformation of habits of thought.

Conclusion

The funerals in which Celestials are involved today in southern Benin take place in the context of a differentiated society, albeit one in which important continuities can still be found, among these the way in which burials are generally organized "beyond one's means." Lavish funerals, however, are often considered a heavy burden to support, as much among Celestials as in southern Benin in general (Noret 2010). The psychic and social tensions they often cause (inside both individuals and households committed to these expenses) are only partially grasped by the expression "funerals for the living," used by S. van der Geest (2000) some years ago to stress the contrast between the conspicuous dimension of funerals (and the huge amounts of funeral expenses) in southern Ghana and the simultaneous regular neglect of old people (see also de Witte 2001: 76–80).

Along with the important social investment in funerals, breaking points, however, also appear in southern Benin society, such as in the attitudes that the different religious worlds adopt towards the "traditional" lineage funeral rites. Celestials indeed often try to break in a rather radical way with the "traditional" ritual forms still accepted by the majority of the population while incorporating into their ritual system in a more or less conscious and declared way certain principles of these traditions, particularly the local longstanding ritual density of the handling of death and the calling of the deceased's spirit into an artifact (namely, the *catafalque*) in order to ritually (try to) ensure its transition to a stable position in the afterlife. Moreover, since they were not really socialized into a Celestial doctrine when they entered the Church, their relationship with the dead bear in various ways and at the same time the marks of habits of thought that evoke traditional schemes of thought (and the pattern of ancestralization) and the imprint of ways of thinking inherited from the historical missionary churches (the Catholic Church in particular) with their emphasis on redemption and salvation. Such entanglements of "traditional" and Christian habits of thought are of course very common phenomena across Africa and may probably be considered as a general trait of African religious modernities. The Celestial stroke of genius is to have imagined, with the eighth-day services, a visually powerful ritual synthesis through the invention of a Christian temporary receptacle for the souls of the dead.

Notes

This chapter was first translated from an original French manuscript by Chiara Giordano, then revised by the author, and finally edited by Michael Jindra.

1. This presentation of the Celestial Church of Christ is of course very short. For more general studies on the church, see Adogame 1999; de Surgy 2001; and Henry 2008. And for more detailed studies of the recent history of the church and of its developments in Europe, see Mary 2005 and Henry and Noret 2008, respectively.
2. For a perspective that emphasizes the importance of "entente" as a moral category in the making of arrangements between social groups in West Africa, see Pierre-Joseph Laurent's analysis of the place of Pentecostal Assemblies of God in contemporary Burkina Faso (Laurent 2003).
3. In an earlier paper (Noret 2003), based on less important fieldwork, I have presented a slightly different view of the status of the dead in the Celestial Church of Christ, where I tended to overestimate the systematization of the diverse religious synthesis of the Celestials. Today, I no longer agree with all the views expressed in that paper. For a more detailed description of the Celestial funerary rites, and a critique of my 2003 paper, see the chapter "Naître et mourir en Chrétien céleste" in Henry 2008.

Bibliography

Adogame, Afeosemime U. 1999. *Celestial Church of Christ. The Politics of Cultural Identity in a West African Prophetic-Charismatic Movement*. Frankfurt: Peter Lang.

Astuti, Rita. 2007. "What happens after death?" In *Questions of Anthropology*, eds. R. Astuti, J. Parry and C. Stafford. Oxford: Berg.

Bähre, Erik. 2007. "Reluctant solidarity: Death, urban poverty and neighbourly assistance in South Africa." *Ethnography* 8, no. 1: 33–59.

Bastide, Roger. 1970. "L'acculturation formelle." In R. Bastide, *Le prochain et le lointain*. Paris: Cujas.

Boltanski, Luc, and Laurent Thévenot. 1991. *De la justification. Les économies de la grandeur*. Paris: Gallimard.

Bourdieu, Pierre. 1980. *Le sens pratique*. Paris: Minuit.

———. [1982] 2001. "Les rites d'institution." In *Langage et pouvoir symbolique*, P. Bourdieu. Paris: Seuil.

de Surgy, Albert. 2001. *L'Eglise du Christianisme Céleste. Un exemple d'Eglise prophétique au Bénin*. Paris: Karthala.

de Witte, Marleen. 2001. *Long Live the Dead! Changing Funeral Celebrations in Asante (Ghana)*. Amsterdam: Aksant Academic Publishers.

Englund, Harri. 2001. "The Politics of Multiple Identities: the Making of a Home Villagers' Association in Lilongwe, Malawi." In *Associational Life in African Cities: Popular Responses to the Urban Crisis,* eds. A. Tostensen, I. Tvedten and M. Vaa. Uppsala: The Nordic Africa Institute.

Giordano, Rosario. 2001. "Missionnaires catholiques et 'Brésiliens' à Ouidah (1861–1871)." *Miscellanea di Studi Storici* XI—1998-2001: 161–180.

Guran, Milton. 2000. *Agudás. Os "brasileiros" do Benim*. Rio de Janeiro: Nova Fronteira.

Henry, Christine. 1998. "Le discours de la conversion." *Journal des Africanistes* 68, nos. 1–2: 155–172.

———. 2008. *La force des anges. Rites, hiérarchie et divination dans le Christianisme Céleste (Bénin)*. Paris: BEHE-SR.

Henry, Christine and Joël Noret. 2008. "Le Christianisme Céleste en France et en Belgique." *Archives de sciences sociales des religions* 143: 91–109.

Herskovits, Melville J. 1938. *Dahomey. An Ancient West African Kingdom*, vol. 1. New York: Augustin Publisher.

Lahire, Bernard. 1998. *L'homme pluriel. Les ressorts de l'action*. Paris: Nathan.

———. 2002. *Portraits sociologiques. Dispositions et variations individuelles*. Paris: Nathan.

Laurent, Pierre-Joseph. 2003. *Les pentecôtistes du Burkina Faso. Mariage, pouvoir et guérison*. Paris: IRD-Karthala.

Lévi-Strauss, Claude. [1962] 1990. *La pensée sauvage*. Paris: Plon.

———. 1971. *L'Homme nu*. Paris: Plon.

Mary, André. 1999. "Culture pentecôtiste et charisme visionnaire au sein d'une Eglise indépendante africaine." *Archives de Sciences Sociales des Religions* 105: 29–50.

———. 2000. *Le bricolage africain des héros chrétiens*. Paris: Cerf.

———. 2005. "Histoires d'Eglise : héros chrétiens et chefs rebelles des nations 'célestes.'" In *Entreprises religieuses transnationales en Afrique de l'Ouest*, eds. L. Fourchard, A. Mary et R. Otayek. Ibadan-Paris: IFRA-Karthala.

Noret, Joël. 2003. "La place des morts dans le christianisme céleste." *Social Compass* 50, no. 3: 493–510.

———. 2004a. "De la conversion au basculement de la place des morts. Les défunts, la personne et la famille au Sud-Bénin." *Politique Africaine* 93: 143–155.

———. 2004b. "Morgues et prise en charge de la mort au Sud-Bénin." *Cahiers d'Etudes africaines* 176: 745–767.

———. 2004c. "Les Assemblées de Dieu du Burkina Faso en contexte." *Civilisations. Revue internationale d'anthropologie et de sciences humaines* 51, nos. 1–2: 171–181.

———. 2005. "Négocier le changement culturel? L'évolution des funérailles en pays *asante* (Ghana)." *L'Homme* 174 : 261–268.

———. 2006. "Autour de 'ceux qui n'existent plus'. Deuil, funérailles et place des défunts au Sud-Bénin." PhD diss., Université libre de Bruxelles and Ecole des Hautes Etudes en Sciences Sociales (Paris).

———. 2010. *Deuil et funérailles dans le Bénin méridional. Enterrer à tout prix.* Brussels: Editions de l'Université de Bruxelles.

van der Geest, Sjaak. 2000. "Funerals for the living. Conversations with elderly people in Kwahu (Ghana)." *African Studies Review* 43, no. 3: 103–129.

Vidal, Claudine. 1986. "Funérailles et conflit social en Côte d'Ivoire." *Politique Africaine* 24: 9–19.

———. 1994. "La solidarité africaine. Un mythe à revisiter." *Cahiers d'Etudes africaines*, 136 : 687–691.

CHAPTER 8

Of Corpses, Clay, and Photographs

Body Imagery and Changing Technologies of Remembrance in Asante Funeral Culture

Marleen de Witte

Introduction

Nana Abena Fosuwaa was an old lady in Trede, an Asante village just south of Kumasi, Ghana.[1] On a Tuesday morning in November 1995, Auntie Joana, the community nurse, and I went to visit the sick Nana Abena at home.[2] We found her in a miserable state. She was left alone in a dark and sultry room where she was lying on a mat on the floor, crouched amidst torn and soiled pieces of cloth. The open wounds on her hands, legs, and feet clearly had not been dressed for days. I was shocked by this degrading image of suffering, this image of a human body on the edge of life. That same afternoon she died. She was taken to the mortuary in Kumasi, where she would stay until the big funeral ceremony that her family would organize for her. This would take some time, since a ceremony for someone of her status requires a considerable amount of preparation. She had reached the admirable age of 115 years, had ten children and over a hundred grandchildren and great-grandchildren.[3] She was a highly respected woman.

Forty days later, the main funeral celebration (*ayie pa*) for Nana Abena was held. The day before was spent on preparing her body, which was brought back from the mortuary that morning.[4] Joana, being a good friend of Nana Abena's daughter, assisted the relatives while I assisted Joana. In the same room where we had visited Nana Abena, we now tried to beautify her body. One of Nana's daughters worried about the damaged skin on the hands and forearms, as these would be decorated with gold and thus would attract attention. Joana and I went out to look for the right color of clay to camouflage the damaged skin. Meanwhile, a commercial "body decorator" from Kumasi arrived to decorate the "display room" and Nana's body. Her relatives had already painted the room electric blue and vivid pink. The ceiling and the walls were lined with lace and colored plastic flowers were put all over. In the center of the room the body decorator put a big golden bed with china ornaments and small electric lights. A rented generator provided the necessary power, as Trede did not yet have electricity.

When Joana and I came back to apply the clay to the skin, a quarrel developed between two of the daughters, Yaa and her sister. The sister had bought only one piece of *kente* cloth to decorate the corpse and Yaa said that she should have bought two. Within a few minutes the room was filled with shouting women. Another decoration item was brought up: gold dust. Nana Abena, and for that matter her daughters too, was related to a chief, meaning the family has "royal blood."[5] This chief had sent the gold dust and demanded that the body be smeared with it, as is the custom for royals. But he had also said that he would not contribute to the funeral expenses and that Yaa should negotiate a loan to pay for the funeral. Yaa did not accept this, saying that he sent the gold dust only to show off his own status. Her sister had agreed to use the gold dust on the body, but Yaa was determined to take it back, and in the heat of the struggle she furiously walked away with it. Meanwhile, the "body decorator" dyed Nana Abena's hair black, painted her lips red, wrapped her body in a beautiful piece of *kente* cloth, and abundantly decorated it with gold necklaces, precious beads, bracelets, and rings. The gold dust was not used. Still, the display of her body was a display of grandness and glamor.

Gorgeously dressed and decorated, Nana's dead body was the central showpiece of the celebrations. Endless numbers of mourners filed past the body to pay her their last respects, to cry, and to admire the way in which she was laid out. Photographers and video men came to shoot the body, the decorations, and the visitors. In front of the body, gifts of cloth, schnapps, and money were presented to Nana Abena to take along to *asamando*, "the land of the dead," and these gifts were shown and announced to the mourners. But Nana Abena was not only visibly present by way of her beautified body lying in state. Two large portrait pictures of her were framed and put on display in the house and later at the public funeral grounds. All over the village, her image featured on the obituary posters pasted on walls. The same picture had been reproduced on T-shirts, handkerchiefs, pinup prints, and key rings/bottle openers that were distributed among the mourners. In the public spectacle following Nana Abena's death, the production and mass reproduction of images of her body, both dead and alive, had to safeguard her "future remembrance" (Wendl and du Plessis 1998) among the living so as to immortalize her.

Abusua ɔ funu, a family loves a dead body, says the Twi proverb that critiques the amount of time and money people spend on the dead to wrap them in an overwhelming luxury they have never enjoyed in life. *Abusua ɔ funu* sang "the Asante Brothers" highlife band in the 1970s.

Mete ase a	When I am alive,
abusua kyiri me tan me,	my family dislikes me,
nanso mewu deɛ ara	but when I die,
ɛnyɛ anka ɛsɛ w'ani.	you would witness it,
Na anka wɔbɛnya adagye	they would get much time
ayɛ m'ayie frenkyim oo.	to make my funeral very fine.
M'awieeɛ oo.	O my end,
Abusua dɔ funu oo.	The family loves a dead body.
Menni sika	I don't have money
ena mennya ntoma,	and I haven't got cloth,
Nanso mewu da ara hɔ	but the very day I die,
anka wadeda me 'adwenasa.'	they would lay me out with adwenasa[6]
Mennya kɛtɛ nna so mpo,	I haven't even got a mat to sleep on,
Nanso meda hɔ a	but when I lie in state,
yɛde dadeɛ mpa bɛsi ho.	they put down a metal bed.[7]

Like the Asante Brothers, many other social commentators complain that people in Ghana, and especially Asante people, care more about their dead than about the living. Despite widespread and longstanding critique from various sides on the extravagance of Asante funerals (de Witte 2001), their exhibitionist nature only increases with every newly available technology. The image to be created of the deceased and the bereaved family matters so much that people today spend fortunes on mortuary fees, body decorators, photographers, video makers, and even television airtime. The immense contrast between the image of Nana Abena Fosuwaa's struggling and suffering body before death and the image of her dead body at the funeral celebration, when it was spectacularly exhibited, made me return to Ghana to conduct ethnographic research on funeral celebrations in the Asante town of Bekwai. This chapter examines the production and reproduction of images of the deceased and the changing modes and technologies of remembrance this process entails.

Funerals have long been grand events in Asante. Early twentieth-century observers (e.g., Rattray 1927; Shaw 1925) described how funerals for "ordinary" people lasted for several days, were characterized by displays of wealth, exchanges of gifts, and "revelry," "drunkenness," "jollity," and "show," and were accompanied by high expenses.[8] Since these early descriptions of Asante mortuary practices, many things have changed in the ways Asante people mourn their dead and celebrate their funerals. One might expect a traditional ritual centered on the extended family and on beliefs about ancestors to fade with Christianization, individualization, urbanization, and the growing influence of the market economy. Indeed, many studies of mortuary rituals in Africa have described them as traces of a disappearing world (e.g., Owusu-Sarpong 2000;

Thomas 1982, 2000). Such a perspective, however, cannot account for the fact that funerals—in Asante as elsewhere in Africa—only seem to be increasing in scale and significance. To understand the dynamics of contemporary funerals in Asante, I have found it more productive to approach them as an open field of interaction where people combine local and globalized ideas, practices, and things to develop new, local styles of celebrating life and death (de Witte 2001). Although practices such as shaving off hair, fasting, firing of musketry, and widowhood rites have greatly diminished in importance and others, such as the use of funerary terra-cotta, have disappeared entirely, funerals appear to be highly absorptive of new forms, practices, and technologies. Christian burial, instead of reducing the grandness of the event, has been incorporated in the overall funerary process as an essential ingredient of a prestigious funeral. Media such as newspapers, radio, television, video, and photography have added new dimensions to the public nature of funerals. Many tasks that were in the past carried out by family members may now be contracted out to a myriad of small scale entrepreneurs active in the "funeral industry" (de Witte 2003). Funerals have thus become more professional, more commercial, and hence, more expensive (Arhin 1994), a development made possible in part by financial contributions from relatives living abroad (Mazzucato et al. 2006; van der Geest 2006; Arhinful 2001). But the change that is the focus of this chapter is the presence of the dead body at the center of the funeral activities coupled with the mass reproduction and public dissemination of images of the living body.

The display of the dead body in the family house for all visitors to come and see has become the major feature of most Asante funerals. This has by no means always been so. In precolonial times as well dead bodies were put on display and, according to social status, decked out in fine cloth, beads, and gold. In contrast to present-day practices, however, this "laying-in-state" ceremony was a rather small-scale event that occurred immediately after death.[9] The body was buried the following day and the major, public funeral celebration (*ayie pa*) was held weeks later, with numerous visitors and without the dead body. As van der Geest (2006) has also pointed out, the advent and gradual spread of mortuary technology has made delayed burial possible for increasing numbers and categories of people and thus allowed for the current custom of combining laying-in-state, burial, and funeral celebrations in one weekend, usually several weeks or more after death. The presence of the dead body at the center of an elaborate celebration has become so valued that average families are willing to spend huge sums on preserving their "stiffs," as corpses are colloquially termed. Financial resources and distance to towns allowing, bodies are kept in mortuaries for weeks, months, even nearly a year in rare cases of rich or royal dead, while families prepare for a celebration that impresses everyone. Much more than in the past, then, the public display of wealth and status has come to be connected to the body of the deceased.

This chapter analyzes such elaborate displays of luxury and wealth focused on the dead body and the mass reproduction of pictures of the deceased as part of the changing modes of creating personhood, ancestorship, and remembrance. Understandings of personhood and afterlife change with cultural, religious, and socioeconomic developments. Funerary practices of producing memories of the person after death change accordingly. This chapter discusses how at contemporary Asante funeral celebrations images of the person are created for future remembrance. I argue that at death, *imaginations* of good life are turned into *images* of good life, represented by the body of the deceased—images in flesh and in photographs, but also in cloth, paint, plaster, and cement. To examine how these practices diverge from or continue historical modes of remembrance, I discuss some sources on ancient terra-cotta funerary heads from archaeology and art history. Comparing these images in clay to contemporary image production sheds a new light on changing conceptions of ancestors and changing modes of relating to the dead.

Asante notions of person and death

Asante people do not hold a singular, unambiguous, and collectively shared notion of personhood, death, and afterlife. These ideas vary from person to person and from situation to situation. As in many parts of Africa, a longstanding religious heterogeneity has produced a plurality of schemes and habits of thought that may conflict and intermingle and may be activated differently according to context and individual socializations. Behind the many practices and expressions that surround the death of a person thus lies a complex of ideas and beliefs, informed by an interaction between two "grand discourses" on death: "traditional" Akan cosmological beliefs about ancestors and *asamando*, "the land of the dead," and Christian teachings about heaven and hell and judgment day.

Akan cosmology has it that a person is composed of three elements: blood, a spirit, and a soul, coming from three different sources. *Mogya* (blood) one acquires matrilineally, from the mother. It is through one's blood that one is related to all living *and* dead members of one's (matrilineal) family, one's *abusua*. *Mogya*, then, is essentially the shared or common part of the person. The *sunsum* (spirit) derives from the father at the moment of conception through his semen and gives a child his personality and character. The *sunsum* is first of all a person's individuality. The soul (*kra*) is a small particle of God (*Onyame*), making the person a human being and giving him or her a destiny (*nkrabea*).[10] The soul is also said to be the stranger (*ɔkra ye ɔhɔhoɔ*), which implies the notion that there is a third dimension of personhood not defined by "commonality" or "individuality" alone. When a person dies, his body goes into the ground "to be the food of ants" (Sarpong 1974: 22); his *kra* returns to

God, while the *sunsum* joins the ancestors in *asamando,* where it continues to live much the same way as the integral person has lived on earth. The state of being an ancestor is closely connected to the concept of blood relationship, as it is above all else kinship ties that continue after death. Ancestors are more often referred to and addressed (in libation) in the plural (*nananom*), as the community of family ancestors, than individually. This is also expressed in the funeral dirges collected and analyzed by Nkètia (1955). In dirges that refer to ancestors, kinship affiliations of the deceased with his ancestors and lineage or clan history are mentioned to bind the group together and to give the deceased a place in the ancestral community. When particular ancestors are named, it is because of their contribution to the corporate life of the group. By mentioning glorious ancestors' names and accomplishments, the dirge establishes the living members' pride in their lineage. The notion of ancestors, then, expresses the continuity of the family group across the boundary of death, rather than the continued life of the individual person.

Death, then, is perceived as the transition to the position of ancestor, as a journey to *asamando.* One's existence in *asamando* will be very much like one's existence on earth. One will have the same position one has had in life and the same material needs. Therefore the deceased is given consumer goods and money ("burial things") to enable him or her to provide for him or herself after arrival in *asamando.* Ancestors retain a functional role in the life of their relatives and their influence may be positive as well as negative. It is important therefore to maintain a good relationship with them by showing them respect. A big funeral and the subsequent memorial celebrations are essential to this end.

Not everybody, however, will be admitted to the land of the ancestors (see Jindra 2005 on Cameroon). Only those who meet certain criteria concerning a successful life can enjoy the position of ancestor after their death. Deceased persons who are not admitted will be roaming about as ghosts (*saman twentwen*) and come back to trouble people, especially their relatives. With the "burial things" (*adesiedeɛ*) and money the deceased take with them in the coffin, they will be able to prove their success in life upon arrival in *asamando.*[11] Likewise, the scale and performance of the funeral are a measure of success in life and thus influence the position and power of the deceased in *asamando.* The number of visitors is very important, but also, among other things, the availability of food and drink, the kinds of music or bands, and the quality of the dancing. In the evaluation of a funeral, these things are counted. *Ayie no bae,* "the funeral came," people say about a successful funeral with plenty of people. Lastly, the way one dies influences one's position after death. Like many African traditions, Asante tradition distinguishes between a "good death" and a "bad death." A good death is a natural death at high age after having brought forth many children and contributed significantly to the family wellbeing.

When one dies young, in an accident, in childbirth, or of an "unclean" illness, this is considered bad. People who die a bad death (*ɔtɔfoɔ*) bring shame upon their family and do not get an elaborate funeral. Burial is supposed to be concealed, private, and silent. All is about forgetting. By contrast, the funeral of someone who died in dignity after a long and successful life that can serve as an example for others is characterized by visibility, publicity, and noise. It is remembrance that matters. Such a person will be admitted to *asamando* and remembered and honored as an ancestor. In practice, however, the distinction between good and bad deaths has become blurred, since families now sometimes organize big funerals to conceal bad deaths, and notions about success in life are changing.

The grounds on which one will be admitted as an ancestor are thus ambiguous and open to different interpretations. Moreover, one is dependent upon others, especially one's family, since the way one's funeral is celebrated also influences one's position in *asamando*. The question of whether one will be admitted to *asamando* after death, then, is a source of great insecurity. Christian teachings about life after death as preached in churches (especially during burial masses) and in popular Christian literature offer people a clearer view in the face of this insecurity. Without being able to do justice to the diversity of Christianities in Ghana within the scope of this chapter, and at the risk of oversimplification, I dare say that popular Christian ideas about death converge around heaven (*ɔsoro*), hell (*ɔbonsam kurom*), and judgment day (*atemmuo*). The promise of a straight way to heaven, if only one is a good Christian (and the criteria for this qualification clearly vary between denominations), gives people something to hold on to, a kind of security. At the same time churches put out the fearsome prospect of eternal damnation of those not found to have been good Christians on judgment day. The message is clear: death is inevitable and irreversible, but after death one can have eternal life in Jesus. But take care: only if you follow Jesus will you be rewarded in heaven; the unsaved will end up in hell. Popular Christian images and tracts thus simplify the complexity and diversity of Christian doctrines to provide people with a clear-cut framework for their ideas about the hereafter. This kind of security is attractive and may explain why, in the context of the growing pervasiveness of Christianity in general, ideas about judgment day, heaven, and hell in particular have gained such a strong foothold.

In contrast to traditional concepts of death, Christian discourses stress the individuality of persons. Whether one's soul will be sent to heaven or to hell depends only on one's personal relationship with God and individual deeds on earth. One's destiny after death is independent of any behavior of family members; it is one's own belief and righteousness that will be rewarded with eternal life "in the bosom of the Lord." Particularly in the very popular Pentecostal churches in Ghana there is a spiritual "battle" to preserve the soul of the person independent of ancestral (blood) relations. Conversely, the dead are not believed to have any direct power over the lives of their descendants on earth. In this sense living and dead relatives are separated; one can only hope for personal reunion with loved ones in heaven.

Christianization and modernization have transformed traditional belief in ancestors. The felt presence of dead forebears as spirits and the real fear of and respect for their power have greatly diminished under the strong influence of Christianity. Living on by way of being actively and collectively remembered as a successful person by one's family members and the community, however, is still very important (Stucki 1995: 120) and a major preoccupation of elderly people. Ancestorship today, then, may be better understood as access to active and collective remembrance and as a reconfirmation of shared norms and values concerning good life. Partly, this understanding of ancestors diverges from earlier anthropological understandings of ancestors as spiritual entities constructed by a whole cycle of rituals. As will be argued, however, access to collective remembrance equally requires a series of transition rituals. The rituals described below facilitate the transition from being a person in the community to being remembered as a person by the community. At the same time, they reconfirm the main criteria for success in life, and thus the conditions for being remembered as an ancestor: accumulation of wealth and resources and accumulation of people and their labor.

Wealth accumulation and redistribution are deeply embedded in the local psyche as central constituents of personhood, achievement, and authority (McCaskie 1983). The public aspect of it is crucial, and especially so at funerals, when a person's success in life is evaluated and publicly represented (and often exaggerated) to establish the deceased as a successful person with, among other things, a nicely painted and decorated house, a corpse covered with expensive cloth, golden jewelry, and beads, as well as a large supply of beer, minerals, and sometimes food. The valuation of what has been termed "wealth-in-people" as an important marker of social success finds expression, for example, in the numerous names of people on obituary posters: first a whole list of people announcing the death of so-and-so, followed by a picture of the deceased, his or her full name, and the funeral arrangements, and then a long list of "chief mourners," children, grandchildren, nieces, nephews, uncles, aunts, and other relatives, their places of sojourn, and their occupations. Some names appear twice or even thrice among the "announcers," the "chief mourners," and some category of relatives. Such obituaries make clear that a person's social esteem, especially at death, consists largely of the number and quality of people related to the person. It is also in the number of mourners, the clothes they wear, and the donations and gifts they bring, then, that one's success in building a network of dependents becomes publicly visible. But if one has not been successful in either of these respects, it is at death that the family may try to mask this failure with a big funeral. More than providing a "true" representation of the accomplishments of the deceased person, then, "funerals provide explicit displays of the ideals of ancestorhood" (Stucki 1995: 23).

Person, imagery, and future remembrance

"If you don't photograph yourself and you die, you have died forever. Nobody will remember you. Nobody will know you." With these words the Ghanaian photographer Joseph K. Davies expresses (in the documentary film *Future Remembrance*, Wendl and du Plessis 1998) the importance of being remembered after death and the need for images, especially photographs, to this end. If for the Asante being a person has much to do with visibility, with being seen by others, this concern becomes most pressing after death, at one's funeral. As death is a key moment for the creation of future remembrance, in the public spectacle following a person's death images of the deceased abound. How you appear at your own funeral will influence how you will live on in the collective memory of the community.

The person lying in state

A successful funeral and lying in state beautifully is a concern of many of the elderly. On the last day of my stay in Bekwai, Nana Agyapomaa, the old lady I stayed with, asked me to send her a watch from Holland.[12] "I need it when I die. I will lie on the bed like this [she bent backwards and put her arms across her chest] and they will put the watch around my wrist and I will look very fine!"[13] The highlife song Owuo Deɛfoɔ ("Merciless Death") by Alex Konadu expresses the hope of a mother on being laid in state beautifully by her children:

Nea ɔbaatan biara pɛ ne sɛ	What every woman wants
ɔwɔ ne ba,	is that she gets a child,
daakye ɔwu da no,	so that on the day she dies,
ɔdeda ne fɛfɛɛfɛ	s/he will lay her out beautifully
akyekyerɛ adosoa	to show adosoa[14]
ansa na yɛsie no.	before they bury her.
Nea ɔbaatan biara pɛ no no.	That is what every woman wants.
Ade nti me maame awɔ me a,	So when my mother gave birth to me,
ɔwɔɔ me sɛ,	she did that so that
daakye ɔbɛwu no,	when she will die in the future,
madeda ne fɛfɛɛfɛ	I will lay her in state beautifully
ansa na masie no.	before I bury her.
Nti owuo ee, me srɛ wo ɛda,	So death, I beg you for time,
ma mensie no ansa na mewu.	let me bury her before I die.[15]

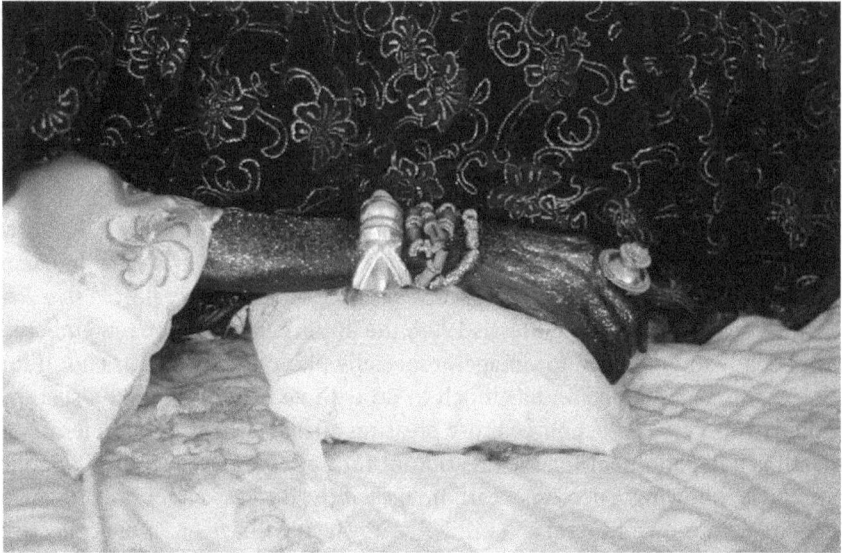

Illustration 8.1. Dead man's hand adorned with gold, Bekwai. Photo by Marleen de Witte.

The elderly people Sjaak van der Geest spoke with in Kwahu (1995) also appeared to be more anxious about their funeral than about death itself. They may worry about the state of the house and feel that they "cannot die like this," meaning their corpse cannot be properly displayed in a poorly maintained house. The dead body is at the center of public attention and evaluation and should thus be "very fine."

Usually, shortly after a person has died, the body is washed by (elderly) female relatives and taken to the mortuary.[16] There the body is kept in what is called the "fridge" until preparations for the funeral have been made. This may take weeks or even months, during which per-day mortuary fees rise and accumulate. Some rich families choose to have their deceased relative embalmed to keep the corpse even better preserved, but this is even more expensive.[17] Normally the frozen body is taken from the mortuary to the family house one day before the "laying-in-state" ceremony to allow it to defrost and to prepare and decorate it, that is, to transform the dead body into a "showpiece," an image of beauty and good life. In the olden days elderly women in the family prepared and decorated the body. Nowadays, especially in towns and cities, it is very common to contract this job out to professional, specialized people who call themselves funeral undertakers, morticians, or body decorators. They do not organize and direct the whole funeral as do their European colleagues, but first of all take care of the presentation of the body and the display room. Sometimes they engage in additional services such as the sale of coffins, wreaths, gowns, or suits. Usually they bring all the materials needed, but families may also provide their own things.

Cloth is the first essential item: one or more pieces of silk-woven *kente*, the traditional textile symbol of riches and royalty, gold-embroidered velvet, brocade, or other expensive types of (imported) cloth. Men can also be laid in state in a suit and women in a white bridal gown, the modern symbol of female beauty and good life and a symbol of rebirth into the next world in traditional color symbolism. Both women's and men's corpses are abundantly decorated with jewelry and beads. Big golden necklaces and strings of precious beads adorn neck and chest. Bulky rings and bracelets are put around wrists and fingers. Specific items symbolizing the life of the deceased may be placed on the body: a typical Fante wig for a woman who had lived on the coast, a judge's gown for a deceased judge, and ceremonial swords and other regalia for chiefs and queen mothers. Of equal importance is the display bed. People who have slept on a mat on the floor for all their life are laid in state in luxurious beds, hired from funeral undertakers when they die. These are normally fancy beds, golden, silver, or white, with china ornaments, flickering Christmas lights, or Perspex pillars filled with colored, bubbling liquids. The bed is placed in a decorated "display parlor." Many houses in Bekwai have a kind of alcove or platform at the courtyard for this purpose, or else a room is used. The walls and ceiling are lined with lace and *kente*. Plastic flowers and plants, framed portrait pictures of the deceased, religious pictures, and wreaths decorate the

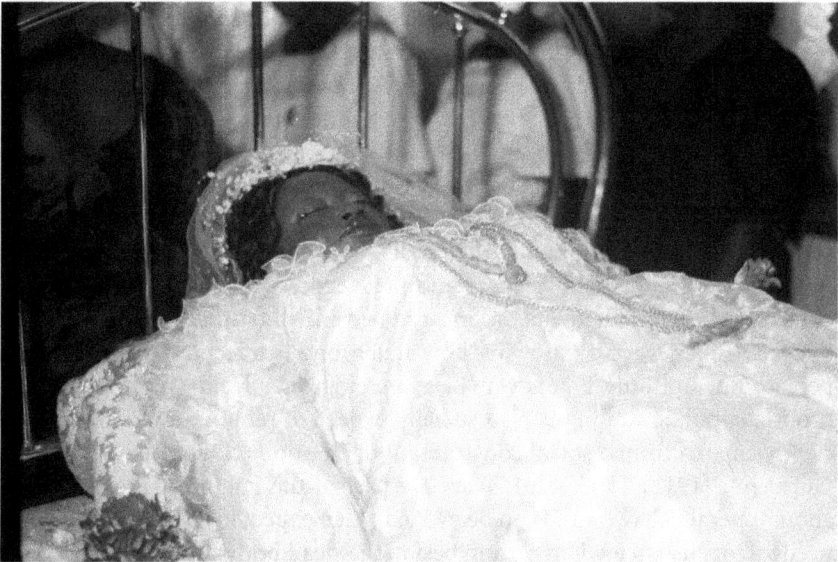

Illustration 8.2. Agnes Ankobiah laid in state, Bekwai. Photo by Marleen de Witte.

room. After the burial, people often leave the room decorated for one more day "for people to come and look at it." Often the whole house is painted and new lace curtains are hung in the doorway of every room. Electricity may even be connected for the occasion or a generator hired to provide power for light, music, and a public address system. Ironically, a freshly painted house with bright lights is often a sign of death.

For the laying-in-state ceremony, the dead body is thus made into an image of good life. It is the showpiece of the celebration. That the image matters much to people may be clear from the struggles over the decoration of the body between relatives, as I witnessed when Nana Abena Fosuwaa was being laid out. The quarrel about the gold dust revealed a struggle between family elders and dignitaries and the deceased's children over the "property" of the dead body. It is often at death that different parties with conflicting interests and agendas clash over the image to be created out of the dead body (see also Appiah 1992, epilogue). Behind the scenes, the image of riches and beauty may be fiercely negotiated.

The main activities taking place around the displayed body are wailing, the presentation of burial gifts (*adesiedeε*), and the taking of pictures or video shots that fix this image of success projected on the dead body.[18] During one of the first laying-in-state ceremonies I visited, I reluctantly asked the sister of the deceased for permission to take a picture of the dead body. "Yes, of course," she replied, "but wait until my sisters and I are ready." A little later she signaled me to follow her and her sisters to the bed with the dead body. They started wailing heartrendingly. "*Nana awu oo, Nana awu oo, yɛn ani abre oo!*" (Our grandmother has died, our grandmother has died, our eyes are red.) They threw their arms up in the air in despair; their eyes became literally red, as tears were flowing across their cheeks. Even though a video man was recording all this from close by, the camera in my hand felt out of place. "*Twa no!*" (snap her!), the woman sitting beside the corpse whisking away the flies urged me to take the picture of the body and the weeping women. As soon as I had done so, they stopped crying and returned to their seats.

Theatrical wailing and weeping, dramatic expression of emotions, and uncontrolled body movements around the bed in which the dead body is laid out are proper ways of showing how much one is affected by the loss of a person. But not only is this way of expressing one's feelings considered appropriate; public wailing is also socially expected, required even. Tears here clearly emerge from a social construction of emotion (cf. van der Geest 1990; Durkheim [1912] 1965: 443). Tears are part of the cultural pattern of rules about funeral behavior and can be evoked when expected and produced when needed, for instance when posing beside the dead body for a camera. This is not to say that the emotions people show are not real, or that their tears are not "genuine." Of course, people do have feelings of deep grief, and many people stressed the importance of not keeping these inside. But the fact that public tears are considered more appropriate for women than for men indicate that crying at funerals is ritual behavior as much as personal emotional expression. In contrast, when a child dies, the parents, however deeply grieved, are not allowed to shed even one tear in public. When they do so, people urge them to stop, because else "the spirits will come and take another one." One should not mourn a dead child, but forget the death as soon as possible and focus on the living children. The taboo on tears in this case points to the importance of remembering successful persons as ancestors and forgetting those who died too early, as well as to the close link between crying and remembrance. Not crying is supposed to make one forget; crying makes one remember. This association between crying and remembrance, then, clarifies why it is so important that, in case of an adult person, people cry at his or her funeral. Wailing and weeping prove that the deceased was someone special. Tears make the life of the deceased important, maybe even more important than it actually was. They show that the deceased has been able to bind people to himself, people who come to his funeral to mourn his death. Families may even hire professional mourners to come and cry at the funeral because tears and lamentations make a funeral successful; they make the dead person a successful person and thereby create remembrance. This cultural meaning of weeping also explains why filming and photographing weeping people around the dead body is so common and so much appreciated. Pictures and video fix the tears that mark the successful life of the deceased and are thus much welcomed by the family.

Before the advent of mortuaries the funerary process looked very different, as laying-in-state ceremonies and funerals were separate events. A deceased person was prepared and laid out very shortly after death had occurred. In the early colonial period, Rattray (1927: 149) described how the body "was dressed in its best cloths and adorned … with every available gold ornament." When a deceased was lying in state, food offerings were placed beside the body and later put on the grave (Ibid.: 151, 163). A "wake" was kept day and night that consisted of gun firing, drumming, dancing, singing, weeping, and formal presentation of gifts, including cloths, gold dust, and sheep, to the dead. Burial was usually performed on the third day. Traditional techniques were applied to preserve the body for these few days, as is still done by rural herbalists sometimes. The main or final funeral rites (*ayie pa*) were celebrated later without the dead body. Until fairly recently, funerals were thus characterized by a separation of burial ceremony and the public and generally more elaborate final funeral rites on the eighth day (*nawotwe da*), fifteenth day, or fortieth day (*adaduanan*). This "second funeral" allowed many more visitors to come from far away and be present at a public spectacle of drumming, dancing, and the display and exchange of gifts.

With the advent and popularization of mortuary technology it has become customary to postpone the burial, including the laying-in-state ceremony, and to combine it with the final funeral rites. Normally a Saturday is chosen and the laying-in-state is done in the morning in the family house and the final funeral celebration in the afternoon in a public open air space in town. The great number of visitors that would in the past only witness the final funeral now also attend the activities around the dead body. The use of broadcasting technologies to announce the funeral has even increased their number. As a result, the laying-in-state ceremony has enormously increased in scale and value as a source of prestige and has thus become the target of much expenditure (cf. Arhin 1994). While in the past the dead body played a role only during the first and much more modest phase of the funerary process, it has now become the centerpiece of the celebrations.

The person in pictures

The importance of visibility and visual technology is evident not only in the practice of hiring professionals to photograph and/or film the dead body and the living bodies of the guests. Portraits of the deceased abound at most Asante funerals: on the obituary posters all over town, enlarged, framed, and displayed in the family house and at the public funeral grounds, and printed on paper, textiles, and small giveaway objects. At funerals, then, pictures of the dead body are taken while pictures of the living body are displayed and distributed.

An important function of photographs at funerals is the realization of a dead person's transition from being a living person to being remembered as a person. Tobias Wendl remarks about photography and rites of passage: "As a ritualized practice, photography stands close to those rites of passage that mark the end of life and thereby reconstitute the social person in a new way" (Wendl 1998: 45; original in German, translation MdW). Photographs are used at funerals to reconstruct the deceased person in such a way that he or she can live on in the memories of the living.

Photography forms part of what Wendl calls a "culture of remembrance" (*Erinnerungskultur*). During their lifetime people already start immortalizing themselves with pictures as part of the process of growing older, dying, and becoming an ancestor. In almost every house a photo album lies on the saloon table and is given to guests to glance through as an integral part of the visiting ritual. Such albums contain portraits of the owner of the album, of family members and friends, usually in beautiful clothes, taken at special occasions or in photo studios. There is no chronology or other logic in the arrangement of the pictures. They are scattered through the album arbitrarily; some are double (for exchange purposes) or upside down. Pictures have come to serve as family chronicles that support oral genealogy. Nana Agyapomaa did not have an album, but kept her photographs in an envelope. She was very delighted when I gave her an album and she showed me her pictures again and again, indicating her relationship to all the persons portrayed. Her two dearest pictures, however, were two old black and white pictures of her mother and her eldest brother, enlarged and glued on a piece of cardboard. The picture of her mother was taken not long before she died. Nana explained:

> She didn't want to be photographed at all, but we, the children, we wanted to have her picture for when she would die. She was old, you see. So then my brother called someone to come and take the picture and we made her sit down on this chair, here in the house. Because of that, she is still with me now.

Besides keeping pictures in an album, many people have framed pictures on the walls or on the floor in their room. Whereas an album mainly contains pictures of loved ones, a person's room is often decorated with her or his own enlarged portraits. Such pictures are not mere decoration; they are a person's own strategic contribution to his or her future funeral. Nana Akyeampomaa, another elderly lady in Bekwai, gave me an old picture of herself as a young lady to have it enlarged and framed in Holland. "There the quality is better, so that when I die, and they will do my funeral, they will put it here, at the court-yard, and it will be very beautiful." This process of self-immortalization, initiated by a person while alive, culminates in the funeral practices performed by the family members after his or her death, when a portrait of the deceased becomes almost like an object of worship (cf. Wendl 1998: 46). Framed pictures

Illustration 8.3. Portrait of Akosua Kayeya on display during the one-year commemorative celebration, Bekwai. Photo by Marleen de Witte.

are not just put on display, but addressed in words, song, dance, and tears. In funeral videos, stills of such framed portraits may be edited in so as to increase their emotional impact.

Apart from using a beautiful framed photograph as a kind of altar during the funeral celebrations, a picture is chosen to print on posters, funeral invitations, brochures, donation receipts,[19] calendars, and newspaper obituaries. The obituary posters in town with the portraits of the dead stay on the walls until sun, wind, and rain have made them perish. This may take a few months to a year, depending upon the quality of the paper and the glue used. The obituary photographs in *The Pioneer*, an Asante weekly, fill pages. A fairly recent practice that emerged with the advent of commercial television in Ghana is the broadcasting of TV obituaries. The portrait of the deceased thus appears on numerous television screens throughout the nation. Sometimes funeral brochures containing photographs are printed and distributed to guests. Nana Akyeampomaa showed me her collection of funeral brochures, about forty in five years' time. She keeps them carefully in a box, but cannot read the texts. It is the pictures on the covers and inside that matter to her and remind her of the persons concerned. A person's portrait may also be printed on T-shirts to be worn by the family on an appointed day during the funeral celebrations, handkerchiefs to be used in dancing and in church, or, if a family is rich enough, a special memorial cloth. The practice of distributing small pictures to be pinned on mourners' cloth or headscarf has been expanded to the production of all kinds of items such as buttons, key rings, bottle openers, or mugs with a small picture of the deceased. All these things are distributed among relatives and others for them to keep as a memory. Lastly, photographs (or paintings after photographs) are used on tombstones, to which I will return below. Asante funerals, then, have come to be characterized by mass reproduction of portrait pictures of the deceased, an explosion of images of the person's face into the public funerary sphere.

Between death and burial a person is photographed or filmed for the last time, when he or she is lying in state. In taking such post mortem pictures particular attention is paid to the decorations of the corpse, the bed, and the room. A photographer in *Future Remembrance* (Wendl and du Plessis 1998) explained:

> They [the relatives] will love to stand by the bedside just to have a photograph to prove the body was well decorated. This serves as a memory. We in our culture, we normally take interest in the dead person, more than the live ones. So when someone dies, people try to put up their maximum. As for future remembrance.

In response to the development of the originally colonial studio photography from an exclusivity of the urban elite to a widespread popular culture of remembrance and self-immortalization (Wendl 1998), many Ghanaian photographers took the opportunity to take snapshots at funerals and other celebrations to earn a living. Since the early nineties, it seems that video is catching up with photography in popularity and many photographers are now combining photography with video making. Kwaku Owusu, a young video maker who runs his own business, told me about his work:

> When a family asks me to cover their funeral, I discuss with them which particular events I must shoot. Mostly I have to do the whole thing, first the week celebration, then the funeral day itself, and some-times also the forty days. Usually I go with one or two assistants for the light, in case the body is inside, and maybe a second camera. It is a thing you have to learn. You should know what is important. You must know all the time what is going on and what is going to hap-pen. Sometimes too, two things are happening the same time. Like for instance, they are praying at the bedside and at the same time some important guests are coming and shaking hands. You have to shoot both. That is why I may choose to bring a second camera, but only if they pay more. As for the guests, you have to make sure that every-body appears, especially the important ones. You also have to have an eye for details, for decorations. Like how they have done the room, the *kente*, the flowers, and the jewels they have used for the body. You have to shoot all. After the whole thing we have a lot of material, so many hours. So then I start editing. Sometimes I use special effects, like mixing shots, to make the thing more dramatic. With this one, for instance, I took the shot of the picture of her as a young lady and I mixed it with the shot of the mother, because it was so sorrowful. The point is that I have to make a very fine video out of it. Then I make as many copies as they have asked for, for them to distribute among themselves and to send it abroad. I keep the original here, so that they can come and order more copies if necessary. If it is a very nice video, more people may want it.

What we see in funeral videos, then, is first of all the numerous visitors as they arrive and greet the bereaved family or file past the body, interspersed with shots of the dead body lying in state, including closeups of the face and decorated hands, closeups of the decorations of the display room, and shots of the displayed portrait pictures. Post mortem photographs and videos thus fix the perishable image of the displayed corpse, the image of beauty, success, and good life projected on the body of the deceased. Family members keep the pictures and the videotapes as a memory to look at once in a while or to show to visitors, and they also send them to relatives and friends abroad who were not able to attend the funeral.

The practices, attributes, and images I have described create and fix a new, edited image of the deceased person that transcends boundaries of time and space so as to safeguard his or her future remembrance. This requires a degree of idealization and perfection that sometimes hardly matches a deceased's past life, but suits his or her future as a memorable ancestor. In this ritual process, the reality of everyday life is transcended and the imagination is called upon to generate idealized images of good life. Images of wealth and riches acquired, of beauty and perfection achieved, of people and relationships accumulated. These desires and imaginations are projected on the body of the deceased, as it is in a liminal state between being alive and being remembered. The decorated and ritually displayed dead body on the bed becomes like an altar, mediating between the visible and the invisible. It connects the metaphysical and the physical person. The tears and lamentations at the bedside, then, are like an offering by the mourners to the deceased person, whose spirit is still felt to be present, through the fixed and idealized image of his/her body. The beautified image of the dead body and the ritual tears, both fixed on video and photographs, constitute the deceased as a successful person and make possible the transition from being a living person to being a remembered person. This "production" of memory out of images of the body is a ritual strategy for overcoming futility (cf. Battaglia 1990: 10).

The person buried

At the end of the laying-in-state ceremony the body is put in the coffin and, in about ninety percent of cases in Bekwai, taken to church for a burial service. Given the strong impact of the church in many people's lives, it is not surprising that the church plays an important role in the organization and performance of funerals. It is at death that one's Christian identity and church affiliation are publicly recognized with a Christian burial. For many people being accorded a Christian burial is a major concern and may be a reason for converting to Christianity (cf. Gilbert 1988), sometimes only a few weeks before death. Access to a Christian burial service is by no means a given, however. It may be a source of tension between families and church authorities. Church leaders also use church burial as a pressure mechanism, threatening people that only if they are "good Christians," regularly attend service, and pay their church contributions, will the church bury them. Not infrequently families have to pay outstanding church dues for their deceased relative in order to secure a church burial.

Having the body brought into the church building before burial is considered highly respectful and, moreover, understood as a "ticket to heaven." The church building itself is of particular importance, providing the perfect setting for a "fine funeral." The coffin is put in the center, covered with a piece of *kente* or white lace. The service follows a standard order with a sermon, prayers, the singing of hymns and psalms, and the reading out of a biography that summarizes the deceased's accomplishments and successes in life, and the presentation of tributes and eulogies that praise the deceased for his or her good character, outstanding qualities, and exemplary deeds. In front of the assembled mourners and sympathizers, the deceased's life is reconstructed as a great success, even if this life has not been so successful at all. The burial service is the last chance to publicly "create" the person. Not only the content but also the number of eulogies is a marker of success. Resources allowing, the family will print a funeral brochure, including the order of service, hymns, the biography, tributes, and photographs, and distribute this among the mourners just before the burial service starts.

After the burial service all sympathizers join the procession to the cemetery for burial. Upon reaching the cemetery women disperse and stop at graves of loved ones, wailing, moving their bodies in grief, and even throwing themselves onto the graves. At the Bekwai municipal cemetery all churches have their own section. One small and less well maintained piece of land is for the "pagans," and nobody wants to end up there. On the plot of the church in question people gather around the grave. Families who can afford it cement and whitewash the inside of the grave and make sure this appears in the photo or video reportage. After the "rites at the graveside," including, in the case of a Catholic burial, the blessing of the grave by sprinkling holy water and waving the censer, prayers, and hymns, the pastor casts the first scoop of earth into the grave, the family head (*abusuapanin*), a brother, uncle, or another male relative the second. The pastor then presents the wreaths, reading out the names and maxims on the ribbons, and places them on the coffin. Some people throw coins or leaves into the grave to "pay the transport fare to the other world" and to protect the spirit on the way. The *abusuapanin* then closes with a short word of thanks to the sympathizers.

In the olden days, people were buried at a burial ground at the edge of the village or in the house, a practice abolished by the colonial government. When the dead person was buried at the burial ground in the bush, there were no rites at the graveside and no identification sign was put on the grave. The grave site was not a memorial spot. Remembrance was through libation and the ancestral stool was considered the dwelling place of the spirit of the deceased (Vollbrecht 1978: 308–309). Although being buried in one's hometown was important, the precise location of the dead body was thus not of much concern. Today still, some people, including Christians, never visit the grave of a loved person. Nana Agyapomaa never went to her late husband's grave, neither that of her brother. She doesn't know exactly where it is. It will be overgrown with plants by now, she told me. But for many people, the burial of someone else is an occasion to visit the graves of relatives. Others combine a visit to the

Illustration 8.4. Grave portrait painted on metal by "Almighty God," Kumasi. Photo by Marleen de Witte.

grave with pouring libations to dead parents and informing them about life's developments.

Under the influence of Christian churches and colonial rule, people came to be buried in cemeteries, in graves with a tomb, cross, or another memorial sign. Christianity has thus provided new ways of remembrance, ones more linked to the individual person. Whereas libation was directed mainly at the community of family ancestors as a whole, Christian remembrance is through a grave tomb with a photograph and through written biographies and memorial services in church. For Christians, burial in the cemetery became a grand affair, with all mourners marching in procession and the coffin conveyed in a hearse. Coffins, first introduced by the churches for all Christians, became objects of prestige and are often put on display during the laying-in-state ceremony.

Until recently, most graves were indicated by just a small sign that mentioned the name of the person buried there, but nowadays many who can afford it choose to have a tombstone erected on the grave of their deceased relative. This is usually done one year after the death, when the official mourning period has come to an end, which allows for raising additional funds to finance an elaborate tomb. A new ceremony has taken root: the unveiling of the tombstone and the laying of new wreaths as part of the anniversary celebration. Not only does this ceremony provide the occasion to collectively remember the deceased, but it also adds to the grandness of the affair and the prestige of the family. Many of the tombs at the Bekwai cemetery display portraits of the dead: painted, in plaster or cement relief, or photographic print. In the film *Future Remembrance* (Wendl and du Plessis 1998), attention is paid to the making of a representation of the deceased to be put on the grave in the form of a full statue, a bust, or a large painting. All types of portraits are copied from a photograph of the living person. The sculptors in the film express great concern for resemblance as well as for the beauty of the image they create. "What we want is beauty; it must look attractive," one of them says. Another important aspect of visual representations of the person on the grave is their relative immunity to time. Unlike coffins, which will be beautiful only on the day of the funeral, grave sculptures or tombs should last very long and thus be durable. The grave tomb is the most lasting, tangible proof of the deceased's status and it is visible anytime people visit the cemetery for the burial of another dead.

Precolonial pictures in clay

Interestingly, the production of images of a deceased person as a part of funerary practice is not as such a practice that emerged from the interaction between Africans and Europeans. In precolonial Asante, long before the advent of photography, people gave visual expression to their beliefs about death and the afterlife through the medium of clay. The use of terra-cotta heads and figures in funerary rites has long been reported in Akan territory. Platvoet (1982) gives a useful discussion of the literature on Akan funerary terra-cottas, providing evidence from late nineteenth- and early twentieth-century observers and from archaeological research. He distinguishes between three types of terra-cotta sculpture that played a role in Akan funerary rites: *akua* (heads, singular *nkua*), *abuasua nkuruwa* ("family pots"), and *ahode* (statues). Archaeological research has pointed out that since at least the seventeenth century, terra-cotta heads and full figures were commonly found in burials of chiefs, queen mothers, priests, or other important persons. They continued to be produced until well into the second half of the twentieth century in some Akan areas (cf. Quarcoo 1973), but in Asante the tradition seemed to have long died out already in the 1930s, "owing to the advance of European influence and the consequent sophistication of the people" (Wild 1934: 1). Fashioned to be a large, idealized representation of the deceased, an *nkua* consists of an individual clay head mounted on a hollow cylinder that can be pushed into the earth. Varying widely in size and style, these sculptures combined individualized features with idealized traits, such as an oval head, a high forehead, and a ringed neck.[20] They thus presented the deceased as a unique person who embodied valued principles of beauty and leadership. These portraits were generally not placed on the grave, but in a part of the "grove of the ghosts" (*asamanpow*) known as the "place of pots" (*asensie*), where also pots that contained food offerings for the deceased and "family pots" (*abusua kuruwa*) were placed (Rattray 1927).[21] Such terra-cotta "family pots" featured similar ancestral portraits (but ones much smaller in size) and were used in royal and ordinary burials alike (Wild 1937; Rattray 1927). The lids of such vessels were modeled to represent an idealized human head with features considered to be attractive, which symbolized the portrait of the deceased. Family members shaved their hair and placed it in the *abusua kuruwa*. Hair being believed to contain part of the spirit of the person, this practice expressed the continued bond between the living members of the family and the deceased member (Platvoet 1982: 116). The family then carried the vessel to the "place of pots" in the forest, placed food and poured libation next to the vessel as an offering for the deceased, and informed the deceased that his funeral rites have finished.

Descriptions of the use of terra-cottas during the final funeral celebrations (Platvoet 1982; Quarcoo 1973) present a striking resemblance to today's practice of laying-in-state and use of photographs. Quarcoo writes that in the case of a death of a chief, priest, or "very influential man," terra-cotta heads "may be commissioned for their commemoration" and displayed and carried around during their final funeral rites "for purposes of visualizing the dead whose funeral are being celebrated" (1973: 55). He describes how, during the final funeral rites for a deceased chief or queen mother,

> the main figure [of a group of terra-cottas representing the deceased and his attendants] was dressed and adorned with rich ornaments befitting the status of the deceased. The objects were placed in a large brass pan or wooden bowl stuffed with rich *kente* and silk. The figures

Illustration 8.5. Memorial head (Nsodie), Ghana, Twifo-Heman traditional area; Akan peoples, 17th–18th century. New York, Metropolitan Museum of Art. Terracotta, roots, quartz fragments, h.w.xd.: 8 x 5 5/8 x 5″ (20.3 x 14.3 x 12.7 cm). The Michael C. Rockefeller Memorial Collection, Purchase, Nelson A. Rockefeller Gift, 1967 (1978.412.563). © 2010, The Metropolitan Museum of Art/Art Resource. /Photo: SCALA, Florence.

were carried to the venue of the funeral and placed in view on a decorated bed or seat on a raised platform.

Interestingly, the terra-cotta representation of the deceased was thus "laid out" similarly to a dead body. Reports given by J. B. Danquah and Margaret Field and discussed by Platvoet describe how "after the procession through the town, the statues were placed for a time under the palmleaf awnings in the square where everyone came to salute them and bid them farewell" (Platvoet 1982: 118). Pots and dishes containing food and drink were also placed by the statues as offerings for the deceased, as used to be done during the laying-in-state. In the absence of the dead body during the final funeral rites, terra-cotta representations of the deceased took its place. As the corpse expressed the presence of the deceased among the mourners during the burial rites, the terracotta expressed his or her presence during the later funeral rites. And as the spirit of the deceased "possessed" the bearers of its corpse during the *funu soa* ritual so as to point out the witch responsible for its death (Rattray 1927: 167–170), during the parading of its statue through the streets much later it was "not uncommon to see the bearers of these statues suddenly obsessed [sic] with the spirit of the dead person and ready to make themselves mediums of communication between the living and the dead" (Danquah 1928: 237, quoted in Platvoet 1982: 117). During the different phases of the funeral, "the corpse and the terra-cotta are both treated as incorporations of the deceased," Platvoet (Ibid.: 123) argues. Hence, he concludes: "Akan funerary terra-cottas are not meant to commemorate the dead … which supposes their not being present, but [to] communicate with them as persons who are actually present among [the living]" (ibid.).

Quarcoo provides an interesting account that points to an emic analogy between terra-cotta heads and portrait photographs and to the interchange-ability of these different media of visual representation after the advent of pho-tographic technology in Ghana:

> Recently, a chief in the Assin area attempted to persuade his people to use a life-size photograph of his mother's brother for the final funeral rites of this man—whom he succeeded as Omanhene [paramount chief]. The disapproval was unequivocal and he had to yield to the tradition of providing an *Nkua* (terracotta head) from an old special-ist in Kwahu area. A piece that was made to cost not less than £200.00 (Quarcoo 1973: 56).

In this case, it was primarily the high cost of a terra-cotta figure that made the chief concerned want to substitute the old tradition with a much cheaper photograph. Also, Quarcoo describes the "emotional attachment to these ter-racotta figures" when they "are displayed and or carried around during the end of final funerals" (ibid.). This too, is very similar to the way enlarged and framed portrait photographs of the deceased are treated and invested with emotions at present-day funerals.

Very different technologies were used to produce images of the dead in past and present times. And whereas terra-cottas were reserved for specified cat-egories of people, photographs are available to anyone independent of social status. Yet despite these differences, the use and function of terra-cotta and photographic body images during the final funeral rites was alike: both mediate the presence of the deceased among the mourners. Their use after the funeral, however, differs entirely. Funerary terra-cottas were generally abandoned in the places of pots to be overgrown by the forest and "no care was paid to the preservation of these images which remained in their places till they crumbled to pieces" (Platvoet 1982: 113). Their significance was limited to their role during the funeral rites. Photographs and video recordings of deceased persons, by contrast, both premortem and post mortem, are carefully kept in albums, boxes, or frames. They are shared among family members and friends, watched at later times, and shown to visitors as a way of commemorating not only the deceased person, but also—in the case of post mortem pictures—the grandness of the funeral, and hence also a way of glorifying the family.

Conclusion: changing technologies of remembering the dead

This chapter has explored changes in the production, reproduction, and use of images of deceased persons in Asante funeral culture. It has analyzed different image carriers or visual media: first, the dead body itself, as it is transformed into an image for the laying-in-state ceremony, second, photographs of the deceased while still alive and their reproduction after death in print, painting, sculpture, video, and television, and third, clay portraits as they were made and used in precolonial times. Relating these various types of funerary imagery to changing ideas about being an ancestor and changing modes of relating to the dead, I argue that the historically changing roles of these images during and after funeral celebrations involve a partial shift from communication with to commemoration of the dead.

In traditional Asante funerals, practices such as putting items into the coffin, shaving hair and putting it in a family pot, or pouring alcohol and placing food items for the dead are ways of interacting with the ancestors, who are part of a lineage community which stretches across the boundary of death. This implies the continued presence of the dead among the living. Many of these practices that served to strengthen the bond between living and dead lineage members have been rejected by churches as "heathen" or "immoral." Instead, Christianity has provided new instruments for the commemoration of the individual person that imply his or her functional absence from among the living. In continuity with Asante notions that one's funeral influences one's destiny after death, however, local Christians themselves have come to see Christian burial with its specific objects and practices as a ticket to heaven.

Images of the deceased have always played a role in relating to the dead. In the past, both the interaction with the dead body during the laying-in-state ceremony and the use of terra-cotta portrait heads formed part of the interaction with the presence of ancestors. Both kind of images were believed to embody (some of) the spirit of the deceased and could thus function as a medium for communicating with him or her. At contemporary laying-in-state ceremonies the dead body may still be addressed directly, as may be the displayed portrait picture. Yet what is at stake is foremost the commemoration of the deceased person as well as the glorification of the family. With the popularization of mortuaries and the general practice of delaying burial, the dead body has become the prime medium on which to project an image of success and wealth. This image concerns both the life of the deceased, which is reconstructed and represented as successful, and the family, which displays its own success by lavishly laying out its deceased member amidst grand funerary spectacle. Fixing this image on photographs and video is crucial "for future remembrance."

Having highlighted the increased importance of remembrance, I do not want to argue, however, that Christianization entailed either a total shift from communication with to commemoration of the dead or the disappearance of the dead from among the living. Rather, in the context of vague and conflicting ideas about death, ancestors, and afterlife, communication with ancestors through their images may mingle or alternate with the remembrance of deceased persons with images. Funerary photography ties into an African visual culture in which images do not so much *represent,* but rather contain—and thus render *present*—something of the person or object depicted. This power attributed to images is evident not only in "traditional" visual media such as the ancient funerary terra-cottas discussed here or the effigies of gods in traditional shrines, but also in a variety of practices with more "modern" visual media, ranging from the use of photographs in healing practices (de Witte 2010; cf. Behrend 2003 for Kenya) to the precautions taken to prevent roaming spirits from taking abode in prop shrines on film sets (Meyer 2006) and the transmission of the Holy Spirit through television images of "anointed Men of God" (de Witte 2003b, 2005). In this context, the power of photographs of the dead is that they can embody a part of the deceased, and as such they can be media for communicating with his or her spirit. In some respects, they can thus assume a function similar to that of ancient terra-cottas, as was most clear in the case of the chief who wanted to substitute one for the other. At the same time, funerary photographs form part of a widely popular culture of remembrance, which includes specific practices of treating, keeping, sharing, and using photographs of persons. This postfunerary use of photographic images thus differs entirely from the use of terra-cotta images, which were generally abandoned in the forest after their use during the funeral. The general popularization of visual technologies such as photography and video since colonial times has included the visualization of the ways in which people relate to the dead. The increased connection between images and remembrance seems to have produced a longer afterlife in visual form and the devaluation of oral forms of commemoration such as libation prayers.

The advent and proliferation of new technologies in the context of Asante funerals has resulted in a paradox: on the one hand, they greatly increase the amounts that people spend on funerals. This is a point that is well established throughout Africa. At the same time, however, the relatively low cost of and easy access to photography and print technologies in comparison to older visual technologies combines with changing social hierarchies to make visual representation possible for many more dead than before. This has led to a proliferation of mass reproduced images of dead people in the public sphere of funerals. While in precolonial and early colonial times, being immortalized with a terra-cotta portrait was restricted to chiefs, queen mothers, and other very important persons; the mass reproduction of images of almost any deceased person today entails what we could call a "democratization of immortality" (cf. Jindra 2005). In addition, the adoption of print and broadcasting technologies for funeral announcements tied into the already public character of Asante funerals to greatly expand their spatial dimension.[22] The image and name of the deceased together with the names of relatives circulate in a much larger space and reach a much vaster and, importantly, more anonymous public. For this public, the images of unknown dead in the media are neither a way of communicating with the deceased nor of commemorating him or her. Ironically, then, the visual technologies of mass reproduction that expanded and popularized the public visibility of the dead made the dead increasingly anonymous to those who see their image.

Notes

1. Her name has been changed.
2. From October 1995 to March 1996 I worked as a volunteer in the community clinic in Trede. Material for this article was collected during that stay and during ethnographic fieldwork in Bekwai (Asante) from July 1998 to March 1999 and return visits to Asante in 2001, 2002, and 2004.
3. Being sources of prestige, age and the number of grandchildren and great-grandchildren are often exaggerated.
4. See van der Geest (2006) for a description of the treatment of corpses in mortuaries in Kwahu.
5. Historically the distinction between "royals" (the lineage that "owns" the ancestral stool of the town and from which the chief is chosen), "commoners," and "slaves" divided the society into three segments for whom different rules counted (Rattray 1929). At present, the difference between being a royal and not being a royal is very small in daily life, but at death one's royal status becomes crucial for the ceremonies performed.
6. *Adwenasa* is the name of a particular woven *kente* pattern. It means 'all ideas have been used up' and refers to a story of a weaver who was ordered by the king to make a *kente* cloth which was more beautiful than any existing *kente* design. He used all known pat-

terns and combined them into one design, hence the name *adwenasa*. In this context it also refers to the singer's dismay at the situation.

7. Song 'Abusua Do Funu' from CD Asante Brothers led by Osei Vasco, *The best of Asante Brothers*. Den Haag: Agyenim Video Productions. Transcription and translation: Joana Gyau and MdW.

8. Of course, not everyone was accorded a grand funeral. The distinction between "royals," "commoners," and "slaves" (see note 5), but also the distinction between a "good death" (*owupa*) and a "bad death" (*ɔtɔfoɔ* or *owubɔne*) determined whether a person would receive a funeral at all and if so, what kind. Such distinctions get blurred, however, as the both the concept of "royalty" and the qualification of a death are ambiguous and subject to social and political maneuvering (van der Geest 2004).

9. Although the action of laying the body out is always concealed, the public ceremony in the family house around the dead body lying in state is commonly referred to as "laying-in-state." I have therefore chosen to use this term instead of the linguistically correct "lying in state."

10. Like the very notion of "traditional religion," the notion of a traditional (High) God was the product of missionary encounter and translation and can thus not be taken for granted. Instead of dismissing such notions as "inventions" and looking for "pure" traditional beliefs, I recognize that missionary translations have profoundly influenced people's ideas about and knowledge of "traditional religion" (de Witte 2008: 229–230).

11. Not all "burial things" are actually buried with the deceased. This might have been more common in the past, as people told me, but now some people said that it is the "spirit" of the things that goes to *asamando* with the spirit of the deceased, while the "body" of the things is shared among the living (i.e., the family).

12. In many ways, I was myself inserted in my informants' funerary aspirations: I contributed to their aims of visual distinction in death by indeed bringing the desired watch on my next visit, by enlarging and framing portrait pictures, by making funeral donations, and by taking and reprinting photographs at funerals, often on demand. Even my mere presence at funerals became a source of prestige sometimes and was deliberately captured on photos or video. One could say that my research methodology thus directly altered the "results" of the study. Instead of masking or minimizing such influence in pursuit of an illusion of "neutrality," I have found it more fruitful to include my own presence and interactions in my analysis of how Asante people innovatively and strategically shape their funerals in an era of increased globalization and foreign connections.

13. All citations from conversations with people in Bekwai are translated from Twi by the author.

14. *Adosoa* is a public presentation of gifts by the in-laws to the bereaved family.

15. Song from CD Alex Konadu (One Man Thousand), Classic Highlife, Akuboat Music, 1998. Transcription and translation MdW.

16. Ghanaian law does not allow independent mortuaries. All mortuaries are thus attached to hospitals. As mortuary fees are lower when a person dies in the hospital, relatives may bring their dying parent to the hospital just before death, contrary to the earlier ideal of dying at home (van der Geest 2006).

17. In the three mortuaries in Kwahu described by van der Geest, embalming (injection of the whole body with formalin) is obligatory.

18. See Gott 2007 for an insightful analysis of the public shows of (rented) *adesiedeɛ* and *adekyeredeɛ* gifts at Kumasi funerals as aesthetic strategies of status-seeking visual display.

19. Visitors make donations, which are written down in a notebook and announced through a public address system. Donors are given a receipt.
20. Although some authors attribute the "ringed neck" to influence from the practice of wearing necklaces of beads or metal rings by other West African tribes (Wild 1934: 2), the similarity to the practice of retouching in studio photography so as to add rings of fat, a symbol of status and beauty, to a woman's neck (Wendl and du Plessis 1998) is remarkable.
21. Wild (1934), however, stresses that these objects were placed on graves, which is significant considering the separation in Asante of burial ground and the place of pots.
22. See Lawuyi 1988 for an analysis of Nigerian obituaries as symbolic manifestations of the tradition of ancestral belief in a new cultural form.

Bibliography

Appiah, Kwame Anthony. 1992. *In My Father's House: Africa in the Philosophy of Culture.* New York and Oxford: Oxford University Press.

Arhin, Kwame. 1994. "The Economic Implications of Transformations in Akan Funeral Rites." *Africa* 64, no. 3: 307–322.

Arhinful, Daniel K. 2001. *"We Think of Them": How Ghanaian Migrants in Amsterdam Assist Relatives at Home.* Leiden: African Studies Centre.

Battaglia, Debbora. 1990. *On the Bones of the Serpent: Person, Memory, and Mortality in Sabarl Island Society.* Chicago and London: University of Chicago Press.

Behrend, Heike. 2003. "Photo Magic: Practices of Healing and Harming in East Africa." *Journal of Religion in Africa* 33, no. 2: 129–145.

de Witte, Marleen. 2001. *Long Live the Dead! Changing Funeral Celebrations in Asante, Ghana.* Amsterdam: Aksant Academic Publishers.

———. 2003a. "Money and Death: Funeral Business in Asante, Ghana." *Africa* 73, no. 4: 531–559.

———. 2003b. "Altar Media's *Living Word*: Televised Charismatic Christianity in Ghana." *Journal of Religion in Africa* 33, no. 2: 172–202.

———. 2005. "The Spectacular and the Spirits: Charismatics and Neo-Traditionalists on Ghanaian Television." *Material Religion* 1, no. 3: 314–335.

———. 2008. "Spirit Media: Charismatics, Traditionalists, and Mediation Practices in Ghana." PhD thesis, University of Amsterdam.

———. 2010. "Religious Media, Mobile Spirits: Publicity and Secrecy in African Pentecostalism and Traditional Religion." In *Travelling Spirits. Migrants, Markets, and Mobilities*, ed. Gertrud Hüwelmeier and Kristine Krause. New York: Routledge.

Durkheim, Emile. 1965 [1912]. *The Elementary Forms of the Religious Life.* Translated from French by Joseph Ward Swain. New York: The Free Press.

Gilbert, Michelle. 1988. "The Sudden Death of a Millionaire: Conversion and Consensus in a Ghanaian Kingdom." *Africa* 58, no. 3: 291–309.

Gott, Suzanne. 2007. "'Onetouch' Quality and 'Marriage Silver Cup': Performative Display, Cosmopolitanism, and Marital *Poatwa* in Kumasi Funerals." *Africa Today* 54, no. 2: 79–106.

Jindra, Michael. 2005. "Christianity and the Proliferation of Ancestors: Changes in Hierarchy and Mortuary Ritual in the Cameroon Grassfields." *Africa* 75, no. 3: 356–377.

Lawuyi, Olatunde B. 1988. "Obituary and Ancestral Worship: Analysis of A Contemporary Cultural Form in Nigeria." *Sociological Analysis* 48, no. 4: 372–379.

Mazzucato, Valentina, Mirjam Kabki and Lothar Smith. 2006. "Transnational Migration and the Economy of Funerals: Changing Practices in Ghana." *Development and Change* 37, no. 5: 1047–1072.

McCaskie, Thomas C. 1983. "Accumulation, Wealth and Belief in Asante History." *Africa* 53, no. 1: 23–40.

Meyer, Birgit. 2006. "Impossible Representations: Pentecostalism, Vision and Video Technology in Ghana." In *Religion, Media and the Public Sphere,* ed. Birgit Meyer and Annelies Moors. Bloomington: Indiana University Press.

Nketia, Kwabena. 1955. *Funeral Dirges of the Akan People.* Achimota: University College of the Gold Coast.

Owusu-Sarpong, Christiane. 2000. *La Mort Akan: Étude Ethno-Semiotique des Textes Funéraires Akan.* Paris: L'Harmattan.

Platvoet, Johannes G. 1982. "Commemoration by Communication: Akan Funerary Terracottas." *Visible Religion: Annual for Religious Iconography* 1: 113–134.

Quarcoo, A. K. 1973. "Akan Visual Art and the Cult of the Ancestors." *Institute of African Studies Research Review* 9, no. 3: 48–82.

Rattray, R.S. 1927. *Religion and Art in Ashanti.* Oxford: Clarendon Press.

Sarpong, Peter K. 1974. *Ghana in Retrospect: Some Aspects of Ghanaian Culture.* Accra: Ghanaian Publishing Corporation.

Stucki, Barbara R. 1995. "Managing the Social Clock: The Negotiation of Elderhood among the Rural Asante of Ghana." PhD thesis, Northwestern University, Evanston, Illinois.

Thomas, Louis-Vincent. 1982. *La Mort Africaine. Idéologie Funéraire en Afrique Noire.* Paris: Payot.

———. 2000. *Les Chairs de la Mort: Corps, Mort, Afrique.* Paris: Institut d'Édition Sanofi-Synthélabo.

van der Geest, Sjaak. 1990. "Culturele tranen op Begrafenissen in Ghana." In *Dodendans: Ontdekkingsreis rond de Dood in Verschillende Culturen,* ed. Pauline van de Klashorst. Amsterdam: Koninklijk Instituut voor de Tropen.

———. 1995. "Old People and Funerals in a Rural Ghanaian Community: Ambiguities in Family Care." *Southern African Journal of Gerontology* 4, no. 2: 33–40.

———. 2000. "Funerals for the Living: Conversations with Elderly People in Kwahu, Ghana." *African Studies Review* 43, no. 3: 103–129.

———. 2004. "Dying peacefully: Considering good death and bad death in Kwahu-Tafo, Ghana." *Social Science and Medicine* 58, no. 5: 899–911.

———. 2006. "Between Death and Funeral: Mortuaries and the Exploitation of Liminality in Kwahu, Ghana." *Africa* 76, no. 4: 485–501.

Vollbrecht, Judith A. 1978. "Structure and Communitas in an Ashanti Village: The Role of Funerals." PhD thesis, University of Pittsburgh.

Wendl, Tobias. 1998. "'God Never Sleep': Fotografie, Tod und Erinnerung." In *Snap me one! Studiofotografen in Afrika,* ed. Tobias Wendl and Heike Behrend. München, London, New York: Prestel.

Wendl, Tobias and Nancy du Plessis. 1998. *Future Remembrance: Photography and Image Arts in Ghana.* Color, 55 minutes. Göttingen: Institut für den Wissenschaftlichen Film.

Wild, R. P. 1934. "Baked Clay Heads from Graves near Fomena, Ashanti." *Man* 34 (January): 1–4.

———. 1937. "Funerary Equipment from Agona-Swedru, Winnebah District; Gold Coast." *The Journal of the Royal Anthropological Institute of Great Britain and Ireland* 67 (January–June): 67–75.

CHAPTER 9

Funerals and Fetish Interment in Accra, Ghana

Jonathan Roberts

In Accra, Ghana, in 2004, a young woman named Amele died of a mysterious illness. Amele was born into a working class family in Bukom, a neighborhood inhabited mostly by Ga-speaking fishermen and petty traders. When she was a teenager, she had an illicit sexual relationship with a schoolmate and became pregnant. Fearing the disgrace of having a child out of wedlock, she aborted the baby using a home remedy recommended by a friend. Amele was free of the stigma of bearing an illegitimate child, but she feared that the abortion medicine had made her barren.[1] In her early twenties, she moved from boyfriend to boyfriend, trying to get pregnant again, but failed repeatedly. According to her friends, she began to lose her self-respect and started associating herself with some unsavory characters that lived in her neighborhood. Her last boyfriend was a known criminal who asked her to steal him some money from her mother, which she did by sneaking into the family compound and snatching the money from her mother's room. When Amele's mother discovered that the money was missing, she hired a "fetish priest" to exact vengeance on the person who had stolen it.[2] Bukom is the religious center of Ga culture, so she hired a female spirit medium who lived nearby to conduct a ceremony that would unleash one of the most infamous forms of fetish magic in Accra, *agbalegba*.[3] The medium gathered together the components of the ritual, including a small figurine and a tiny wooden coffin, and instructed Amele's mother to write a letter to the thief to tell him or her to return the money or face the consequence of death. She took the letter, wrapped it around the effigy of the thief, and placed it in the miniature coffin along with some gruesomely symbolic components, including human body parts. In a midnight ceremony at Awudome Cemetery, the largest graveyard in Accra, the mother looked on while the spirit medium poured libation to consecrate the curse fetish, charging it with the duty of taking revenge on the thief. They buried the tiny coffin in a small hole in the ground and departed. A few days later, Amele fell sick and quickly began to lose weight. While she was bedridden and delirious, she confessed to stealing money from her mother, and begged her mother to remove the *agbalegba* curse. In a panic, the mother paid the spirit medium to exhume the coffin, but it was too late. Amele's condition worsened and she died shortly afterwards. At her funeral ceremony, there were two separate explanations circulating about the cause of her death. Some said she had died of AIDS, a consequence of her high risk sexual lifestyle. Others gossiped quietly in corners about the *agbalegba* curse.

On one level, this story is a commentary about the stigma of AIDS in Accra in the twenty-first century, a cautionary tale about the perils of a sexually promiscuous lifestyle. Though Ghana has a relatively low HIV/AIDS rate of approximately 3 percent (Duda *et al.* 2005; Adjaye 2004), the disease is a danger to youth in Bukom and is sometimes considered as a punishment for an amoral lifestyle. On another level, the story follows the West African literary trope of the "bad death" caused by sorcery, a storyline that is recognizable to many people who have attended Ghanaian funerals where mourners speculate about the cause of death (van der Geest 2004). Many Ghanaians harbor deep fears of supernatural forces that can interfere with normative transitions to the afterlife, and if someone dies young or by accident, there are often rumors that the death was caused by poison, witchcraft, sorcery, or on rare occasions, *agbalegba*. There is rarely an investigation to uncover the truth behind such allegations, and direct evidence of a curse like that found in the case of Amele is almost impossible to come by. Yet people continue to hypothesize about the existence of devious "juju" practitioners who can mimic and twist the symbolism of funerary customs for nefarious purposes, and it is widely accepted that ritual experts like shrine priests, spirit mediums, and herbalists (collectively known in the Ga language as the *won hegbemei*) can produce consecrated religious objects that can harness wandering souls to kill.[4] This chapter will first discuss the protocols and changes of funerary customs in Bukom and their relationship to rituals of fetish interment. Second, it will describe the practice of *agbalegba*, a set of obsequies that expose uncertainties about the integrity of the human body and manipulate spatial relationships between the dead and living.

In Accra, as in other parts of Africa, funerals have become lavish events with food, drinks, DJs, and dancing (de Witte 2003; van der Geest 2000; Arhin 1994). Saturday is the preferred day for funeral ceremonies, and it is rare for a weekend to arrive without an invitation to a wake or memorial party.[5] Some people even go to more than one funeral per weekend, because it is assumed that if you do not attend the funerals of others, nobody will come to your own funeral.[6] A sparsely attended funeral is a nightmare for many Ghanaians who still hold beliefs that one must be remembered by the living to exist in the afterlife. Funeral expenses can reach into the thousands of dollars, and some insurance firms have created special investment funds to help families defray the costs.[7] The celebrations are sometimes so excessive that mourners sometimes bankrupt themselves with open demonstrations of wealth to publicly display their love for the deceased (van der Geest 2000).

Recent scholarship has emphasized the way that extravagant funeral ceremonies have become expressions of the social, political, and economic power of the living. Kwame Arhin (1994: 318) has argued that migration, cash crop exports, and urbanization have transformed funerals in Ghana "into an institution of economic and social rather than religious significance." Sjaak van der Geest (2000) has recounted the extravagances lavished upon the dead in Ghana, and has shown how funerals can emphasize revelry for the living rather than reverence for the dead. Michelle Gilbert (1988: 291–314) described the grand funeral of a wealthy merchant in the Akwapim Region of Ghana as an expression of the tensions between the political power of the traditional chieftaincy, the religious power of the Presbyterian Church, and the economic power of commercial elites. And in a study of masculinity in Ghana, Stephen Miescher (2005: 184–91) contrasted the extravagance of contemporary funerary customs with the beliefs of elders who hold that a "moral legacy" is more important than a political or economic legacy. This current focus on funerals as articulations of social cleavages is apposite considering that Ghanaians often express concerns about the profligacy of funerals, a lament pithily expressed by the Akan proverb *abusua do funu*—"the family loves a corpse."

However, though the social stakes for the living are high at any funeral, the interment of the deceased continues to have a religious significance based on Ga beliefs. The funeral, as understood by Ga-speakers, is a time when the soul of the departed makes its transition to the realm of the ancestors, a parallel world where past generations watch over and care for their living descendants. It is paramount then that the soul of the departed is respectfully guided towards the afterlife by the mourners because the power of the departed spirit can help them prosper in the world of the living. Though the majority of residents of Bukom identify as Christians and subscribe to Christian notions about the progress of the soul to the afterlife, they continue to respectfully adhere to historical patterns of funerary convention.

Ga funerary ritual and practice

When Ga-speakers attend funerals, they understand themselves as replicating ritual forms devised by the ancestors that preceded them. Funerals are part of Ga *kusum*, meaning the inherited practices of the ancestors. The observance of *kusum* is important because these remembered funerary rites have the explicit religious purpose of transitioning the soul of the departed into the afterlife. Though the logic here is circuitous, mourners do not see it as such. They assume that since there is already a world of ancestors filled with their forebears, the ancients must have already devised effective practices to open a route for the soul to transition to the world of the dead. Those practices have now accumulated together as *yara*, or Ga funerary tradition.

Though mourners recognize the customs of *yara* as having a special historical legitimacy, changes to the content of funeral rituals occur every time one is held. In order to honor the individual personality of the deceased, there must be flexibility in interpreting funerary tradition in a special way each time someone dies. The mourning family may also reinterpret tradition according to their needs and desires. This means that *yara* includes both rote performances and improvisation. The scholarship of the late twentieth century has emphasized the substantial changes to funeral rituals wrought by technology and increasing affluence in West Africa. Marleen de Witte, Sjaak van der Geest, and Michelle Gilbert have commented on how funerals have become as much an arena for the individual expression of material wealth as a time to reinforce kinship and social solidarity. While mentioning that funeral expenses have become a serious impediment to economic growth in Ghana, Paul Gifford (2004: 52–53) also recently noted that Pentecostal churches have started to become more involved in the obsequies of their congregation members. The families of Bukom are making continuous adjustments to the *kusum* of *yara* in order to adapt to recent innovations in technology and changing religious beliefs. This section will elaborate on funeral customs as they are practiced in contemporary Bukom, including the preservation and dressing of the body, the display of the cadaver, the burial, and the wake.

Prior to the mid-twentieth century arrival of refrigeration and western embalming technologies, elderly women were responsible for bathing and dressing dead bodies (Daniell 1856: 16; Adjei 1943: 87, 89). They were vocationally known as the *gbonyohetsuulo*, the corpse (*gbonyo*) purifiers (*hetsuulo*), people with expertise in using local herbs to prevent a body from rapidly decomposing.[8] Today, bodies are embalmed and preserved at hospital mortuaries by morticians trained and employed by the Ministry of Health. Refrigeration at a morgue allows the funeral to be delayed for weeks, even months, while a committee made up of the immediate family, the *kɛtrɛ*, plans the upcoming ceremonies.[9] According to the resources at their disposal, they send out notice of the death by word of mouth, by phone, by postering a neighborhood, and, if possible, by taking out an advertisement in a newspaper. All family members and friends are obligated to attend out of respect for the deceased and as a form of social reciprocity with the families of friends and relatives.

Once the cadaver is taken from refrigeration, it is washed and prepared for display, usually by the elderly women of the household.[10] They begin by "dividing the sponge," a sharing of the bundles of dried grass that will be moistened and used to scrub the body. The family members then remove the clothes from the body, tearing them into strips and wearing these around their wrists in solidarity with the deceased. They trim the fingernails, cut the hair, and shave excess hair from the body, placing these removable parts, or exuviae, inside the coffin with the corpse.[11] Then they sponge down the corpse with soap and water, sprinkle it with lime juice, dry it with towels and cotton, and powder it with talcum and crushed camphor. The attendants then dress the body in funeral garb, usually fine cloth or a suit. After the body is dressed, the family places it out on a bed or props it up in a chair for viewing in the household or compound. A container, known as the *kɛtrɛ* bowl, is placed alongside the body, and mourners are asked to pay their final respects to the deceased and place a gift of money in the bowl.[12] At this point they might speak directly to the body of the deceased, telling them to take their gift to help them "cross the river," "climb the hill," or "climb the ladder" to the afterlife, or more practically to use the money to buy water for the long (and presumably thirsty) journey ahead. There is no particular dogma that determines the process that the soul of the deceased takes in the afterlife, but mourners do believe that it will join an aggregation of ancestral spirits capable of influencing the world of the living. As the mourners pass by the corpse, they may improvise in their communication with the deceased, telling the dead soul that their friendship in the world of the living has now ceased, and that they should take their gift and move on toward the realm of the ancestors.[13] Ga speakers claim that it is dangerous to speak ill of the dead, sometimes quoting the proverb "ghosts carry a cudgel."[14]

On the following day, the body is placed in a coffin, which can be as simple as a wooden box or as elaborate as a designer casket from Paa Joe's famous workshop at Teshie.[15] Because of the modest incomes of most residents of Bukom, coffins are usually rudimentary affairs with rope handles, though people with higher economic status might be buried in moulded and painted coffins with glass windows. Inside the coffin, next to the body, the mourners place things the immediate family thinks the deceased will need in the afterlife such as toiletries, jewelry, and mementos.[16] After everyone has had an opportunity to view the body, the family members close the coffin and bear it on their shoulders to the burial grounds at Awudome near Kwame Nkrumah Circle.

Occasionally, the mourners may argue over who will carry the deceased to the cemetery because it is an honor to carry the body of the dead. As the pallbearers carry the coffin through the air, it may occasionally lurch about as they shift its weight on their shoulders and heads. Some believe that if the deceased was murdered, poisoned, or killed by foul means, they will purposefully move their coffins toward the killer. This can lead to anxiety amongst the onlookers, who might interpret a weight-bearing shift by the pallbearers as a deliberate movement by the deceased.[17] In the past twenty years, it has been a more common practice to load a coffin into a hearse equipped with sirens and a loudspeaker to announce the movement of the deceased.

Once the coffin arrives at Awudome, the head of the immediate paternal line, a grandparent or a prominent uncle, calls upon the ancestors as a group to accept the new family member into their midst, then pours a libation of gin or palm wine and makes incantations to speed the soul of the deceased into the afterlife. A Christian pastor or a Muslim cleric may lead prayers at this point, but their presence is not required. At a Muslim funeral, a mallam may recite passages from the Koran at the grave site. At Christian funerals, a clergyman might recite a version of the funeral rites found in the Book of Common Prayer, and each person will take turns casting dirt onto the coffin. At this point friends, church members, or work colleagues might also choose to speak before the body is interred, but the time spent by the graveside is kept to a minimum because the mourners are usually out in the midday sun, crowded around the grave on the piles of excavated dirt.[18] The casket is then buried by grave diggers employed at the cemetery and is sometimes sealed with concrete to prevent grave robbery.

After the burial, the mourners depart and later reassemble at appointed spot in Bukom for a wake, usually on a cordoned side street.[19] The extravagance of the party held at the wake grounds depends on the wealth of the family of the deceased. In Bukom, where most people are employed in fishing or petty trading, families have to pool their money and take out loans to make certain that they hold a memorial party that befits the status of the deceased. This money is spent on rental fees for canopies to keep out the sun and the rain, plastic chairs to seat dozens of guests, and a DJ with an accompanying sound system. The wake is a time when friends and associates can greet and console the family of the deceased, as well as enjoy some food, drinks, and dancing.[20] These festivities often run late into the evening and are known as times when young people gather to meet each other. Youths sometimes even meet their future spouses at funerals.

Though Muslims form a minority of the population of Bukom, it is worth mentioning that Muslim funerals differ slightly from *yara* convention in that the family of the deceased will dress the body with white calico and bury it on the same day. Only the male kin will take the body to the graveyard, and forty days after the burial the family will reassemble for a ceremony where the elderly kin of the deceased break kola nuts and hand them out to family, friends, and acquaintances. There is normally no wake or drinking at Muslim funerals, but it is common for the nonMuslim friends of the deceased to hold a party to celebrate the life of the departed.

It is also important to mention that Christian rituals are starting to be incorporated into *yara* customs. If the deceased was an active member of a Christian congregation, the body may be brought to the church in a closed casket for a special service to pray for the deceased, but this sort of service was not practiced in the past and is still uncommon today, making it part of a Chrstian layering that has only recently been added to *yara* conventions. Christian prayer is usually reserved for the Sunday after the funeral, when mourners can attend church to pray for the soul of the deceased. A well planned and well attended postfuneral church service can enhance the prestige of the family holding the funeral, but it is an addition to rather than an alteration of funerary custom. Though Christians are probably aware of the contradictions in believing in both a world of ancestors and heaven, this has not dramatically changed funeral practices in the city. Despite the increase of public Christian discourse and street preaching in Accra, priests and pastors do not play a role during postburial gatherings unless specifically invited to do so, and the wake held in the street is not considered to be a church event. Because of the rapid growth of charismatic churches in Accra, there may come a time when funerary customs will be absorbed into church services, but today it is still very common to attend funerals in Accra that have no Christian ritual and that leave prayer to the priests of the local shrines.[21] If a member of the *won hegbemei* passes away, the funeral service will include a congregation of spirit mediums dancing to a local drumming troupe and will attract shrine priests from the Ga-speaking suburbs of Accra.[22]

Among the major changes to Ga funerary custom in the past two hundred years has been the dwindling role of exuviae in burial ritual. Oral tradition in Accra holds that it is Ga funeral *kusum* to remove the hair and fingernails of the deceased for burial in the family compound (Reindorf [1895] 1966: 116), a practice that may have been developed to deal with the growing mobility amongst merchants and soldiers along the west coast of Africa during the slave trade and the colonial period. Ludewig Rømer ([1760] 2000: 184), a Danish slave trader on the coast of Africa, noted that corpses were buried in private locations in family compounds. Willem Bosman (Bosman 1705: 232) observed that while the family was expected to bury the whole body of the deceased, they could compromise by burying removable body parts when it was impossible to bring the entire corpse home from a distant location:

> [They] are strangely fond of being buried in their own country; so that if any person dies out of it, they frequently bring his corpse home to be buried, unless it be too far distant; in which case they bury him there; and if he have any friends or acquaintances there, they cut off his head, one arm, and one leg, which they cleanse, boil, and carry to his own country, where they are interred with fresh solemnity . . .

The continuity of this practice is also evident in Carl Christian Reindorf's 1895 history of the Gold Coast, which includes a passage describing the way that "a finger, toe, hair or finger nail" from the body of a Ga warrior slain in a battle outside the city was often returned for interment at home (Reindorf [1895] 1966: 116). Despite the absence of the complete cadaver, the funeral would proceed as usual at home, with a full-size coffin containing exuviae "buried as if it were the entire body" (Reindorf [1895] 1966: 116) so it could be worshiped as a part of the ancestral lineage.

The practice of burying removable body parts continues today, but they are usually placed within the coffin along with the corpse, and are sometimes discarded altogether. The interment of exuviae in the soil of the family compound is no longer part of the public funeral celebration, and if it is still practiced in Accra today, it is done secretly. In cases when the entire body is unavailable for burial (for example, if a person dies in the UK or the US and the family cannot afford to send the body home) the dressers of the body might indeed decide to send the hair and fingernails back to Accra. In this case, the exuviae will be placed inside a coffin along with heavy objects like cement bricks and given a closed casket funeral.[23] Some of the funeralgoers may know that the corpse is not in the coffin, but it will make no difference in the way that they openly mourn for the deceased.

Another major change in Ga funerary custom has been the location of burial. Before Accra became the capital of the Gold Coast, families buried their dead within their ancestral compounds (known as *adebo shia*) because to bury them in a cemetery was to abandon them to the spirits of the bush. The land beyond the limits of the city was known as the *kose* (Parker 2000a: 208–9), a metaphysical borderland where the bodies of the wretched, such as witches and women who died in childbirth, were cast.[24] This practice was altered at the end of the nineteenth century when the British prohibited intramural sepulture, spurring innovations in the use of cemeteries outside the city. Wealthy Ga families established mortuary complexes outside the city, but continued to bury body parts separately in the ancestral compound. Today, all burials are conducted at cemeteries, and the majority of bodies are interred at Awudome. Established in the 1960s by the Accra Metropolitan Assembly in an area that was mostly open bush, the Awudome Cemetery was designed as a burial ground for all of the citizens of the city. Anyone can be buried there, regardless of class or ethnicity and irrespective of the cause of the death. But though Awudome was regarded as a secular space by urban planners, it is still regarded by many residents of Accra as a place teeming with spiritual activity, making it ideal territory for fetish interment.

Mirroring funerals: the practice of fetish interment

Though ritually divorced from their association with *yara* convention, miniature coffins are still widely used in the rituals of the *won hegbemei* that mirror funeral customs. The coffin remains a powerful symbol when incorporated into fetish ceremonies, and it is notorious when included in *agbalegba*, a type of high stakes "deep play" (Geertz 2005) that utilizes the symbolism and the meanings of Ga funeral practice to curse and kill. Of course, studying *agbalegba* is not as easy as outlining Ga funerary conventions. The reasons for this are many. First of all, it is difficult to define what exactly *agbalegba* is. I have chosen to describe the practice of fetish interment, the ritual of burying a wooden figurine in a miniature coffin, as *agbalegba*, but the term is popularly used to refer to any secret fetish practice. Secondly, it is a clandestine practice. The ritual experts who conduct such ceremonies do not perform them out in the open for fear of exposing their secret knowledge of supernatural forces. They will also not conduct *agbalegba* ceremonies indiscriminately. The way that fetish interment kills is analogous to murder, and its practitioners will not conduct the rituals unless their client can show a legitimate reason for seeking revenge against a living person. Thirdly, *agbalegba* rituals are expensive. The components used to fabricate *agbalegba* fetishes are rare and obtainable only on the black market. There is a fetish market in Accra that sells herbs, roots, and animal parts, but many of the components used in *agbalegba* are illegal, which increases their cost because they must be sourced on the black market. Hiring a ritual expert who is willing to conduct *agbalegba* is also costly. In the case of Amele's *agbalegba* curse, her mother paid over $120 to the *woyoo* over the course of several weeks, the equivalent of two months salary for the average worker in Accra.

Because *agbalegba* rituals are rare, expensive, dangerous, and secret, few people will ever witness them.[25] But despite these obstacles to research, there are many Ga-speaking ritual experts living in the old city quarter of Bukom who are willing to demonstrate some of the charms that they make to seek vengeance for their clients. Not all curse medicines are composed literally. Some do include fishhooks or knives that represent the physical agents that will wound or kill, but since the victim is always at a distance and unaware of the impending curse, evoking the spirits to kill is not always enacted with material reagents. A curse can also be evoked simply through incantations that name the target and call on the power of the god to kill. Fetish interment differs slightly in that the repertoire of ingredients and practices are formulaic because they are a micro-reflection of the enduring burial rites of the Ga people. Over the course of several years of research, I was able to observe a handful of *agbalegba* rituals. Though each ritual had significant variations, each contained common elements that demonstrated its operation as a shadow ceremony of Ga funerary traditions.

Every *agbalegba* ceremony takes place in a private domestic setting, usually at the home of a spiritualist, a member of the *won hegbemei*. The Ga-speaking ritual experts who live in Accra are mostly locally born, and trained in the fetish arts by elder specialists in outlying villages.[26] They occupy modest homes, and their revenues are meager because they compete with dozens of other ritualists in the city. The setting for an *agbalegba* ceremony is usually innocuous (a corner of a family compound or a small bedroom), but the ritual is always conducted next to a shrine. The shrine can be comprised of a small cluster of consecrated medical or religious objects, or can be a more elaborate structure with carved images dedicated to the deity. In front of the shrine, the practitioner will assemble the mundane reagents that go into the construction of an *agbalegba* fetish. These are mostly items from the average stand at a night market in Accra, such as soaps, sponges, straw, square camphor, talcum powder, limes—the usual goods associated with cleansing a dead body. Standing in for the cadaver is a six-inch genderless figurine, fashioned on request by a wood carver at a timber market a few blocks north of Bukom. There is no *kɛtrɛ* present during the ceremony, nor is the extended family present to wash the body. The ritual expert alone consecrates the fetish by individually reproducing a conventional funeral ceremony that includes the cleansing of the body with a herbal bath, washing with soap and lime, and the burning of incense. Once the ceremony is complete, the "body" is placed in a miniature wooden coffin, carpentered at the same timber market where the figurine was carved.

At this juncture, the ritual deviates significantly from funerary convention. When the figurine is laid in the coffin, it becomes a representation of the person who is the target of the *agbalegba* curse. To direct harm against this person, an initial volley of incantations is uttered, including prayers in Ga that call upon local occult forces (like local gods and spirits) to attack the person. The victim's name is mentioned and repeated, sometimes in the form of a chant, in a manner that sympathetically associates the person with the figurine in the box. To intensify the curse, deadly new reagents are added, expensive items that can only be found on the black market through suppliers accessible via references from established ritualists.[27] The most powerful of these are human body parts from the intended victim, including the conventional types of exuviae. Fingernails and hair are the most commonly included reagents, but rumors abound about the use of human blood in *agbalegba* ritual.[28] Improvised additions, such as the letter written by Amele's mother, can be included to declare the target of the curse and to create an occult channel through which harm can be directed towards the victim.

Another component added to the coffin is *otofo mama*, strips of torn clothing taken from the dead body of a victim of violence. This is not meant to represent the clean cloth normally used to wrap the body of someone who has died a "good death," one that comes peacefully, at home, in old age. Rather, the *otofo mama* is the negative of the funeral shroud; it symbolizes a "bad death," one that happens when people die prematurely by accident, in childbirth, through suicide, or by infectious disease. The shoes, clothing, hair, fingernails, or blood from the corpse of someone who died violently are assumed to carry the power of the misfortune with them, thereby making them powerful material agents in the production of magic and sorcery. Sullied, stained, and encrusted with blood, *otofo mama* is included in the *agbalegba* ritual with the purpose of harvesting the spite of the *otofoi*: the ghosts of suicide victims, the angry souls of the murdered, and the wandering spirits of people killed in car accidents. The *otofoi* roam the world of the spirits, hungry for revenge, and the *otofo mama* is meant to attract their attention so that their anger can be focused on the target of the curse.[29]

When the material components of the *agbalegba* curse have been enclosed in the coffin, it is nailed firmly shut. At that point, the object is fully consecrated and it becomes a beacon that attracts the hatred of wandering spirits and re-directs them toward the target of the curse. To maximize the possibility of at-tracting such dangerous occult forces, the practitioners of *agbalegba* bury their coffins at Awudome Cemetery. Today Awudome is completely surrounded by highways, warehouses, and residential development, and is considered by most to be just an urban cemetery, a common component of a twenty-first century African city. However, to the practitioners of *agbalegba*, Awudome is fertile spiritual ground because bodies are buried collectively there, outside the space of the lineage compound and outside the spaces dominated by the major Ga deities. There is no longer a distinction between those who have died honorably and the circumspect dead who have passed away as a result of vio-lent deaths or infectious disease. Moreover, the admixture of ancestral spirits at Awudome has been intensified by the practice of stacking burial spaces; ac-cording to its caretaker, the cemetery has been full for over a decade, which has forced gravediggers to dig fresh graves on top of old and forgotten grave sites (Peace FM 2010). It is during midnight ceremonies, among the clutter of head-stones at Awudome, that the *won hegbemei* bury their miniature coffins. The ceremonies are summarily conducted, with a short incantation and a hastily poured libation to fix the curse. There is no mock wake after interment, only a slow deathwatch. Those who have participated believe that they only need to wait until the curse seizes upon its chosen target.

The scope of *agbalegba* activity at the graveyard is difficult to measure, but it is probable that many forms of ritual interment are conducted there. It is illegal to trespass on the grounds of Awudome at night, but the cemetery stretches nearly a square mile and is neither well enclosed nor guarded, making it ap-proachable from almost any direction. Under the cover of darkness, almost anyone can enter and exit without being noticed. Gravediggers and security personnel are also willing to turn a blind eye for a small bribe, and interviews reveal that perhaps dozens of ceremonies a month take place here.[30] Though no one I interviewed was willing to dig up a buried coffin to provide material evidence of the scope of ritual activity at the cemetery, I was directed to a min-iature box that had been exhumed to negate a prior curse. The box had been deconsecrated, emptied, and discarded on an old grave site, and it sat partially

Illustration 9.1. An altar for the preparation of an *agbalegba* fetish burial, including a wooden figurine, calico shroud, soap, limes, talcum powder, pomade, square camphor, perfume, and a grass scrubbing sponge. Photo by Jonathan Roberts.

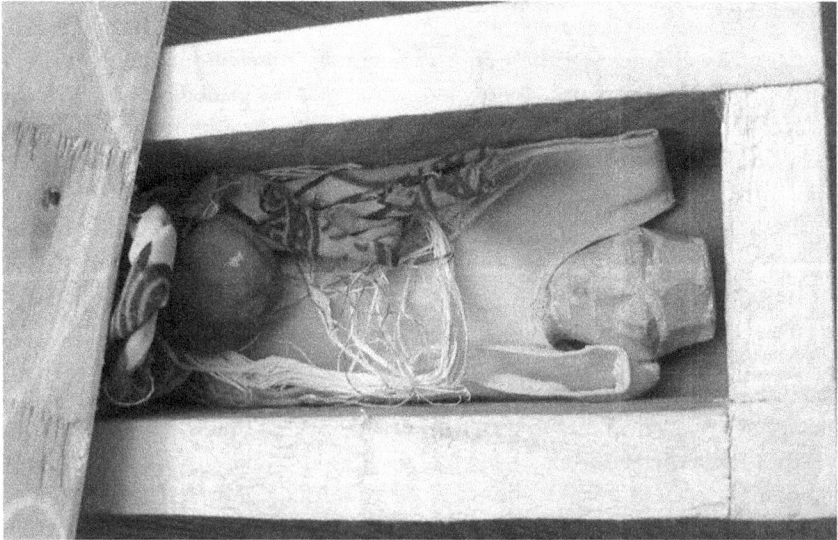

Illustration 9.2. An *agbalegba* curse medicine ready for interment. Photo by Jonathan Roberts.

Illustration 9.3. An exhumed and abandoned miniature coffin at Awudome Cemetery. Photo by Jonathan Roberts.

buried with leaves like a piece of fetish debris, an unearthed beacon that had lost its spiritual charge.

Agbalegba as a funeral shadow ceremony

The practice of fetish interment mirrors Ga funerary ritual in a number of ways. Firstly, it is a genre of terror that draws on deep-rooted fears within the popular consciousness of many Ghanaians. The rumor of the "secret fetish burial" crops up in discussions at the funeral grounds, reverberating as gossip well after the deceased is buried. Layers of secrecy and fear prevent the average resident of Bukom from seeing and understanding a ritual of *agbalegba,* so the popular image of the ritual has become that of the evil fetish priest chanting above a coffin in a hole in the ground at Awudome Cemetery. Few will ever witness a ceremony of fetish interment but the idea of *agbalegba* alone can evoke phobias of occult terrorism in the minds of the general public.

The nightmarish ideas found within *agbalegba* are akin to tropes of horror found in witchcraft beliefs. Witches are terrifying because they are parasites that cannibalize their own families, the very social unit that is supposed to be a haven of trust and fidelity. They cause illness and death as they devour the flesh of their cognates and even their own children, rotting the social order of the kinship group from within. As Peter Geschiere (2000: 11) has emphasized, witchcraft stories expose the "dark side of kinship" and thereby pose a challenge to the norms of ethical partiality towards the family. So too does *agbalegba* expose the fears of the mourner. A funeral is supposed to sooth the bereaved as they unite to send the soul of their loved one to the afterlife, but even as they perpetuate the funerary customs, mourners are aware that the same rituals can be appropriated and transformed into deadly forms of fetish power.

Agbalegba is also terrifying because it perverts the assumed outcome of funerary *kusum*. It is not a public ceremony that facilitates the movement of the soul into the afterlife, but a private, shadow ceremony that indexes the privileged context of funerary symbolism and manipulates it in ways that deviate from its socially accepted uses. The revered customs of *yara* seem easily rendered down into a microcosmic prototype, one that can have as much significance as a real burial involving a cadaver and hundreds of mourners because *agbalegba* can kill the living and harvest the souls of the dead. Moreover, since fetish interment is for sale, even close kin and family members can make each other the targets of a secret *agbalegba* curse.

Interestingly, *agbalegba* is not a form of colonial mimicry. There are instances of European influence in the practice, such as the use of a coffin, but the ritual contains no other notable derivations twentieth century Ga funeral *kusum*—no imitation of a frozen body, no imitation morgue, and no Christian or Muslim imagery. The economic and religious changes of the twentieth century that have changed funerals in Ghana simply do not appear in this ritual. Rather, the ingredients used to compose an *agbalegba* curse medicine are drawn from commonplace items used in daily activities like herbs, cloths, toiletries. The figurine is not unique either, as anthropomorphic carvings are stock in trade for the *won hegbemei*.[31] At the fetish market in Accra, one can find stacks and stacks of figurines waiting to be purchased by ritualists, who utilize them in innumerable ways.

Nor does the practice of *agbalegba* reflect the sorts of of double vision that Bhabha (1994: 889) has commented on or the appropriation of European symbols found in Taussig's (1993) Cuna figurines. This may change. As new brands of charismatic Christianity begin to play a larger role in the urban center of Accra, there may be a greater inclusion of Pentecostal practice and Christian symbolism, but as a practice passed down through generations of the *won hegbemei*, *agbalegba* operates within ritual framework that shows little recent innovation. In fact, *agbalegba* draws much of its power from components of *yara* that are considered obsolete. Its aesthetic emphasizes an earlier layer of funeral practice that placed emphasis on the use of removable body parts that are used as a form of sympathetic magic to extend the self beyond the corporeal. The incorporation of body parts into an *agbalegba* ritual operates according to Frazer's (1940: 37) principles of magical contagion, which dictate that things once conjoined must ever remain in a sympathetic relation with each other. It treats the body as the starting point of a continuum that begins with the bodily self and extends outward through removable body parts and gossamer emanations like the *otofoi*. This distributed personhood (Gell 1998: 1045) provides the physical and occult reagents necessary for the fetish magics composed by the *won hegbemei*.

Fetish interment also draws on lingering anxieties about the geography of burial. As John Parker (2000b: 6) has shown, the dyadic relationship between city (*man*) and bush (*kose*) is a way of reckoning how the world of the supernatural interlocks with the world of the living. In the past, families interred their dead within their ancestral compounds; to bury them outside the city was to abandon them to the spirits of the bush. And the cemetery was considered a dangerous space beyond Ga urban space where the bodies of the wretched were discarded. This has changed dramatically in the twenty-first century as Awudome Cemetery has become a place where anyone can be buried regardless of birthplace and regardless of the cause of death. This has left the topography of the spirit world decidedly underdetermined in the minds of mourners. Though the cemetery is now surrounded by urban sprawl, it continues to be regarded as a haunting ground, an interstitial space between the *kose* and the *man*, where the souls of the deceased who died good deaths mix with the *otofoi* of the condemned. This makes it a resource of spiritual power waiting to be exploited by practitioners of *agbalegba*, who have unlimited access to the cemetery and are known to visit it regularly.

Conclusion

After Amele's funeral in 2004, her mother left Accra to live in Amasaman, a suburb several miles north of the city. In 2007, I traveled there to meet her and gently broached the topic of the death of her daughter.[32] During our brief chat, she refused to speak of the matter, but just as I was leaving she admitted that she would never return to Accra because of the shame of knowing that she had killed her own daughter. The stigma of AIDS in Ghana is severe, but not enough for someone to exile themselves from their home. Amele's mother was giving herself a life sentence in exile for evoking the power of *agbalegba*, showing how seriously people continue to treat fetish power and the world of the spirits.

Accra continues to be famous for extravagant funerals that celebrate the lives of the dead and help the soul make a transition toward the afterlife. But Accra is also home to rituals of fetish interment, secret ceremonies that operate in parallel to Ga funerary custom to Ga funerary custom, and that trigger horror and revulsion amongst the population of the city. The *won hegbemei*, the most powerful ritual specialists in the city, have copied and refined some major aspects of funerals into a miniaturized fetish form that has become known as *agbalegba*. Though the practice draws on antiquated notions of the relationship between the body and spirit, and outmoded understandings of the geography of burial, it continues to survive as a way for people to express hate and demand vengeance. No matter how extravagant or innovative the funerals of Accra may be, can always be mimicked in fetish form by the power of *agbalegba*.

Notes

1. Interview, Nii Oshiu Codjoe, February 17, 2003. The abortion medicine was a mix of malt drink and sugar, but its exact application was not explained.
2. When this story was recounted, the term "fetish priest" was used, but it was most likely a *woyoo*, a female spirit medium, who initiated the curse medicine. In local parlance, a fetish priest is anyone who derives religion and healing from lesser gods and spirits. They are also known as the *won hegbemei*, the Ga term for the "people of the gods." Using the terms "fetish priest" to describe groups of ritual experts is common, but accusing someone of being a "fetish priest" is normally an insult. A "fetish" can be glossed as a consecrated medicine, an aggregated collection of objects that is ritually imbued with the power of local gods and spirits. For a detailed investigation of the history of the fetish, see a series of articles by William Pietz (1985: 5–17, 1987: 23–45, 1988: 105–23)
3. The orthography of the Ga terms used in this chapter are consistent with Kropp Daku-bu's *Ga-English Dictionary* (1999), with the exception of the character representing the o sound in "hot" and of the character *ŋ* for the ng in "long". These have been changed to *o* and *n* respectively to prevent gaps in the formatting of paragraphs.
4. The pidgin terms of "juju" and "fetish" are used along the west coast of Africa as catchall terms that refer to local religious practices. In Accra, Christians and Muslims use fetish to describe any rituals, magics, or medicines created by indigenous practitioners.
5. In Ghana, the commonly used term for a gathering by family and friends after the burial to celebrate the life of the deceased is "wakekeeping," but in this article the term "wake" will be used.
6. A common saying in Accra is that "Saturdays are for funerals, Sundays are for church."
7. For a recent journalistic account of funerals in Ghana, see Colleen Ross, "How much is the afterlife worth?" CBC, November 2, 2005, accessed March 31, 2008 from http://www.cbc.ca/news/viewpoint/vp_ross/20051102.html.
8. For a parallel group of traditional morticians in Benin, see Noret (2004: 757).
9. Though there is usually time for an autopsy or an inquest into a death during this interval, they are rarely held because of a lack of trained coroners and a dearth of funding for post mortem operations and record-keeping. For details on the changing temporal frameworks of funeral rituals in neighboring southern Benin, see Noret (2004: 745–67).

10. Interview, Mary Otabil, January 22, 2007.

11. It is possible that the hair and the fingernails are trimmed because they tend to lengthen as a corpse dries out, but no interviewee mentioned this as a reason for trimming them. Most just pointed out that the body had to be made presentable for viewing. There does not seem to be any spiritual significance embedded in the hair and nails.

12. Kwame Arhin (1994: 310) describes the lineage head giving a dying family member water so that he will be able to "climb the steep hill between the lands of the living and of ghosts." Arhin also notes that charms and gold dust (known as *kra sika*) were tied to cadavers during Akan funeral rites. This practice is not followed by Ga speakers today, nor is there a specific name for the money given to the deceased.

13. Margaret Field (1937: 200) quotes a statement by a mourner who gives a gift of money to the deceased, and says "*ke fo ohe fa*—take it to cross the river." Arhin (1994: 311) claims that during Akan funerals, the mourners give messages to the deceased for delivery to other dead relatives. Interview, Abigail Quaye, April 2, 2008 and Interview, Nii Oshiu Codjoe, March 15, 2008.

14. Field 1937: 203.

15. The Ga adopted the *adeka,* the coffin, for burial in the nineteenth century, and had previously wrapped their dead in woven mats (Parker 2000a: 210). For information on the coffin industry in Ghana, see Secretan 1995.

16. Interview, Abigail Quaye, April 2, 2008; Interview, Nii Oshiu Codjoe, March 15, 2008.

17. Field 1937: 200; Interview, Mary Otabil, March 15, 2008; Interview, Nii Oshiu Codjoe, March 15, 2008.

18. Interview, Nii Oshiu Codjoe, March 15, 2008. The common prayer at the graveside is normally an appropriately edited version of: "In sure and certain hope of the resurrection to eternal life through our Lord Jesus Christ, we commend to Almighty God our brother _____, and we commit his body to the ground, earth to earth, ashes to ashes, dust to dust. The Lord bless him and keep him, the Lord make his face to shine upon him and be gracious unto him and give him peace. Amen."

19. An added expense to funerals in Bukom is the cost of a permit to block a street for a wake, which must be paid to the Accra Metropolitan Assembly.

20. Interview, Nii Oshiu Codjoe, March 15, 2008. The food served at funerals is usually comprised of "small chops" for acquaintances and larger meals of chicken and fish for closer relations and friends. The traditional Ga drink is a sweet nonalcoholic wine made from corn, but most people serve beer and soft drinks. The most common music at funerals today is recorded popular music like gospel and hiplife, but occasionally music is provided by local drumming troupes.

21. Bukom is not an upwardly mobile part of town, and therefore does not attract the class of worshipers who attend the growing charismatic churches based in the suburbs of Accra. The largest churches in the neighborhood are the more conservative Anglican, Presbyterian, and Methodist denominations, which were established in the city at the end of the nineteenth century. Paul Gifford (2004: 52–3) argues that the new churches of Accra have young congregations, so they have not had to deal with handling funeral arrangements for people who worship in their churches. He also notes that "death has always been something of an embarrassment in these churches" because their pastors often preach that no Christian should die before the standard biblical lifespan of seventy years. Life expectancy in Ghana according to UNICEF was fifty-nine years in

2000. See UNICEF, accessed March 31, 2008, http://www.unicef.org/infobycountry/ghana_statistics.html.

22. Some people in Accra claim that remembrance of the deceased must last for one full year. After that point, the mourning period is over, and should be celebrated with *faafo*, a final mourning party. After the *faafo* gathering ends, it is assumed that the soul of the departed had joined the world of the ancestors. People in Accra no longer celebrate *faafo* publicly. If they do gather to remember the one year anniversary of the death of a loved one, they do so in a family setting, without advertising the event to the public. In the twenty-first century, *faafo* seems to have disappeared, as it is not common to hear about one-year mourning events. This may be because so many emotional and financial resources are spent on the funeral, or it may be just a withering away of an extraneous form of funerary *kusum*.

23. Interview, Nii Oshiu Codjoe, January 22, 2007.

24. John Parker (2000a: 208–9) has noted that because of the division of the ritual topography of the city between the *man* and the *kose*, conflicts about burial locations were common among the urban elites in Accra. A British ban on intramural sepulture led to an era of "mortuary politics" that expressed Ga anxieties about the relationship between burial location, ancestral power, and political authority.

25. As a parallel from the region of the Congo, Wyatt MacGaffey (1988: 188) noted that ritual artifacts called *minkisi* are also difficult to study because they are "multitudinous, secret, and expensive."

26. The caste of ritualists known as the *won hegbemei* is drawn either from a mostly undereducated working class community in the center of Accra or from fishing and farming villages in outlying Ga-speaking areas. None of them choose to become healers; rather, they are chosen, either by a clan to fulfill the role of a shrine priest or spiritually by a god that resides within them. They are trained to manage their relationship with the gods during several months of apprenticeship with elders, sometimes in outlying farming areas like Pokuase (which is rapidly becoming a suburban part of Accra.) For more on the *won hegbemei*, see Field 1937: 100–134.

27. The trade in illicit ingredients such as cloth stained with blood or human body parts is illegal in Ghana according to adopted statutes of British law that prevent the use of "obnoxious medicines." The availability of such items is rare and the knowledge of their sources is usually unverifiable. Prices are not set either, but in one instance a strip of *otofo mama* was priced at around $20. Interview, Thunder, December 22, 2006.

28. Interview, Nii Oshiu Codjoe, January 22, 2007. Interview, Thunder, December 22, 2006. Like the *kusum* of *yara*, each *agbalegba* ritual is an individualized ceremony and is subject to a high degree of personal interpretation by the ritual expert who conducts it. What the practitioner includes in the coffin can be idiosyncratic and varies on a case by case basis. Margaret Field (1937: 129) noted the use of human body parts in acts of sorcery.

29. Margaret Field (1937: 202) describes the *otofoi* in a visceral manner, as a tortured soul roaming purgatory: "When any violent or premature death takes place the spirit wandering about for forty days is called an *otofo*. It is savage and resentful of being snatched away and is very jealous of anyone partaking of pleasures such as dancing, feasting, and especially sexual pleasure. If it catches any one returning late at night from pleasure it will kill him by chasing him till his heart gives out. Any one bent only on business is not harmed if he sees an *otofo* so long as he pretends he has not seen it.

It is easy enough to recognize because its breath is fiery and its mouth is red inside, its blood groans and cries and with shrill whistling calls other *otofoi* to come to its help. It greatly dislikes white and can be kept away by the wearing of white clothes ..."

30. Interview, Yao, gravedigger at Awudome Cemetery, January 31, 2008. Interview, Muhammed, gravedigger at Awudome Cemetery, January 29, 2008.
31. Figurines are used improvisationally in the practices of the *won hegbemei,* and so can be put toward any particular ritual use, but they are commonly found in love medicines (bound together with cloth) and curse medicines (with the name of the accursed attached to the figurine through incantation.).
32. Interview, *Elizabeth Quartey,* December 28, 2006.

Bibliography

Adjaye, Angela Evelyn. 2004. "HIV/AIDS Situation and Impact in Ghana and Accra Metropolitan Assembly (AMA)" *ALGAFIV—Local Government Responses to HIV/AIDS, Accra Metropolitan Assembly Response to HIV/AIDS among High-Risk Groups.* (Feb.).

Adjei, Ako. 1943. "Mortuary Usages of the Ga People of the Gold Coast." *American Anthropologist* 45, no. 1: 84–98.

Arhin, Kwame. 1994. "The Economic Implications of Transformations in Akan Funeral Rites." *Africa* 64, no. 3: 307–22.

Bhabha, Homi. 1994. *The Location of Culture.* New York: Routledge.

Bosman, Willam. 1705. *A New and Accurate Description of the Coast of Guinea, Divided into the Gold, the Slave, and the Ivory Coasts.* London: James Knapton.

Daniell, William F. 1856. "On the Ethnography of Akkrah and Adampe, Gold Coast, Western Africa." *Journal of the Ethnological Society of London* 4: 1–32.

de Witte, Marleen. 2003. "Money and Death: Funeral business in Asante, Ghana." *Africa* 73, no. 4: 531–559.

Duda, Rosemary B., Rudolph Darko, Richard M.K. Adanu, Joseph Seffah, John K. Anarfi, Shiva Gautam, and Allan G. Hill. 2005. "HIV Prevalence and Risk Factors in Women of Accra, Ghana: Results from the Women's Health Study of Accra." *American Journal of Tropical Medicine and Hygiene* 73, no. 1: 63–66.

Field, Margaret Joyce. 1937. *Religion and Medicine of the Gã People.* London: Oxford University Press.

Frazer, Sir James George. 1940. *The Golden Bough: A Study in Magic and Religion.* New York: MacMillan.

Geertz, Clifford. 2005. "Deep play: Notes on the Balinese cockfight." *Daedalus* 134, no. 4: 56–86.

Gell, Alfred. 1998. *Art and Agency: An Anthropological Theory.* Oxford: Clarendon Press.

Geschiere, Peter. 2000. *The Modernity of Witchcraft: Politics and the Occult in Postcolonial Africa.* Charlottesville: University Press of Virginia.

Gifford, Paul. 2004. *Ghana's New Christianity: Pentecostalism in a Globalizing African Economy.* Bloomington and Indianapolis: Indiana University Press.

Gilbert, Michelle. 1988. "The Sudden Death of a Millionaire: Conversion and Consensus in a Ghanaian Kingdom." *Africa* 58, no. 3: 291–314.

MacGaffey, Wyatt. 1988. "Complexity, Astonishment and Power: The Visual Vocabulary of Kongo Minkisi." *Journal of Southern African Studies* 14, no. 2: 188–203.

Miescher, Stephen F. 2005. *Making Men in Ghana.* Bloomington: Indiana University Press.

Mullins, Leith. 1984. *Therapy, Ideology, and Social Change: Mental Healing in Urban Ghana.* London: University of California Press.

Noret, Joël. 2004. "Morgues et prise en charge de la mort au Sud-Bénin." *Cahiers d'études africaines* 44, no. 4: 745–67.

Parker, John. 2000a. "The Cultural Politics of Death & Burial in Early Colonial Accra." In *Africa's Urban Past,* eds. David M. Anderson & Richard Rathbone. Oxford: James Currey.

———. 2000b. *Making the Town: Ga state and society in early Colonial Accra.* Portsmouth, NH: Heinemann.

Peace FM Online "No Place For The DeadOsu, Awudome Cemeteries Full" accessed January 28 http://news.peacefmonline.com/health/201001/37137.php.

Pietz, William. 1985. "The Problem of the Fetish, I." *Res* 9 (Spring): 5–17.

———. 1987. "The Problem of the Fetish, II." *Res* 13 (Spring): 23–45.

———. 1988. "The Problem of the Fetish, IIIa." *Res* 16 (Autumn): 105–23.

Reindorf, Carl Christian. 18951966. *The History of the Gold Coast And Asante: Based on traditions and historical facts comprising a period of more than three centuries from about 1500 to 1860.* Accra: Ghana Universities Press.

Rømer, Ludewig F. 2000. *A Reliable Account of the Coast of Guinea.* Oxford: Oxford University Press.

Ross, Colleen. 2005. "How much is the afterlife worth?" CBC, November 2, 2005. Accessed March 31, 2008. http://www.cbc.ca/news/viewpoint/vp_ross/20051102.html.

Secretan, Thierry. 1995. *Going into Darkness: Fantastic Coffins from Africa.* London: Thames and Hudson.

Taussig, Michael. 1993. *Mimesis and Alterity: A Particular History of the Senses.* New York: Routledge.

UNICEF. 2008. Accessed March 31. http://www.unicef.org/infobycountry/ghana_statistics.html.

van der Geest, Sjaak. 2000. "Funerals for the Living: Conversations with Elderly People in Kwahu, Ghana." *African Studies Review* 43, no. 3: 103–129.

———. 2004. "Dying Peacefully: Considering good death and bad death in Kwahu-Tafo, Ghana." *Social Science & Medicine* 58, no. 5: 899–911.

World Bank. 2008. Accessed March 14. http://info.worldbank.org/etools/docs/library/134438/ALGAF/Algaf_cd/algaf_docs/Resources/Country percent20Specific percent20Presentations/ALGAF percent20Countries/Ghana/Assignment percent20for percent20Accra percent20Ghana.pdf.

Notes on Contributors

de Witte, Marleen

Marleen de Witte (PhD, anthropology, University of Amsterdam) is a postdoctoral researcher at the University of Amsterdam. Her research interests include religion (Pentecostalism, African traditional religion) and media, cultural heritage, the anthropology of death, popular culture, and Ghana and Africa overall. She has published *Long Live the Dead!: Changing Funeral Celebrations in Asante, Ghana* (Aksant, 2001) and articles in *Africa, Journal of Religion in Africa,* and other international journals.

Droz, Yvan

A social anthropologist (PhD, University of Neuchâtel), Yvan Droz did extensive fieldwork in Africa, Latin America, and Europe. From 2003 to 2007, he was deputy director and head of the research department of the Graduate Institute of Development Studies (now the "Graduate Institute of International and Development Studies"). Today, he heads a team of researchers on religious mobility in Kenya and Brazil and is developing a political anthropology of agriculture (Switzerland, France, and Quebec).

Jindra, Michael

Michael Jindra is an adjunct associate professor in the department of anthropology and a visiting research scholar at the Center for the Study of Religion and Society at the University of Notre Dame (USA). He has published in journals such as *Africa, Sociology of Religion, Anthropological Forum,* and *Society,* and has also contributed chapters to a number of books. His current research focuses on the connection between lifestyle diversity, culture, and inequality in the U.S. His PhD is from the University of Wisconsin-Madison.

Lamont, Mark

Mark Lamont is a lecturer in anthropology at Goldsmiths. His PhD was from Edinburgh in 2005, and he most recently worked as a research fellow on an AHRC funded project, "Death in Africa, c. 1800 to present," organized between Goldsmiths and Cambridge. He is currently researching a book on car crashes in Kenya and the global road safety lobby.

Langewiesche, Katrin
Katrin Langewiesche holds a PhD in Social Anthropology from the Ecole des Hautes Etudes en Sciences Sociales, France. She is a research associate at the Johannes Gutenberg University of Mainz, Germany. Her main research is on religious anthropology in Europe and modern Africa and in the socioanthropological analysis of missions in West Africa. She is currently coordinating a research project on the confessional health system in Burkina Faso and its collaborations and tensions with the public health system. She is the author of *Mobilité religieuse: Changements religieux au Burkina Faso.*

Noret, Joël
Joël Noret is assistant professor in anthropology at the Université libre de Bruxelles, Belgium. He has been conducting fieldwork in southern Benin since the beginning of the 2000s. His publications include the co-edition of a special issue of Gradhiva on "Mémoire de l'esclavage au Bénin" (with Gaetano Ciarcia, 2008), and his monograph *Deuil et funérailles dans le Bénin méridional: Enterrer à tout prix* has recently been published at the Editions de l'Université de Bruxelles (2010).

Ranger, Terence
Terence Ranger is professor emeritus at St Antony's College, Oxford. He first went to Rhodesia (Zimbabwe) in 1957 and has been involved in African history ever since. He has been a professor in Dar es Salaam, UCLA, Manchester, Oxford, and at the University of Zimbabwe. He has written nine monographs on the history of Zimbabwe, the latest being *Bulawayo Burning: The Social History of a Southern African City, 1893–1960* (James Currey, 2010.)

Roberts, Jonathan
Jonathan Roberts is a historian of medicine and religion in West Africa, with a particular focus on the history of healing in Ghana. He is currently completing his PhD at the University of Toronto and is a faculty member at Mount Saint Vincent University in Halifax, Nova Scotia.

Index

www.ingramcontent.com/pod-product-compliance
Lightning Source LLC
Chambersburg PA
CBHW072105040426

42334CB00042B/2328